Tales of the Mekong Delta Bluesman

Autobiography of Son Vo

By Son Hoang Vo

Edited by Sara B Ware

Table of Contents

Tales of the Mekong Delta Bluesman

"I been in the blues all my life. I'm still delivering 'cause I got a long memory."
- Muddy Waters

"Muddy water is best cleared by leaving it alone."
– Alan Watts

"The meaning of life is just to be alive. It is so plain and so obvious and so simple. And yet, everybody rushes around in a great panic as if it were necessary to achieve something beyond themselves."
- Alan Watts

"I'm a fan first. I believed Duke Ellington when he said there's no bad music, just some of it is presented badly. As a kid, hanging around Church Street, the presentation of music was so powerful, I couldn't help but jump for joy. I had discovered art, or truth, or whatever you want to call it; I had seen a light I'd follow forever."

- B.B. King, Blues All Around Me: The Autobiography of B.B. King

INTRODUCTION

The Blues

Mekong Delta Bluesman was born on a night where I must've felt really clever, combining my birthplace (Saigon, Vietnam) with my biggest influence, which was the blues; BB King mostly. It's stuck with me ever since. I don't take that title lightly. Many blues musicians who should've been living a life of opulence were ultimately oppressed and struggled to the very end. They weren't singing and writing about the blues because they were trying to become famous. They were baring their souls to whoever was listening and knew they'd feel better after shedding their day's pain, even if it helped but for only a few moments. Many legendary bluesmen made very little money from music during their lifetimes, and many of them only got recognized because of pop rock figures like the Rolling Stones, Eric Clapton, and Peter Green. It took the most popular English bands and radio play to open the world to discovering how integral the blues were in shaping the world of popular music. Blues, besides folk music, is the root of all American music from 1920 to the present. Even the die-hard jazz artists and connoisseurs will admit to that. After all, jazz is sophisticated blues at its roots, according to my guitar teacher, Val Mollineux.

Not to get all dark and dingy, but what I endured as a child, I surely felt like I'd already lived the blues by the time I was eight years old. "Mekong Delta Bluesman" felt very fitting, a perfect marriage of East meets West blues. Sure, I'll never be able to sing like BB King or the other Son, Son House, nor play guitar like them, but I feel the blues in every lyric; in every song I sing and write. The sincerity of the blues will never leave me. It's my heart and soul.

The blues is about telling your stories through music, no matter how painful those stories are. It's about releasing what hurts and feeling better afterwards, simply because you don't feel so alone once your stories are shared. Everybody's got some blues in them, some more than others. But through sharing the blues, everybody connects with it and walks out feeling better, recharged for a new day.

CHAPTER 1
SAIGON 1971-1975

January 14th, 1971, St. Paul Hospital in Saigon. I arrived. My mom's birth name was Vo Thí Nguyet Van, and she told me, years later, that my father was an Air Force pilot name Jimmy Soto. As the story went, he took an interest in my mom, then left to go back to war before I was born.

When I was three, my mother left for the United States with Frank Muccio, Jr. to free herself from what I can only consider the shackles of the Vietnam War. Frank, a Naval officer, fell head-over-heels in love with her, helped bring her to America, and shortly thereafter they married.

While that happy little fairy tale was happening in the U.S., my older sister Hien and I were left behind and sent to separate families to be raised. Hien went to a working-class family with many boys, while I was sent to a middle-class family with no kids. I can only assume my mother wanted her first-born son to "have all the best opportunities" while my sister was thought of as "not the first-born son" and a second-class citizen. It was cruel, but that was the reality. Confucianism still influenced the mindset of Vietnamese culture.

I have only the vaguest memories of being introduced to the family that was to look after me, specifically remembering the staircase of their home. It wasn't that it was this incredibly epic staircase, it's that I had never seen one before, especially a stained-wooden one! When I looked up the stairs, it was as if they just extended up and up; the ceiling was so tall. That first day I must've stared at the top of those stairs for minutes before I climbed up a quarter of the way, then shoved my head between two banisters to gaze down on the enormous room below. I had never seen a house so huge, let alone so grand. Even though it was just a middle-class house in American terms, it was much fancier than where we had been living before that. There's a photo that still exists of my sister and I at this house. I remember my front foot was blurry because I was fidgety. How long I lived there, I can only estimate. Maybe a year, two at most.

Perhaps my big sister, Hien, knew more than I did about our mom's empty promises to return and retrieve us. I only know that even though we were separated for that time, my sister still managed to visit me as often as she could. Perhaps she made a vow with my mom to keep watch over me, because she did. She took it upon herself to be my protector, even at such an early age. I'll always be grateful for her. Our fractured souls needed each other during that uncertain time, and she made sure we didn't lose our connection.

She made sure our bond was only made stronger during those days, because all we had now was each other.

MY EARLIEST MEMORIES

One of my earliest memories is quite odd, but it kind of ties into my life as somebody who relies on their ears as a musician. It obviously left an impression on me.

I was going to some daycare, or maybe preschool? Nevertheless, during naptime, we all slept on thin, bamboo mats lined up side by side in this big room. There were probably twenty other kids in the room. I honestly don't remember. I just remember bamboo mats lined up in a small room with other kids sleeping all around me. As I lay on my right side with my head down on the mat, something suddenly just plopped out of my ear. I looked down to see what it was and saw this huge piece of earwax! As a child, it seemed a lot bigger than what it actually was. All I know was that I was intrigued. I picked it up, turning it about to view it at every angle, wondering how something like that could've come out of my ear! I also noticed that I could hear better. The blanket muffling audio had lifted, and the world sounded different. It sounded *full*.

After I stopped rolling the wad of earwax around in my fingers and my curiosity abated, I finally put my head back down to nap. Or maybe I was caught awake and told to go back to sleep?

I forget. All I know is that one of my earliest memories is of a fairly substantial wad of earwax falling out of my ear, being curious about it, looking at it, then noticing that, suddenly, my hearing had improved. I could hear the clock on the wall ticking and the other kids breathing while they napped. I became aware of how it *feels* to hear. I consider my hearing to be the most valuable sensory perception I have, and this being a first memory speaks volumes.

MILITARY TRUCKS

Another vivid memory I have is of military trucks filled with American soldiers driving by the place we lived, with huge cannons attached to them. Tanks and jeeps were never far behind. They'd leave a trail of dust that looked humungous to a young kid's eyes. I was never afraid of them though. They seemed like a natural part of the environment. I'd watch them come through and knew it was just part of whatever was going on around us.

THE CRICKET FIGHT

One morning, my sister and I were walking around the bustling streets of Saigon, as we probably did quite often. She was, as usual, tightly holding onto my hand, making sure I didn't run off. It was very easy to lose somebody among the crowd, especially a curious three-year-old boy. As we walked down this one street, I noticed a commotion coming from a group of men to my right. They were all hunched over, shouting and passing money around, watching something that I couldn't quite see from where I was, but stirred my curiosity enough that I just had to get closer.

I was able to escape my sister's grip and ran off towards them, around and under people's legs, until I finally got close enough to see what all the commotion was about.

There I was, peering into a little cage with a small wooden dowel going from end to end, and as I peered even closer, I saw two crickets, one on each end of the dowel, waiting to wage battle. It was a cricket fight! This was an age-old tradition brought over from China. Each cricket owner would bring their prized cricket towards the middle of the little pole, then release them when commanded, and the cricket battle would begin.

The first cricket to fall off the pole would lose. When a cricket won, the men would scream loudly in unison. Some would grumble, some would laugh, and money was passed around. Then the next cricket contenders would enter the cage and the whole process would repeat. A new fight would begin! I was completely mesmerized, plus I had front row seats, and the men didn't seem to mind me being there. Meanwhile, my sister had been searching for me and, eventually finding me, dragged me away. She was relieved that she found me but also reminded me that I couldn't go off running like that again. I knew I shouldn't have, but it was worth all the worry in the world. I never got to see another cricket fight, but I got an up-close experience for that one cricket fight, which will last a lifetime.

THE SOUND OF BULLETS

One final memory I have in Saigon is inside a crowded building; lots and lots of other people. The memory is of bullets ricocheting. The sound was distinctive because it created a 'PING', unlike any other sound I've ever heard. We obviously all ducked for cover, as good as that'll do to protect you.

The building itself was made of concrete bricks, from what I remember, so at least we weren't going to get pierced by nearby stray rounds. It's not the best thing to remember, but it was the reality of being in Saigon just before it fell.

LEAVING VIETNAM WITH MY SISTER AND MOM

About a year after my mom left for the United States, my stepfather Frank somehow learned that she had left two kids behind in Vietnam. He was apparently rummaging through some papers and accidentally found proof she had kids. He was astonished, to say the least, that she had never revealed this to him and immediately questioned her about it. She told him she had been too afraid that he wouldn't have taken her to America had he known of us. Her ticket out of Vietnam could've been in jeopardy, a chance she wasn't willing to take, even if it meant leaving her children behind. It was an act of desperation from a young and desperate woman during a time of war. At least, I'd like to think that that's what it was.

So, my stepfather, bless his heart, used his life's savings to help get us out of Vietnam and bring us to the United States. He somehow had expedition papers signed and quickly processed in time for my mom to return and retrieve us. After all, there was very little time to spare - it was April of 1975, a month before Saigon fell. Thank God for his act of kindness. Being an Amerasian, I couldn't have imagined that my opportunities in Vietnam would surpass becoming a petty thief, a victim of child slave labor, or worse. More likely than not, it would've been a living hell. As far as the Vietnamese thought of children born of American soldiers, we were sons of whores, lower than even a dog. Sorry, dogs. I had no future if I had stayed, and my sister wasn't much better off, since she was also born out of wedlock. Two peas in a fucked-up pod.

The time came and my mother rushed back to retrieve my sister and myself to bring us with her to the United States. While waiting for the day to come when we'd be allowed to board the airplane, we had to live in a boarding house, a cement-walled building that housed broken Vietnamese families, all waiting to leave.

During this time, a monsoon occurred, raising the water levels up to my waist. The front door of the building we were staying in was always left open, so we were quickly exposed to the rising water levels, as was the entire neighborhood. There were about a dozen cots lined up along each wall, which most of us stood up on while the water was rising, except for myself. I was waist-deep in the monsoon water in the middle of the room.

Suddenly, I see something fairly large squirming in the water near me and I heard somebody scream "snake!" - in Vietnamese, of course. It was a huge Anaconda. That's when I quickly jumped up onto the closest cot.

People were frantically looking about for the anaconda, wondering where it went as it slid underneath the murky water. We all stood on our cots for a long time, either until the water receded, or until the snake found its way out. Even now, I can see it – about three feet of its body, as thick as me, swimming through the muddy water, trying to find an escape route. What I was able to see was enormous. I'm just glad it left before anyone was harmed.

COMING TO AMERICA

The day arrived for my sister, my mom, and myself to escape Vietnam and fly to America. It was April 22nd, 1975. Granted, we weren't part of the melee that occurred days before Saigon was taken over, but you wouldn't have noticed the difference at the airport. The scene was just short of mayhem, filled with sounds of desperation.

We arrived at the airport early in the morning. It was exactly like scenes you see depicted in movies. It looked more like a military holding facility, with barbed wire-topped fencing surrounding the entrance. Mobs of people were screaming, waving to Vietnamese soldiers, scaling the barriers, crying and pleading to get past the checkpoint, while those already near the checkpoints stayed absolutely silent, frantically hoping they'd get lucky enough to escape the war-torn country.

The tormented looks on their faces told you everything you ever needed to know, and probably even more than you wanted to know, about that hell. I'll never forget this. Right before the three of us started walking towards the checkpoint, my mom stopped, kneeled down, looked at my sister and I, and with an extremely serious expression said firmly to us, "Whatever you do, *DO NOT* let go of my hand!" Message received, loud and clear. We clutched her hands tightly, walked past some soldiers to the right of the lines, through the havoc of screaming people all around us, then finally reached the checkpoint. My mom took out the expedition papers, personally signed by Henry Kissinger, in order to get us out, and the man sitting behind the makeshift table looked at them briefly for a few seconds, stamped them, and allowed us through.

This is where it all became slow motion to me. As we walked towards the airport entrance and past the fencing, I looked back to see all the pleading faces left behind, hearing their desperate cries slowly dissipate. The air changed, and a quiet enveloped us, replacing the chaos with a sense of calm and hope. I guess this meant we passed the test and were going to get onto a plane for the United States.

The next thing I knew, we were on the plane! Once I was buckled in and we were flying, all I could remember was the movie playing, and boy, was I excited! I had never seen a movie, ever in my life. It caught my attention, to say the least. It was a movie with Sinbad the Sailor. He was fighting skeletons and a six-armed, sword-wielding God. It was a little boy's dream come true! I fell asleep shortly afterwards, then woke up to us landing down at the San Fransico airport, in the United States of America. We still weren't home free, as we had to take another flight from San Francisco to Portland, Maine. I don't remember that flight. As far as I was concerned, being in America was all that mattered.

And thank you, Frank, for helping to get the expedition papers signed. He knew time was of the essence. If he hadn't done what was needed to make that happen, I'm quite sure my life would've been drastically different, and not for the better.

CHAPTER 2

THE UNITED STATES, EARLY YEARS

We lived in Wells, Maine, in a modest, cookie-cutter home in a working-class neighborhood. We lived right up the street from a zoo called York's Wild Kingdom, a popular tourist spot. When we passed by in our car, there were these suspended steps where you could see a goat peering out of a little fort. Some days, I would see a chimpanzee looking out from it.

My stepfather carpooled to work at the NAVY shipyard in Portsmouth, New Hampshire. He helped build nuclear submarines. Mom stayed home and took care of Hien, myself, and now also my younger brother, Frankie. I only have vague memories of our time in Wells as it was short lived, but events that occurred shortly after arriving forever shaped my future.

BUMBLEBEES AND MARBLES

My first spring and summer in Wells, Maine I became fascinated with bumblebees. I wasn't afraid of them in the least since nobody ever told me they stung you if you agitated them, which I didn't. I would pick them up and hold them in my hand. I somehow knew to pick them up gently where the wings fold in. Never a sting.

One day, I had this grand idea of collecting as many bumblebees as I could and shoving them into a tic tack container. I showed Henny (my sister's nickname) how I did this; how to pick them up and most importantly, how to gently place them into the Tic Tac container. It didn't translate.

She immediately got stung by the first bee she picked up. So ended her participation in that fun event. I just shrugged it off and continued to shove a couple more bees into my Tic Tac container while my sister ran into the house, crying and mad at me for making her do such a treacherous thing. If she had just followed my instructions, she would've been unscathed. Oh well.

Another activity I enjoyed was digging holes on the side of the road in the sand and filling them with a few marbles, then digging them back up the next day, convinced the sand had magical properties that would make them change colors once I dug them up. I was slightly obsessed with this notion, not even fantasizing that perhaps I was growing new marbles of different colors and patterns. Alas, a child's imagination at play!

MY FIRST WINTER

I woke up one morning and saw nothing but this land of white all around our house and neighborhood, covering everything, even our car. I couldn't see the grass, or the toys littered about the driveway, just this layer of white that looked fluffy and fun.

If you're familiar with "A Christmas Story" and Ralphie's little brother in the snowsuit, well, that was basically me on that first morning after the snowstorm.

I was dressed in layer upon layer of clothes, a snowsuit, boots, a scarf that was wrapped around me about 4-5 times, and a pair of oversized mittens that didn't keep the cold out. Once we were all prepared for the snow, the front door opened for us. I looked around in amazement and a little trepidation, trying to muster up the courage to go out into this new, unknown white wilderness world of snow.

I finally jumped from the front stairs and into the snow, not knowing that I'd sink about a foot, which completely caught me off-guard. I was stuck almost waist-high in snow, hardly able to move. I did not like this situation one bit. Plus, it was cold outside. Then I took off a mitten and touched this new white world – it was cold!! Why on Earth didn't anybody tell me that snow was going to be cold?! I was shocked and kind of pissed off at this prospect. I'm not sure what I was actually wanting from snow, but it certainly didn't include it being cold. Fluffy and fun? Great! Cold? Not cool. In a nutshell, I probably spent about five minutes out there, then enthusiastically trudged back inside. No offense to snow, but I did not like it, and I was mad that nobody told me it was cold. From that day on, snow was something I never even tried to like. If they could only make warm snow, then I would've been just fine with it.

MEMORIES OF MY MOM

There are very few memories I have of spending time with my mom. I hold them dearly in my heart. I was so young, but somehow, I knew those moments were precious.

My mom occasionally took me on evening walks around our neighborhood with her. We were still new to the area, and being the only Asians from Vietnam, I'm sure our neighbors were aware of us. As we were walking, my mom started chatting with a neighbor, in her broken English, and told him how proud she was of me, patting me on my head, telling him that I was such a good boy. I'll never forget that. It made me fill up with pride and I smiled proudly up at her. I knew at that moment that she loved me deeply and I felt what love from a mom should feel like, even if I couldn't articulate it at such a young age. It was a simple moment, but it was also a bonding moment.

The most important memory I have of spending time with my mom was when she decided to take me to Ogunquit Beach. Just the two of us. I was so excited. A *big* trip! Ogunquit Beach wasn't far, but for any kid, a car trip that lasts for fifteen minutes feels like an hour.

Once we arrived, we walked down to the beach, found a spot, and she placed a blanket down on the sand. Being that it was a weekday, there weren't many people there, so finding a spot was fairly easy. Somehow, a bucket of Kentucky Fried Chicken was magically in the picture to make our private time even more special. The day was serene. It was overcast, but that helped make it feel *more* serene. Just the sound of the waves gently crashing in and my mom and I, eating chicken on a blanket at the beach. It was simple, but it was the most important, and only, bonding moment I'd ever have like that with my mom. It also made Ogunquit Beach one of the most magical places in my life, at least in my mind, every time I thought of it. On that day, life couldn't have been better. Just me and my mom.

MY FIRST PUNISHMENT

My mother was strict. Once I had apparently done something that constituted a punishment of going into the corner of the living room couch, sitting on my knees from morning to evening with my head down, and not being allowed to look at anything going on around me. My sister was the appointed babysitter and had to make sure I followed the rules, which I did. Happily? Of course not. It was painful! And for the life of me to this day, I don't know what I did to merit that punishment. I chalk it up to some stupid kid stunt or maybe lying about something, then getting caught.

CUTTING MY EYELASHES AND A CLEAVER THROUGH THE DOOR

My sister was in charge of babysitting me one night, probably Frankie too, and she decided that it would be a great idea to cut my eyelashes. As her younger sibling, I yielded and let her cut them. Apparently, she was jealous of them. They were long and worthy of trimming. When my mom and stepdad returned from their date night, my mom looked at me closely for a moment, then noticed something was off. Once she figured out the situation, she became quite angry at my sister, and also at me.

She immediately brought me into the bathroom, pushing my head into the toilet and flushing it a few times while screaming at me, punishing *me* for the situation. Once she was finished with that, she tossed my head underneath the tub's faucet while running the water on high torque. She couldn't understand why I let my sister cut my eyelashes. She became angry beyond reproach and marched me out of the bathroom, grabbing my sister and slapping her over and over. Unbeknownst to us, our mother had a brain tumor the size of a peach in her brain, making her unable to manage her emotions. Her anger became uncontrollable.

She went into the kitchen, opened a drawer and grabbed a cleaver, screaming at the top of her lungs. Our stepdad, Frank, shoved us into their bedroom and told us not leave, no matter what we heard. He bravely went out to try to calm her down. My sister and I held each other, hoping it wouldn't get crazier, but it did. We heard a terrifying scream, then the cleaver she was wielding went through the bedroom door. Finally, silence. We waited in anticipation for a couple minutes, hoping that Frank didn't get stabbed. He didn't. From here I don't remember what happened. I just know that ultimately, nobody got hurt, at least physically.

TAKEN AWAY FROM MOM

Obviously, the previous night's events captured the attention of our neighbors and within days, the Department of Human Services came to investigate the situation. Once the adults talked, it was agreed that my sister and I were to be placed in a foster home. My stepfather was unable to care for now four children, in addition to a wife who was clearly behaving erratically. Due to a request from my mom, we were not to be separated, so whoever took us in had to agree to take the both of us.

We ended up going to a foster home in Harrison, Maine with Phyllis LaFontaine. She initially only wanted a boy, but agreed to fulfill the agreement made with my mom, the irony being that she ended up adopting my sister but not me.

This was the biggest turning moment of my life, at least on the conscious level. Even though my mom left me and my sister in Vietnam at about age three, I couldn't quite grasp the depth of that moment, but *this* moment shook the very ground beneath me. My heart and soul became untethered, flying without a pilot and with no sense of direction, utterly confused on so many levels. I couldn't understand why any of this was happening. Sure, my sister cut off my eyelashes, which led to my mother's unbridled rage, but as far as I was concerned, I just wanted to be with my mom. It's instinct. But to be *taken away* from my mom? Nobody had a good enough explanation. Like most kids, I thought I had done something wrong, and because of it, I was sent away.

This was explained to us once we were settled in with our new foster parent in Harrison. We soon learned that my mom had a brain tumor, which explained her erratic behavior, which at least quashed the feelings of it being my fault, but it didn't get us any nearer to going back to live with her.

This became a semi-yearly tease. I would ask, "When can I see my mom?" And all I would get were indefinite answers. My sister and I would walk home after school and we would talk for hours about our mom - when we could see her, would we live with her again, etc. It felt at once magical and futile, feelings I tried to balance as a kid, but futility pretty much won every time. We would go through scenarios; imagining being picked up by her and driving back to a place where she'd be back in our lives.

This went on for a couple years, until I stopped asking that question of my sister and Philly, since it always left me feeling lost, without settling the confusion that surrounded me. I felt like a ghost, living in purgatory, unable to live a life that made sense or felt grounded.

I didn't know how to explain how I felt at that age, but looking back, that is exactly how I felt – like an empty vessel forced to accept that questions I asked about my mom could never be answered. A sense of futility and suppressed rage were the unfortunate emotions that I clung to for years. But it also made me think about life on a deeper level than most kids my age. I don't know if I'm particularly grateful for that, but I'm sure it led to helping me write songs in the future.

CHAPTER 3
HARRISON, MAINE

EARLY YEARS IN HARRISON

We came to Harrison, Maine right before the school year began, so we had a little time to acclimate to our new surroundings. Looking back, it was a beautiful place to be raised. The house was a classic white farmhouse with a long breezeway that went to this huge unpainted barn, and an enormous maple tree towered in the front lawn with a tire swing. There were two cherry trees beside the barn, plus two apple trees and a pear tree in the back yard. The property ran down the street a way, fenced in with antique lumber. At the furthest end of the property stood the last surviving operational windmill in Harrison, although it wasn't actually being used, officially making it a historic landmark. It was a beautiful farm and home, dreamlike really, perfect to raise a couple kids. So apparently, this was where my sister and I were going to be living from now on, away from our mom. It didn't really sink in until the days and months went by with no sign of our mom around. Being kids, and living in such a nice place, we were easily distracted.

SPIDER AND STRING

On the first morning I woke up there, I was introduced to the horses - a sweet Palomino named Spring and her son, a beautiful brown horse named Strider. Because I couldn't quite get the pronunciation right, I called them 'Spider' and 'String'. I'm sure that pulled on the heart strings of those who heard me and made me extra adorable. I remember that morning vividly.

LEARNING TO SPEAK ENGLISH

While in Wells, my sister and I learned the English language fairly well, and fairly quickly, before we got to Harrison, Maine. Our mom tried to speak in English as much as she could, so our Vietnamese vocabulary diminished quickly. I can only remember speaking Vietnamese when I was in Saigon, never in America.

When we moved to Harrison, Maine, my sister and I watched a lot of Sesame Street, Zoom, and Electric Company. They taught us to annunciate and create more complex words and sentences. It might not have been the most ideal way to learn English, but we learned fast, and we learned some slang along the way.

When we moved in, Phyllis asked us to write down a bunch of words in Vietnamese that we remembered and could translate into English. We remembered about 30-40 words, which we wrote on a piece of lined paper, which was then put on the refrigerator. After that, our Vietnamese language quickly left us. Since we were no longer exposed to any Vietnamese-speaking people, and English became a necessity, Vietnamese became obsolete. I could've been saddened by that prospect, but I was busy trying to learn English.

MY FIRST DAY OF SCHOOL

I was starting my first day of kindergarten, but I didn't know where to go to meet the school bus or what time it was coming. I was new to all this school stuff and a little nervous about everything. I ended up missing the school bus but I didn't dare wake Phyllis up to tell her. Once she got up and realized the situation, she immediately drove me to school.

Harrison Elementary School was a classic red shingled, slanted roof building with five classrooms, kindergarten to third grade. The entrance had a tall set of stairs with double doors. The stairs *seemed* tall, at least to a five-year-old. I don't remember if I was nervous or not, I just knew I had to go to school.

Once Philly dropped me off, I went directly to the bathroom, which was immediately to the right and down a flight of stairs from the entrance. I only knew this because I ran into the janitor, Walter. He was the first person I met when I entered, and he was very kind. He had the classic janitor look – a burly guy with big plastic rectangular-framed glasses and that default faded janitor-green shirt and pants, wheeling around a mop and yellow mop bucket.

I walked down the stairs to the bathroom. As I'm about to enter, I look up the stairs and see this kid coming down the stairs to use the restroom as well. I thought he looked kinda strange. He was blonde with a Little Lord Fauntleroy haircut. So, I asked him directly, in the way most kids do, "Are you a boy or a girl?" Yup, that was my very first sentence to the very first kid I met in Harrison. I honestly didn't know! He replied, "I'm a boy." Well, I still had my doubts, so I said to him, "Then prove it." So being a kid, with little inhibition, he pulled his pants down and immediately proved he was a boy. What would've been an uncomfortable scene for any adult was just a natural event for two five-year-olds. It was just a question, and nothing more. And my question was answered! And since I asked him that question, he asked me the same thing. I told him I was a boy, pulled my pants down and proved it, put my pants back on and that was that! From that day on, we became best friends for many years! What a hoot! In hindsight it might embarrass us, but in that moment, we were just innocent kids.

THE FIRE ALARM AND WALTER THE JANITOR

Right after meeting my "new best friend" I walked out of the restroom and my attention shifted to a white handle that read *PULL*. It was the fire alarm. As I had just met Walter, the janitor of the school, right before I saw that alluring lever at the bottom of the boys' room, I asked him what it was. He told me that it was a fire alarm, and not to touch it. I believe he was quietly adamant in how he told me; not being aggressive but being very assertive as to the importance of not pulling it unless the building was on fire.

Well, his words obviously didn't convince me. Too late. With him midsentence, I pulled the fire alarm. Oh, that poor janitor's face. He couldn't scold me but he certainly wanted to. The ringing that came out at the school was very loud. I walked up the stairs to the hallway and saw all these kids going outside, wondering what was going on. I soon realized it was because I pulled that lever. Let's just say I never again pulled another fire lever. I'm quite certain Walter made it clear I was never to touch that lever again unless the school was on fire. Duly noted!

MY FIRST CHRISTMAS

I remember decorating the first Christmas tree my sister and I ever saw. It was quite magical. We'd never seen anything quite like it. All these amazing ornaments, and then this silver tinsel we'd just toss onto the tree to make it sparkle even more. And all the presents! All these huge boxes wrapped in colorful paper, waiting to be ripped open. I'm sure we had a tree when we lived with our mom, I just don't remember it that well, if at all, so I consider Harrison, Maine as my first true Christmas tree experience. We also didn't know the tradition of it all: the stockings, the leaving out cookies and milk, and going to bed early to be woken at the crack of dawn for the opening of presents. It was all so exciting.

When Phyllis woke us in the morning, we flew down the stairs to the living room, and saw even more presents! First, we opened our stockings, which were filled with so many amazing things – mostly candy, of course. Then we went to the Christmas tree and started passing around the presents. I'll always remember what I got: a GI Joe doll, a Six-Million Dollar Man doll, and this open jet with seats that the both of them could sit down on. I pulled the string on GI Joe's back to make him talk and was blown away. Then I proceeded to take out Steve Austin's bionic eye, which blew me away even more.

The best part? My sister got The Bionic Woman, so we got to play with the both of them for what seemed like hours, but was most likely fifteen minutes. It was the best Christmas I've ever had to this day.

What I didn't know, and Phyllis only recently told us, was that many of those presents were donated by Philly's friends and residents of Harrison. They knew we had escaped the Vietnam War and felt for us. I wish I had known this before – I would've reached out to each one of them and personally thanked them.

HOUSE RAISING-PARTY AND MY FIRST KISS

Phyllis had bought an old cape-style house in Lewiston, Maine, that was built in 1803. It was going to be torn down but the frame itself was in excellent shape, so she decided to keep the frame intact, label each section, then have it shipped to Harrison and rebuild the house around the original frame. A basement and foundation had already been poured on her new property, which was directly across the street from the farmhouse where we were currently living. Once the foundation dried and settled, it was ready for the frame, so Phyllis decided to have a huge celebration, country-style, invite her friends and literally the entire town, and have a party!

On the morning of the party, I was woken up and told to get dressed as it was going to be a very busy day. I was instantly excited. This was when I first met Maureen, who was very close with Phyllis and would come visit her when she was in town, which she was on this day. She was a green-eyed, happy-go-lucky, stout Irish woman who was always ready for a laugh. She helped me to get ready for the big to-do. Once I was dressed, I came flying down the stairs, went outside, and saw all this activity happening. There were people setting up a barbeque station at the end of the property, cars coming in, parking up and down Maple Ridge Road, and carpenters hammering away across the street where the new house was about to be raised. It was a house-raising party!

As the day got going, musicians started setting up beside the barbeque station underneath a huge maple tree on the property's corner. This is where all the action was! By the afternoon, hundreds of people were mingling about, music was being played in high gear, and the burgers, ribs, and hot dogs were being grilled aplenty. In traditional house-raising form, a small pine tree was placed at the top of the roof's arch while a crane lifted it, and the carpenters ceremoniously nailed the arch in place. Afterward, a huge collective wave of celebratory whoops and whistles and clapping ensued. Then the bluegrass music began! I think I spent most of the day running around with my friend, Danny Gray, son of the main carpenter, John Gray. Much of it was a blissful blur.

As the afternoon turned to dusk, I saw a girl who I thought was really cute and asked Danny what her name was. He told me her name was Stephanie. Then I told Danny that I was going to kiss her. He didn't believe me and laughed. We ran around a bit more.

A little later, I saw her again as we almost ran past her but I stopped and knew this was the moment to lay a big smacker on her. So, I ran right up to her, got on my tippy toes (she was much taller than me) and gave her a big ol' kiss, right on the lips!

Her eyes got all wide, she was surprised to say the least, but also smiled, which made me smile, then I ran off giggling with Danny, all proud of myself and full of confidence as she walked away in slight disbelief, but still smiling herself. It was the perfect way to end what was the most perfect day ever.

SEEING TWO TINKERBELLS

The Wonderful World of Walt Disney was just about to come on the TV. I was very excited about this. I was probably almost seven years old. I remember seeing Philly drink this fun-looking drink in a tin can and I asked her what it was. She told me it was a beer and that it wasn't for children. Of course, this made me want to try it even more. I begged and pleaded with her to please, please, let me have one.

After about ten minutes of my foolishness, she relented and grabbed one from the fridge. She cracked it open and handed me the drink. I instantly gulped down a few big swills, then a couple more a few minutes later. It was kind of bitter, not something I liked too much, even though I liked that it was fizzy. When Walt Disney came on, I was looking at Tinkerbell flying around the screen, but then I noticed there were two Tinkerbells! I didn't know which one to focus on. Then I looked around and saw other things in double vision. I started feeling pretty relaxed and put my head down on a couple pillows, watching the two Tinkerbells and other things until I yawned and conked out. I had barely drunk a third of that beer but boy, it sure put me to sleep. Pretty sure it was Schlitz, based on the fancy lettering.

The next thing I knew, it was morning. I never asked for another drink of beer. It wasn't that tasty and after that experience, I knew it would make me see double and put me to sleep. I'm quite sure that was Philly's way of teaching me about the downside of alcohol. Not the best approach, but it worked!

PLAYING DRESS UP, DOCTOR AND PATIENT

My sister and I had some neighborhood friends, the Searles, about a mile up the street on Maple Ridge Road and we'd play together during the spring and summertime.

In the winters, we'd play inside the house. My sister and her girlfriends would recruit me to be their dress up doll, if you will. I knew what this entailed to some extent, but as they kept bringing out *more* dresses and *more* makeup to put on me, I knew I was in for a long haul and would have to endure however long it took. I liked hanging out with girls because I thought they were cute, even at such a young age, so I was willing to put up with certain things, including being dressed up as a doll. Funnier still, once they were finished dolling me up, they'd just leave me like that and run away to do whatever the hell else young girls do who like to dress up boys as dolls.

Come summertime, we started playing patient and nurse out on the lawn. I even "went steady" with our neighbor, Carol, for a few days, then we "broke up" - all innocent! What was really fun was playing doctor and patient with our friends. The patient would be on the grass, feigning illness. I had one of those Fisher Price doctor's kits with the foam stethoscope, which kind of worked. I began by placing it on her upper chest, close to her throat, asking her, "does it hurt here?" and she'd say "No." I'd move it down a little more than say, "how about here?" followed by another "No" and this would proceed to go on a couple more times.

I gotta be honest, I already liked the ladies at a young age. Somehow, this ended with me kissing her in some way, then she'd magically feel better and get up! Miraculous! That stethoscope must've possessed some healing powers, or I was a very good, young doctor. Ahhh, the wonderful, innocent world of child's play.

MY FIRST TIME ON STAGE

I was about six years old, seven tops. Phyllis had a folk singing friend visiting us for a few days named Ginni Clemmens, a legendary blues and folk singer who worked with troubled kids in Chicago. I absolutely adored her. She was so down-to-earth and just had this natural way about her. And boy, she could play the banjo.

Once, while she was staying with us for a few days, my sister and I were told to put on our jackets because we were going out that night. It was way past our bedtime, 9pm (ha!) and so of course we were excited! My sister was five years older than me, eleven years old, so she was a little more excited. We weren't being told where we were going because it was a surprise. More excitement. It must've been a Friday or Saturday night because I don't remember going to school the next day.

Anyways, we get to the end of Route 35 where it meets the 302 in Sebago, and there's this bar on the North East corner. We park and go inside. My sister and I just think we're there to eat some food and drink some cokes. That's more than enough excitement for us! Just as we think we're going to leave, Philly and Ginni tell us that Ginni's going to play some music. The place starts filling up - it wasn't that big; it could hold an intimate crowd of about a hundred people.

How I remember that, I haven't got a clue. Anyways, towards the end of Ginni's first set, she asks my sister and I if we'd like to get up on stage to sing some songs with her, since we already knew her songs. (Note: this was the late 70's and kids could stay in bars after 9pm; more relaxed back then.) I kind of froze at first, but quickly ran up alongside my sister onto that stage once I heard my name. I was so nervous but excited at the same time. Looking at all these people, who I'm quite certain thought we were as cute as can be, and knowing that I had their full attention, gave me an ultimate rush.

The different colored lights, the mood of the people, Ginni cracking jokes because we weren't totally disciplined and ready to sing, until we were. Then she started singing a few tunes, and we sang along with her.

She made us feel so comfortable and made it fun. I remember requesting a refill of Coca-Cola on the stage, which drew fits of laughter from the audience. I really liked that. Then we sang another song. We got to sing my favorite song of hers, which was "Sneaky Snake" which I still remember to this day. She got the whole damn room to sing along with her.

We probably only sang about four tunes tops with her, but I'll tell you, it felt like an hour up there - in the best way possible. We finished our last song and the entire room just clapped and whistled at us.

A standing ovation! It was the greatest feeling I'd ever felt up to that point. Then we all walked off the stage, and on our way back to our table, we received compliment after compliment. I was all smiles, still sipping on my Coca-Cola.

I truly believe that moment rearranged my DNA and subliminally made me become a performing musician before I had any idea what that meant. And I'll always remember Ginni Clemmens as my very first musical idol whom I still cherish. She was very special. And if it wasn't for my foster mom, Phyllis, who was deep in the Chicago folk scene of the 60's and 70's and very open-minded, I would've never had that experience. That moment in time, I'm pretty convinced, began my musical career.

CRYSTAL LAKE AND THE MIDDLE FINGER

I was still a little kid; pretty sure it was the summer after first grade. Crystal Lake (once named Anonymous Lake!) was where all the action was during the summertime in Harrison, Maine. It's kept many people happy for many decades. This was also where Harrison's little league baseball field and basketball court were located, along with a modest-sized, dirt and rock parking lot. I can still hear the sound of the tires rolling over all the small, rounded rocks in the lot. It brings back so many fond memories.

Harrison had organized activities for the kids: baseball, street hockey, basketball, swimming lessons, etc., which I took, along with many other kids of all ages from Harrison and the surrounding towns. Mind you, water and lakes frightened me as a kid. Specifically deep, dark water. I was skinny as all hell and could barely float, but I listened dutifully to the swimming instructor and I got better over time. We started with the back float, which was petrifying at first. But I breathed through it, stopped getting water up my nose, and learned to float just enough to keep my face above water. Then I learned to doggy paddle. That wasn't too bad. I learned other swimming styles but quickly lost interest in anything more than just floating on my back.

Cutting to the chase. It was sometime in July, a perfect summer day, I had a babysitter taking care of me who agreed to bring me to my swimming lessons. She lived down the street on Scribner Mills Road. She was this pretty little blonde woman who reminded me of Clint Eastwood's wife, Sondra Locke, and my sister was friends with her daughter. So, we all arrived at Crystal Lake, I did my swimming lessons thing, then got out of the water and hung out on the little beach. In the brief time I was hanging out, I had learned the phrase "Fuck You!" along with pointing my middle finger up forcefully while saying those two words. I had immediately become enamored by this powerful phrase.

I was so awestruck by its power that I went up and down the beach, excitedly walking up to everyone I saw, putting my left arm out, with middle finger proudly extended, saying, "Fuck You!" to them. Every 'Fuck You' felt better than the one before, so I kept on going, not knowing what it meant at all, just feeling how fun it felt to say to everybody I could possibly say it to.

This obviously horrified my babysitter, not to mention completely embarrassed her. I had totally forgotten that she was even around by the seventh or eighth person (or group of people) who had gotten my 'Fuck You' salute. She quickly scuttled me away, leaving me confused and wondering what was wrong. I was having fun!

Obviously, what I was doing wasn't proper behavior. She grabbed our belongings, hurried us into her car and quickly drove me back to my home, where she told Philly what I had done.

After the babysitter left, Philly walked towards me and explained why the sitter had so suddenly taken me home. She could hardly contain herself while trying to explain to me that what I had done was something I should never do again. The words that I had used are bad words, and words children should never use. Pointing the middle finger to people was also something that I should never do. She was trying to make her point with a straight face, but I could hardly call it a reprimand because there was a smirk behind her every sentence.

Despite my doubts that she was upset at me, I understood afterwards that I couldn't do that ever again, and that she had to punish me by not letting me go to the beach for a week. Maybe two. I actually understood that as a fair punishment. To this day, I've never lackadaisically pointed my middle finger to strangers and said 'Fuck You!' simultaneously. Although I've done each separately, and countless times.

STORIES FROM SECOND GRADE

I don't remember much of kindergarten or first grade, save for meeting my new best friend, the janitor, pulling the fire alarm, and watching the entire school file out onto the front yard. I only have a few memories of Harrison Elementary School during 2nd grade. My teacher was Miss Smart. She had short, curly dark hair, large black-framed glasses, and wore plaid and checkered skirts. She was very kind and had a soft spot for me, something I would discover later. She would let us bring records that we could play on her turntable once a week. I would bring in my Walt Disney record with Davey Crockett and the Bear Necessities song from the Jungle Book. She would also play the Peter and the Wolf album, which I wasn't too keen on. I thought it was a little spooky - because it was.

Most of my second-grade memories were of me either swinging on the swings as high as I could, then jumping as far as I could, and making mud dams with my rubber boots when it was raining. By this time, I had also joined Cub Scouts. One day, I was chasing the girls (already!) in the patch of woods across from the school. I slipped and fell, nearly muddying up my entire Cub Scout uniform. I didn't care. I simply brushed off as much mud as I could and resumed chasing them. Where this went, I have no idea. I just liked chasing girls and they apparently liked being chased; otherwise, I wouldn't have chased them. A win-win situation.

There were also many mornings at this age that I spent playing my plastic recorder along to The Jungle Book and Lady and the Tramp songs, my favorites being "I Wanna Be Like You", "The Bear Necessities", and "The Siamese Cat Song." I'd close the door to the other part of the house and just blow the shit out of that recorder, thinking I was hitting every note perfectly, all proud of myself. I'm pretty confident now that I sounded terrible and made ears bleed, but little kids hardly notice those details.

SLIDING INTO THE CEMETARY AND GETTING DETENTION

During the wintertime, across the street from the school, there was this perfect little hill which we'd all slide down with our plastic slides.

At the bottom of this little hill, there was this hole at the bottom of the property fence that separated the school from a cemetery. It was just the right size to let a little 2nd grader and his plastic slide through if he slid downhill just right. My friend Adam and I would challenge each other to see how far we could glide under and past the hole. This was a forbidden thing to do, being that it was a cemetery and all. The teachers would give us soft warnings but they didn't stick.

Until we met Miss McGillicuddy (her nickname) – the third-grade teacher who warned us that if we ever went under that fence again with our slides, we'd get detention for a week. Miss McGillicuddy was a former Army sergeant, tall and square-shaped, and very intimidating. She spoke like a man and enforced the rules. I'm quite sure she enjoyed being forceful and tough. She didn't have time for any elementary school kids' nonsense. But she could seldom expose a lighter side and joke around, then go right back to sergeant mode. To make the image complete, she always wore this Army Green overcoat, which I'm positive was the same one she'd had while in the service. I'm sure it kept her connected to those roots.

So, Miss McGillicuddy had told us to not ever go past the school property again and into the cemetery, lest we get a week's detention. We nodded our heads in agreement, and said, "Yes, Miss McGillicuddy." Minutes later, we'd be back up on that hill, sliding down through that hole into the cemetery. When I poked my head back into the school's side of that hole, I looked up and saw the hulking, disapproving figure of Miss McGillicuddy, and knew I was basically fucked. She was obviously upset, gave us a tongue-lashing and brought us back into the school. She talked to my second-grade teacher Miss Smart, who begrudgingly gave me a note to give to Philly stating that I needed to serve a week's detention due to my disobedient behavior against Miss Mcgillicuddy's orders.

Miss Smart was sympathetic toward me. I could kind of tell, but she clearly didn't think that what I did warranted a week of detention – no recess, twice a day. She tried to make it as nice as she could. She didn't make me put my head down, as Miss McGillicuddy would've made me do. Miss Smart actually broke down on Friday and let me out for afternoon recess. She just didn't have the heart to punish me any further. I'll always remember Miss Smart.

KICKING KEVIN POWELL IN THE NADS

Winter was passing, the earth was thawing, and the ice was melting. It wasn't quite spring, but the snow was no longer pervasive, and the mud hadn't taken over everything that wasn't a tarred road. It was morning recess time and I was playing with my friend, Kevin Powell. He was almost albino but without the albino eyes. He had white-blonde hair, was a little taller than the other kids, and was basically an obnoxious idiot.

Tough "Miss McGillicuddy" could barely tolerate him. As we were playing, something happened that made us argue. He got me so riled up that I threatened to kick him in the nuts. He had this phrase that he'd say, already mastered at such an early age, that enraged me that involved getting right into your face and saying, "Yah - Uh huh... Suuuuure" while leaning closer into you, and you were forced to watch his stupid lips accentuating the word *suuuure*.

I warned him that if he said that phrase again, I'd kick him so hard in the nuts that I'd make him cry. He laughed at me and said the exact same phrase, even closer to my face. By this time, I was so ready to kick his piece-of-shit nuts to the fucking moon because he was such an obnoxious asshole. He continued to challenge me, "Yah - Uh huh, I dare 'ya. Suuuuure... uh huh, I dare Ya'" and had me seething inside.

I walked backwards about 10 paces, like an angry ram sizing down my nemesis, making sure I had enough distance to do maximum testicular damage, then I ran full throttle towards him while he's still saying, "Yah, uh huh, Suuure."

When I got to him, I brought my right foot up as hard as I could, and after a second of shocked silence I watched his stupid face turn red as hell as he dropped to his knees, screaming in pain while holding his injured groin. I smiled with complete satisfaction, kind of surprised that I followed through with my threat, giggling to myself, and then said, "See? I told you I'd kick you in the nuts. Fuckin' asshole." I just walked away and went to the swings, laughing at him as I went. He tried to get Miss Mcgillicuddy's attention so she would punish me, which scared me for a few seconds, but she seemed completely uninterested in what he was telling her, so I went back to smiling. There weren't any other teachers around to whom he could plead his case, so he just stayed there, keeled over again in pain.

I had never felt so satisfied in my life. Of course, the next day, we were friends and laughing about it. Well, I laughed and he gave me shit, and life went on. Kids will be kids.

FOUR-EYED CHINA BOY AND DAMIEN

Every weekday morning, I would take the bus to school. I'd get picked up at the corner of Maple Ridge and Carson, then we'd take a right on Edes Falls Road about a mile away. That's where Damien lived. For the sake of this story, that's the name I'm going with, which seems much more fitting than his real name. I'd like to say he was just another kid that got picked up for the bus, along with all the other kids, but he really did not seem to like me. I'll forever remember his face because he looked like a Satanic version of the kid from "A Christmas Story." He had these wolf-like blue eyes that pierced right through me, striking fear.

I had just started wearing glasses, which I wasn't too thrilled about, and they always slipped down my nose and fogged up whenever I came in from the outside. I hated how they made me look – a foreign Asian kid with glasses made me stand out even more than I already did. Not fun.

At first, I didn't think twice of Damien. He was just another kid being picked up on the bus. But one day, he decided to express how he *really* felt about me. Damien got settled into his seat a couple rows behind me, something stirred him up, and he started picking on me. He began by making fun of my glasses, looking around at his friends with his piece-of-shit smirk to see if he would get accolades. Then he just came up to my face and started saying, "You're nothing but a slanty-eyed China boy" and smirked that evil smirk of his, looking like Satan's child. He continued from there, spouting "four-eyed Gook" and "chink" or "China boy" and then just the word "Gook" came out of his mouth. He snickered and looked back at his quasi-posse, waiting for affirmation and possibly applause. As he kept it up and I kept I telling him to stop, he became more enticed to lean even closer into me and become more animated, constantly checking to see if others were laughing with him. I don't think they were. They seemed confused as to how to react.

Damien made me acutely aware that I was quite different from everyone else in our school that day, and he wasn't going to stop until he was sure I understood. No matter how many times I asked his satanic face to stop, he just kept going. I was instantly ashamed to be Asian because of this smarmy fucking devil-child. And so began the self-consciousness of looking different. This is where it gets interesting.

This piece-of-shit kid keeps on yappin' racist bullshit to my face, unaware that the bus driver, Mr. Bigelow, has been looking at his rear-view mirror all this time. After what felt like minutes of my pleading for Damien to stop, Mr. Bigelow decided enough was enough.

I'll never forget the look he had before he abruptly stopped the bus and unbuckled his seat belt, and angrily walked back to where we were to take care of business. His face was red and fuming, and as anybody knows, when your bus driver abruptly stops their bus out of nowhere, some potentially serious shit just went down.

Mr. Bigelow is now bent down staring right into the eyes of the Satan-child Damien, and with a very large voice, with an angry finger pointed, he says, "I don't **EVER** want to hear you say those things **EVER AGAIN** to him, do you hear me?! If I ever hear you say those things again, by God, I will stop this bus and kick you out! Do you understand me?!" This obviously confused Damien and put a little scare into his piece-of-shit heart, forcing him to nod obediently. Mr. Bigelow looked at me and, without words, let me know that he was never going to allow anything like that to happen on his bus ever again.

From that point on, we developed a clear understanding. And I developed an instant respect for Mr. Bigelow. He took a deep breath, turned around, walked back to his seat and proceeded to drive us to Harrison Elementary School. The Satan's child, Damien Webster, kept quiet for the remainder of the bus ride.

Mind you, I'm paraphrasing, but it's awfully damn close, because it's a memory that's seared into my brain forever. Even though I felt the pain of looking different, and I held that insecurity with me for a long time, at least in that moment I felt like Mr. Bigelow was some kind of moral soldier who came to my aid so I didn't need to feel bad for being different. Because he felt the pain, too.

It's also safe to say that I never became friends with Damien, nor did I ever wonder what happened to him. After that incident, I didn't see nor hear much about him at all, which was just fine with me, thanks to Mr. Bigelow, who'll always hold a special place in my heart.

HU KE LAO CHINESE RESTAURANT AND MEETING SONNY NG

It was around 1979-80. A funny commercial aired on TV with a Chinese man who called himself Sonny Ng (pronounced "ing"). He sat atop an elephant in front of his restaurant, the Hu Ke Lao, while shouting at the top of his lungs for everyone to come eat at his restaurant, the Hu Ke Lau. Then the elephant raises his trunk, blasts a loud note while lifting and suspending its two front feet…and scene!

You bet your ass I wanted to eat there! He even showed the wishing well in the commercial, with its huge Koi fish in the man-made stream while a woman flicks a penny into the wishing well, smiling afterwards. This was something no other Chinese restaurant in Maine could offer. He also promoted the "Pu Pu Platter", which was huge and had every possible Chinese appetizer that you could imagine on it. The close-up sizzling visuals not only made your mouth salivate, but the name inextricably made every boy giggle and want to order it.

The Hu Ke Lau restaurant was right beside the Maine Mall, located in South Portland, a new and major shopping center that created a culture shift for the shoppers' experience. Chinese chef, "Sonny", or Chan Sun Ng, saw the writing on the wall and capitalized on this new phenomenon. Unbeknownst to me, refugees from the Vietnam war who had moved to Maine, with help from the 1965 Immigration Act, expanded the Asian culture in the state, which in its day was considered the "whitest state in America", and helped the small Chinese community build an identity.

One Friday night, my sister and I were surprised to learn that we were going to eat at the Hu Ke Lau! I was beyond excited. When we arrived, we immediately ran to the wishing well that we had seen in the commercial, then dropped a penny in along with our wishes.

Then we walked into the restaurant with Phillis and Maureen, were seated, handed menus, and the waiter asked us what we wanted, naturally. I couldn't get the words out "Pu Pu Platter" fast enough. The waiter smiled cordially at me, got the rest of the orders and walked into the kitchen.

Minutes later, the waiter comes back with the Pu Pu Platter in tow, piping hot and smelling so delicious. I was overwhelmed with excitement. I couldn't believe that what I saw on the television was right before my eyes. I didn't gobble it do wn like a caveman, I just happily ate from it, picking out each piece and as I went along.

The waiter came back a little while later to ask us how everything was. We replied that everything was great. We kept chatting with him and eventually, we started talking about Sonny, and how much I wanted to meet him. Since my name was Son, the owner's name was Sonny, and I was an Asian boy, a rare sighting in these parts, the waiter quickly made the connection.

He walked back into the kitchen, and seconds later, somebody different bursts out of the kitchen door and heads right over to our table. It was Sonny! He had a huge smile and went right over to me and asked me what my name was. I told him, "My name is Son". His eyes lit up. He told me his name was Sonny! I don't know who was more excited to meet who. He bent down and enthusiastically asked me if I wanted to see the kitchen. Of course, I said "Yes!"

He then took me by the hand, walked me to the kitchen doors, then hoisted me up onto his shoulders and walked through the kitchen doors.

At this point, I was so starstruck, I would've followed him to China! We walked around the kitchen with me still on his shoulders as he introduced me to the kitchen staff. He finally put me down onto one of many stainless-steel tables while the cooks came over and surrounded me, smiling at how damn cute I must've been. Sonny kept talking to me and asking questions, which I asked, with the occasional group laugh. I must've said some funny kid stuff.

All I knew was that I was completely over the moon, blown away that I was getting a kitchen tour by the most famous Asian in Maine. I was being treated like a rock star by a rock star, Sonny Ng, himself! He was so happy just to see an Asian kid in his restaurant. Son and Sonny, a moment I'll never forget.

I wish the Hu Ke Lau could have survived longer, but alas, changes occur. Sonny and his restaurant were an icon up into the late 80's, and I got to experience the most rock star moment with the most famous Asian in Maine. Chan Sun "Sonny" Ng beat the odds as an Asian in Maine during that era. He relied on his instincts, imagination, skills as a chef, and his ability to adapt to a changing landscape, even if it meant waking up with doubt whispering in his ear every day. He persevered through the challenges and took them head-on, with wit on his side, and succeeded.

MISS McGILLICUDDY OR MRS KISH FOR 3RD GRADE?

At the end of second grade, there was a decision to be made about whether students would be in Miss Mcgillicuddy's 3rd grade class, or Mrs. Kish's 3rd grade class. What I'll always remember about Miss Smart is that she made sure I got into Mrs. Kish's third grade class. She knew I wouldn't have thrived under Mrs. Mcgillicuddy's sergeant-like rules. For that, I will always be grateful for her, because Mrs. Kish proved to be everything I had hoped for in a new teacher. She was kind, soft-hearted, and had a lightness to her that I remember to this day. She also had this Dorothy Hamill hairstyle that I'll never forget.

RUTH DIEHL AND PIANO LESSONS

I began taking piano lessons at age 7 with an eccentric former opera singer and pianist by the name of Ruth Diehl. She absolutely loved the color yellow. Her house was painted light yellow, she owned a yellow 1977 Ford Mustang II Ghia (which coincidentally is what Kevin Powell's grandfather owned - but not yellow) *and* most everything in her house was yellow. She wore nothing but bright yellow muumuus and she'd slather equally bright red lipstick well past her lip lines, mostly due to her arthritis. You had to enter her home from the garage then walk up a flight of stairs, which led to her yellow kitchen, which revealed her affection for yellow in detail – her fridge, toaster, oven, kitchen table, counters, curtains, you name it – all yellow. Then you would walk into the living room/piano lesson room, which continued the theme with yellow shag carpeting, long yellow drapes on each window, a 3-piece yellow furniture set, and against the wall on the right side of the room: the yellow piano. She had a very sweet vibe, as if she came from another time and place. She had certainly traveled and seen much of the world as a younger woman, singing and performing opera pieces at a high level, finally settling down once she reached her 60's. By the time she was teaching me piano, she was in her early 70's. I liked looking into her eyes because they always seemed to sparkle and have a little surprise in them. She had a true artist's spirit. Arthritis had gotten the best of her once beautiful hands and long fingers, transforming them into slightly twisted knots. Somehow, though, once she sat at the piano, she could play that thing quite effortlessly. At least as a seven-year-old, I was quite impressed.

She taught me proper classical technique and was a stickler about it. In hindsight, I'm very glad she taught me the correct way, which meant the most efficient way, to get around the keyboard. I began with the basics, "Hot Cross Buns" and then on to tackling all the scales: major, minor, augmented, diminished.

I also learned some classical pieces, but not many. It was mostly scales and learning to read in all keys. It was a lot of work and frankly I hated practicing, mostly because our piano was in the basement, where it was almost always dank and cold, and I always felt like somebody was staring at me as I played. The incentive to practice was lacking, to say the least. But I did an hour each day, grinning and bearing it through the obstacles.

I would also do some minor chores for Ruth since she was old and arthritic, like bringing up firewood from the garage. Once I reached ten years old, I started mowing her lawn and raking leaves. She paid very little, which led to an argument between Phyllis and her, which led to my no longer doing chores. I felt bad about the argument because I knew she didn't mean to be cheap; she just came from a different generation and wasn't aware of what things cost in the current world. By the time I reached age thirteen, the summer of sixth grade, I decided to end piano lessons. I was very thankful to end them, because I was beginning to explore other interests like baseball and soccer, but moreso because I didn't want to practice.

WHEN CAN WE SEE OUR MOM?

Right around this time, I began to wonder more and more about my mom. Pretty much every day. My sister and I were always talking about when we could live with her again. We mostly discussed it on our walks back home from school after getting dropped off by the bus. My sister was really supportive about it all. She was my protector, the one person I had left who made me feel safe while all my questions were whirring about, unanswered. She was my anchor. Our bond was the most important thing to me. We were inseparable. She made sure I knew that she was always going to protect me. I'm sure that also helped her spirit in getting through her own unanswered questions. I hope that I also helped her during those times. I think I did.

We only saw our mom twice a year. Christmas, and for a few days in the summertime. When we asked Philly about her, or somebody from the DHS (Department of Human Services) we'd get polite, washed-down adult replies, telling us we'd see her soon and that everything was fine. This might've given us hope for a couple years, but each year would come and go with no answers and no guarantee that we'd be going back home to live with her. This, of course, created despondency.

My sister did her best to make me feel better, but we both knew the truth - we were never going back to live with our mom again.

The DHS and Phyllis were holding back and we knew it, we just couldn't nail down what the problem was.

The empty feelings of being without my mom made me feel so confused. I thought maybe it was because of me. Did I do something wrong? I just didn't know. That's just how kids think - they bring it back to themselves as the problem. Eventually, this empty feeling became less painful as the days passed by, and the reality of never living with her became numbing. I didn't know it at the time, but I was resentful and angry. I closed myself off from accepting Phyllis as a loving figure, let alone a mother figure, which I'm sure crushed her. I was stiff as a board when she would hug me. I just didn't know how to respond. She wasn't my mom. I *wanted* to feel like she was my mom, but I didn't know *how* to feel about her, if that makes any sense. I walked around questioning life at an age when I should've just been a kid. But those weren't the cards I was dealt. I searched deep for answers that never came. All I was left with was the familiar feeling of emptiness and abandonment, even though my mom promised on the phone that we'd be back together again. It was never going to happen. Of course, I didn't know that at the time, I was still living on hope.

It was during this time that I began lying to Phyllis more often, even over stupid little things that I didn't need to lie about. I never knew why I did that as a kid, but looking back, I realized that I was a little afraid of her because I saw her hit my sister quite a few times in the first couple years of us living with her.

My sister got wise to this and figured out what to do in order to avoid getting hit, but I didn't, so the baton of physical and verbal abuse got passed onto me. Thus began a pattern of distrust. She became increasingly frustrated with me because I lied about needless things. I felt like I had no control over my surroundings, and whatever I said, be it the truth or a lie, resulted in the same outcome - being punished physically or emotionally. What was the point in telling the truth when the chances of getting out of a jam by telling a lie was slightly better? That was a survival skill I developed, if you will, and not the best thing to have cultivated in order to avoid abuse.

Phyllis was obviously quite upset at this behavioral pattern. Regardless of the methods she attempted to stop my lying, nothing worked. It was already too late. The thing is, once a kid gets hit, the first time a kid gets hit, you cannot still expect them to stay in line and say whatever you want to hear. The bond of trust has been broken and is very difficult to rebuild. I was already a broken kid, so she faced a near impossible task. Phyllis was never going to fully regain my trust. Once you know that somebody who's supposed to take care of you will hit you, you know they'll most likely hit you again, so you live in a world of fearful anticipation, waiting for that next blow to come. You watch what you say, how you act around them, trying not to upset them. You start flinching around them when they get closer, thinking they're going to strike you. You become grateful for every day they're in a good mood, because your chances are higher of not being hit. You wake up and walk on eggshells for most of the day when you're around them, hoping you're doing and saying all the right things to make sure that day goes by without repercussions.

At a very young age, I had resolved in my mind that Phyllis didn't deserve the truth from me, much less my trust, since I was just going to get beaten up or slapped around, and told that I was a useless piece of shit and would grow up to be worth nothing.

Harboring hostility towards her was an understatement. I was not only afraid of her, but also carried an inner rage that stuck in my gut like glue for many years, dreaming of ways to either exact my revenge or even kill her. I know that sounds extreme, but I went there as a kid, knowing that killing her in my mind in many imaginative ways was *much* better than being sent away for *actually* killing her. I wasn't a psychopath; I was just angry, vengeful, feeling trapped and helpless, without anybody to turn to ask for help. She of course wrapped it all in a perfect little bow by saying, "If you ever tell anybody that I hit you, I'll beat you up so bad that you won't be able to walk again" or something very close to that. It worked. I never told a soul, even when there was suspicion that I was being abused and I had a possible out. I was also afraid to reveal the abuse because I didn't want to be separated from my sister. She was the only form of strength that I could rely on. If I had lost that bond, I would've collapsed emotionally.

The biggest irony of it all was that Phyllis just wanted me to love her. She didn't know that she could've had that love, but because she wielded so much anger and created an environment of fear, I was too afraid to trust her, which in turn diminished the chance of my loving her. I knew there was goodness and kindness inside of her, but she was too unpredictable and angry. She ruined any hope of having the son she'd always wanted by trying to beat the truth out of me. The beatings and verbal insults only made me go further inside myself in order to escape her anger. With each new beating or slapping around, I vowed to push her out of my heart as each day passed, even though I was still living with her. The hostility and resentment ran deep, and I buried it very well, but not without the vengeance of giving her *nothing* good of myself. Most days, I gave her cold, blank, emotionless stares. I'd walk around like a petrified stick, unbending when she hugged me. It was the only thing I could do to exert control and that I knew would hurt her. Unfortunately, it maintained an endless circle of abuse for many years.

Granted, there were good days, even good weeks, but sure enough, the anger would reappear, or I'd do something that pissed her off and get hit for stupid shit. Then I'd wonder what I did. Did I lie this time? No. If not, what was it? It was an impossible environment to live in. I was fucked. If only I had known that the abuse wasn't singularly created by my actions, but moreso by her lack of control of *her* actions.

OUR LAST VISIT WITH MOM

One morning when I woke up, I was told by Philly to put on my suit because my sister and I were going to see our mom. We knew that she was very ill and that she wanted to see us. Little did I know that this was the very last time we would ever see her again. Truth be told, I was a little nervous. I hadn't seen her since the past Christmas, and it was now October, ten months later. They (my mom, Frank, siblings Frankie and now also sister Zeland) lived in Kittery, Maine so the drive was about an hour away.

When we arrived, I was elated to reunite with my brother and barely two-year-old sister. We walked inside and were told to sit in the living room until we were called to see our mother. She was in an upstairs bedroom.

Finally, I was called, and walked up the stairs not knowing what to expect. When I saw my mom from the hallway, I was shocked. She hardly looked like my mom. She was yellow with jaundice, skeletal and bald in her nightgown, smelling of formaldehyde. I was actually afraid to approach her. She opened up her arms and asked me to come closer to her, which I slowly did. I hugged her, but was in such shock that I couldn't absorb the magnitude of the moment. She said things to me, but I don't remember what they were. I'm sure they were loving words.

As terrible as it sounds, all I wanted to do was run back downstairs. I wished I had never seen her. There was a part of me that wondered if that even *was* my mom, though deep down I knew that she was. We might've only had but a few minutes, then she got tired and I was told to go back downstairs. The entire upstairs had that sickly formaldehyde odor, something that haunts me to this day. Every time I go to the hospital and run into that smell, I go right back to being in that hallway, looking at my sickly, skeletal, balding mom. What I would give to have known that was the last time I'd ever see her. I never even got to say goodbye to her, something I'd regret for years.

During that next Christmas vacation my brother and sister stayed with us, and when they got picked up by my stepdad, Frank, we were told our mom had passed – nearly a month previously. They held onto the information of her death for a *month*, creating an anger I'd hold onto for many years. It was bad enough that she died, delaying the news was like salt in the wound. They said that they'd wanted to lessen the blow, if you will, and tell us when we were all together. I disagreed with that plan.

What was interesting was that I didn't cry or show any emotion when I heard the news. I just felt emptiness, an emotion I was all too familiar with already. We hadn't lived with her for so many years, so in a sense, her death didn't really make much of an emotional impact.

I just didn't know what to feel. I stood there silently, pretending to look sad, but I actually didn't have any feelings about it. I would finally experience the pain of her death when I was eighteen. Until then, I'd just shove the reality down my throat and move on without her, as had been the case for years already. My older sister and Philly cried a lot. I just waited until my younger brother and sister had left with my stepdad, went to my room, and fell asleep. I woke up and still didn't feel a thing. Incredible what coping mechanisms a child can create to survive traumatic experiences.

THIRD GRADE - MRS KISH

Mrs. Kish was everything you'd hope a teacher would be. She was kind, had excitement in her voice, and I felt like every time I went to school, I was going to learn something new – and that I liked. She taught us cursive writing, which I was obsessed with doing correctly, as well as multiplication, division, and geography.

Third grade was also where I learned that I could be funny. I would say things to the kid behind me, Greg Weston, that would make him crack up during class. If this had been Miss McGillicuddy, I would've had detention, but it was Mrs. Kish, who was more tolerant and would just tell me to pay attention. I'd stop joking around because she was nice and I didn't want to make her upset.

Waterford Elementary had a humble little library in the basement, located beside the cafeteria. The class would venture down there every so often. I loved going down there. I was first introduced to classic books like *Super Fudge*, *The Mouse and the Motorcycle*, *How to Eat Fried Worms*, *Charlotte's Web*, and others. However, my absolute favorite book at that time was an overlooked one named *Dominic the Dog* by William Steig, who is also the author of the book *Shrek* before it was a movie. Dominic becomes bored with life, so he decides to leave home and see the world. It's filled with adventures and great tales, comedy, acts of heroism. Just a great book overall, even to this day.

This little library filled my mind with wonderful new worlds, facts and memories. It might not have held many books, but what it had was rich in great stories.

MARY POPPINS PLAY

Mrs. Kish would put on plays every year. With our class, she chose *Mary Poppins*. I managed to get the role of Michael Banks, one of the kids. It was my first experience in having to remember so many lines. I actually memorized them in secret at home, never telling Phyllis until about one week before the play was to be performed.

It was a lot of work. Phyllis was completely shocked that I had learned all of my lines without any help. For whatever reason, I didn't want to tell her nor my sister until I felt I had memorized everything and felt comfortable with my role.

The stars of the show were Ricky Sanborn, Courtney Buganski, Angela Webb (we actually "went out" for a couple months in sixth grade, but that's another story) and myself. We rehearsed a lot and all played our roles quite well for third-graders.

For the night scene, I had to wear my Dallas Cowboys pajamas, as that was all I owned. I'm sure that got a couple laughs from the audience. We sang quite a few numbers, all of which drew positive applause. This was the first taste of what it was like to be in front of many people performing and having to memorize a lot of lines.

THE HAUNTED HOUSE ON SUMMIT HILL ROAD

Philly was assigned to go over to this dilapidated, grey-shingled house on Summit Hill Road by its owner, Buffy Sainte-Marie, a beautiful Native American woman who was a popular and respected folk singer. The house played the part well of looking like it was haunted, because it was.

To the right of the gravel driveway, there were these very tall Italian Cypress trees, overgrown into ominous, over-lording figures that watched the property. Ragged-looking blackberry bushes protected the front of the house, their thorns tearing you up if you decided to pry and peer into the windows without permission of the house.

Legend has it that the first homeowners had just moved in, and their two kids were playing with the front door, tugging at the doorknob from each end. The front steps were actually one huge granite stone. Tragically, when the boy from the inside let go of the doorknob, his brother, who was on the outside, suddenly fell backwards and hit his head on the granite stone, killing him. So it goes that this child haunts the house, along with another spirit, who is thought to be a malevolent male spirit known to play the organ in the living room.

Buffy owned this black velvet painting of herself that hung in that living room. It showed three angles of her face, and her eyes always followed you no matter where you walked. It creeped me the fuck out. The board games were all kept in a closet in that room, and it was always so damn dark in there, with all the drapes closed up, so I'd quickly grab a game and run out of that room before I caught a glimpse of the painting looking at me. It never felt like she was staring at me, it always felt like something was hiding behind her eyes and staring at me.

There was this mini grand piano at the end of that room, with the painting right behind and above that piano. It apparently was owned by Andrew Jackson, the seventh president of the United States. It could apparently be proven; I just forget how.

One time, I went with Philly to inspect the house and we went into the barn. Somehow, we heard a horse neigh from within, but there wasn't a horse in there, nor were there any horses around the property. The sound of the horse was very close, within ten feet. It was unmistakable. So, does that mean there was a fucking ghost horse in that place as well? Who knows! All I know is we heard what we heard, and there wasn't a damn horse near us.

Philly continued the inspection into this little section of the barn that was apparently a secret hatch to get into the house. I had no idea it was there. As she got closer to the hatch and climbed up the little stairs to open it up, she heard the organ playing directly upstairs. She stopped dead in her tracks, listened for a few seconds, then scurried down. Her face was ashen. She said, "Let's get the hell out of here!" and I asked her what was wrong. She told me about the organ playing, and as we proceeded to walk out of the barn, she looked into a window with a direct path to view the organ at the other end of the house. By then, the organ had stopped playing, and there wasn't anybody in the house. It had been playing itself, or some spirit was playing it. You tell me. It certainly wasn't the wind. The house was empty.

There was another time when she'd looked into the windows and saw shit being thrown about in the house – records, books, etc. I mean, tossed from one end to the other, making a mess of the inside. This freaked her out. The basement was also freaky – the only way to get down there was with a rope that was attached to the entrance's ceiling. The stairs had either fallen down or been taken apart.

A couple times, my sister and I were babysat by this woman named Lee, who was the caretaker of the house for a number of years. She was a pretty serious-looking woman, a writer I believe, skinny with a marine haircut. If there was anyone who would be skeptical, it'd be her, but she wasn't -- she knew that house was haunted, because she'd lived there for years and saw what happened there. One evening, when my sister and I were upstairs in one of the bedrooms, we were rummaging around cupboards in the room nearest to the stairs. There were these nifty cubbyholes made of pine boards. When we opened up one of the cupboards, my sister noticed this ring that was hiding in it. She picked it up and put it on. It was a beautiful little diamond ring.

We quickly went downstairs to tell Lee what we found. Looking at it quizzically, she asked us where we found it, and we told her. She appeared dumbfounded, kept the ring, and didn't speak of it further. We just ran back upstairs to see what else we could find.

The next morning, when Philly came by to pick us up, Lee told her what we found, but went into greater detail about its story. Philly soon thereafter told us that the ring we found most likely was the lost ring of the newlywed couple who had been there twenty-five years ago, when the bride mysteriously lost her ring one morning. They frantically searched for it but could never find it. Then *we* found it. Crazy.

On that same babysitting weekend, I came downstairs one morning to have some breakfast. I took the milk bottle out of the fridge and put it on the counter to have with some cereal. But first, I poured myself some orange juice. Ten seconds later, when I went to pour the milk, I noticed that container was half-full. This was impossible – it had been *completely* full and the *seal to the lid hadn't even been broken.* I had no explanation for that. I don't think I ended up having cereal that day, I just walked out of the kitchen and grabbed something else to eat.

You can say what you want about houses being haunted, but I'm pretty certain this was a haunted house. Too many unexplained events happened in there. I'm not sure if it's still there but man, as a kid, that was one of the creepiest places I'd ever had to stay in. My sister would have to agree.

FOURTH GRADE

My teacher was Mr. Schwaner, who was a disciplined though nice man. He was also considered handsome by the other teachers. He had that perfect 70's haircut – parted on the side, slicked back with product and wore classic 70's three-piece plaid suits. It's funny to look back at him as old, when he was probably barely in his early 30's! Hilarious.

I do remember that President Ronald Reagan had begun this national Physical Fitness program and we all had to participate. I didn't mind it too much. One event was doing sit-ups. I partnered up with my friend, Adam Gosselin, who was probably the most athletic fourth-grader in our class. We had one minute to do as many sit-ups as possible. I went first. I was pretty damn fast, actually. I kept doing sit-up after sit-up, tiring out in the last ten seconds, but still ending with sixty sit-ups in a minute. Adam, being naturally competitive, seemed to take that as a challenge and tried to beat me, but he couldn't.

He got pretty close, something like fifty-six sit-ups. I kind of couldn't believe that this scrawny little skinny Asian kid, me, could beat out this strong-as-an-ox kid at something that seemed so easy, but apparently wasn't. What's funny is that I remember how his strategy made him tire out before he should've. He began by trying to go as fast as possible.

I even told him to try to pace himself and not go so fast, but he didn't listen. As the seconds went on, I just saw him lose power, until he didn't have anything left in the tank. Even funnier? I took the record for sit-ups for fourth-graders that year in the state of Maine! Go figure! I had no idea that I was naturally athletic.

CHRISTMAS ART COMPETITION

Mr. Schwaner announced to his fourth-grade class that there was a Christmas art competition and whoever won would get their drawing published on a full page in *The Advertiser Democrat*, the main newspaper located in Norway, Maine. So, I drew a Christmas scene that I thought was a perfect depiction of Christmas, not expecting to win anything. I drew a little town with a snowman, kids playing, a decorated Christmas tree, and Santa Claus flying overhead.

A week later, to my surprise, the announcement was made in the classroom that they had chosen my illustration! I was the winner! It was the first thing that I had ever won, and also suggested to me that I had some artistic talent. Phyllis couldn't have been prouder. Furthermore, the much-read regional newspaper, *The Advertiser Democrat*, got in touch with us and commissioned me to draw a couple illustrations for their newspaper every season that year, all of which they printed.

I sure wish I had those clippings. It was exciting and also a little overwhelming – it was a lot of work to create so many scenes. Prior to this, I had no idea that I had any artistic talent, I just knew I liked to draw. But it was the first glimmer of confidence that I did. Thank you, Mr. Schwaner. You opened up a world I never knew existed.

CROSSING THE PISCATAQUA BRIDGE WITH FRANKIE

I haven't talked much about my little brother Frankie, or for that matter, my little sister, Zeland. They both lived with my stepfather, Frank. My older sister Hien and I would still spend Christmas with my younger siblings after our mom passed away. We would also have the occasional summer visit, but Christmas was the one I looked forward to. We'd stay for about five days, then come back to Harrison.

Frankie and I had a deep connection as kids. I hated leaving him when the visits were over. He'd get visibly sad or angry, also hating the situation. But we knew it couldn't be any other way, so we learned to appreciate what little time we had.

We spent a lot of time looking for arcades or playing video games. We were both obsessed with them, naturally. They were the coolest thing ever invented for young boys. We would also bug my stepdad to take us to Chuck E. Cheese whenever possible. Knowing what I know now, we had no idea how expensive a night out at Chuck E. Cheese was.

Back then, who cares?! We wanted pizza and video games. Forget that stupid enclosure with plastic balls, just give me my Ms. Pac Man, Galaga, Space Invaders! We'd play video games all night!

One winter on a Sunday, Frankie and I must've walked all around Portsmouth, New Hampshire in search of an arcade that could break my hundred-dollar bill. That's what my stepdad gave me for Christmas, but little did we know how difficult it was going to be to change it. Nobody at an arcade wanted to, and I didn't want to spend it on anything but video games.

It was starting to get late and cold. By now, we had been walking for about more than half the day. Somehow, we got to the Piscataqua Bridge and I had the brilliant idea of crossing it. It was the better part of a mile! My brother didn't want to, but I insisted. Mind you, this is the freeway bridge that crosses back into Maine from New Hampshire.

Cars speeding by, and the bridge is mighty tall. Some people were honking at us, some slowed down, wondering why the hell two young boys were crossing the span of the bridge on a freezing, late afternoon. It felt like an hour before we finally got across and took the exit back to my stepdad's home. Boy, Frankie was pissed at me, mostly because he was hungry and tired, but also because we wasted the entire day without playing video games because nobody would break my hundred-dollar bill.

We still talk about that stupid stunt I made us do. Wow, so incredibly stupid. What's more incredible is that within the thirty minutes it took to walk across that bridge, not a single cop drove by. Surely, they would've stopped us and brought us back home. After all, it's illegal to walk on the freeway.

FIFTH GRADE, MR WALDIER, AND THE HOBBIT

Mr. Waldier was a cool dude, easily the coolest teacher I'd ever had, before and after fifth grade. He looked like a more intense version of Alan Watts but with a beard, not a Fu Manchu. He had eyebrows like a hawk. Since he only lived a mile from school, he would bike there because he didn't want to waste gas driving his car.

He was decades ahead of his time. If we were the same age and living in the same town, I'm sure we'd be friends. He was the first Vietnam War veteran that I'd met or known. He had this gift of teaching kids in a way that not only made them feel like learning was exciting, almost mystical, but he also loved reading *The Hobbit* to every class, every year. That was his thing, and he was good at it, because he was a great storyteller, and had enthusiasm in his eyes and soul. He understood the importance of good storytelling in order to bring the best out of a child's mind. He was a gift to this world. I will always remember him with the deepest respect.

We obviously connected because of the Vietnam War. He looked at and treated me slightly differently than other children because he'd been a combat soldier in the field, and somewhat knew my story as a child who came here from Saigon, so we had this unspoken bond. However, I kind of blew that bond a little bit.

Once a year, he would show slides of his time in Vietnam, and since I was the only Vietnamese kid he had ever had in his class since the war, there'd be a little spotlight on me. When the day came to show his slides, I was apparently a little obnoxious in the classroom, to the point where he had to call me out and ask why I was talking over him. I'm sure I disappointed him a little as I was the last kid that he expected to interrupt him. I must've been nervous about the whole thing, feeling uncomfortable in that spotlight.

I felt bad about that moment, and after he spoke to me, I quieted down. I'm sure he knew exactly what was going through my head, but nonetheless I felt bad that I disappointed the one teacher I felt most connected with.

I know he's smiling down on me now, though, waving that moment off, just happy there was one child from Vietnam that made it to his classroom. He could share his experience with me and I would really get it, more than any other child that would ever come into his classroom before and after that day. For all I know, I helped him be able to speak a little more freely about a time in his life that was difficult to talk about.

Regardless, Mr. Waldier left the most lasting impression on me of any teacher that I've ever had. He was top tier in every aspect. He was not only ahead of his time, but able to move forward emotionally after fighting in the Vietnam War, and teaching in ways that naturally expanded minds. He was gentle, clever, wise and fair. He was everything I wanted to become.

A few years later when I was in eighth grade, our school bus somehow got diverted and we went over to Waterford Elementary School, and I got to visit him. I had my break dance outfit on, and he commented with a wry smile, "So … you have quite the outfit on" and looked me up and down in my red parachute pants and checkered Vans. I was actually quite proud of the outfit. He knew it was just a phase, and he was just glad to see me.

I was grateful to at least get a couple minutes with him. By that time, he was either the vice principal or principal of the school. We chatted a bit, then I had to get back on the bus. That was the last time I saw him. I still think of Tony Waldier to this day.

MR WALDIER AND MY PERVERTED DRAWING

This incident in Mr. Waldier's classroom is actually quite embarrassing and graphic, but I'm going to write about anyway. I was just a fifth-grader after all. I'm also going to give shit to my "friend" Ricky Sanborn, who ratted me out. His name deserves full attention, since he was *also* drawing perverted illustrations.

Ricky and I, as well as some other boys, would all draw some fairly deviant drawings. They were simple, of course, not anything worthy of hanging up, just straight-up fifth-grade-kid drawings. I was also reading the book *Our Bodies, Ourselves* at home, which included graphic drawings of female sexual parts which fascinated me. As a boy becoming curious about girls, I began drawing illustrations of a penis inside a vagina, and I would add the most depraved written words I could think of, which I'm not going to repeat here. All I'll admit is that it was shocking, particularly since I was only a fifth grader, but I wanted to be as shocking as I could be when I showed it to the other boys I hung out with.

After I finished drawing this particularly warped piece, I showed it to Ricky Sanborn. His eyes got wide, then he covered his mouth in a fake state of shock, then smirked and decided to suddenly shout out loud, "Hey Mr. Waldier, Son has something to show you!"

I will never forget that moment. I was mortified. I immediately shoved my drawing as deep into my desk as I could possibly shove it, and crinkled it into a ball. There was no way in hell I was going to show this horrific depiction of a woman's private parts, with what I wrote above it, to Mr. Waldier! But since Ricky shouted out with such enthusiasm, Mr. Waldier's attention was now squarely on me. He slowly walked over, asking me what I had drawn. I told him that I couldn't show it to him, shaking my head furiously, while Ricky Sanborn stood snickering. I was so pissed at him, while trying to fend off Mr. Waldier and failing. He calmly asked me again to show him the drawing. I refused, shoving it even deeper into my desk and shaking my head wildly, panicked at the repercussions that might ensue once he saw it. We went back and forth a couple times, and I refused to budge. He finally said, "Son, I promise that you won't get into any trouble if you show it to me. I promise." I said, "Are you sure? It's pretty bad." He said, with a little reassuring smile, "Yes, I promise."

So, I slowly grabbed my crumpled-up piece of pornography I'd drawn out of the desk and handed it to him with great trepidation. I was ashamed at the deepest of levels. Once I handed it to him, I suddenly rushed from my chair, ran from the classroom, and raced to the boy's restroom. I panicked! I opened up a stall, locked the door, and sat up above the toilet so as my feet couldn't be seen. There I sat, knowing that he'd eventually find me. About a minute later, I heard footsteps slowly coming in. It was obviously Mr. Waldier.

He calmly said, "Son? I know you're in here. Will you please come out?"

Me: No.

Mr. Waldier: Well, you're going to have to come out eventually.

Me: No ... I wrote a very bad thing.

Mr. Waldier: I promise you I won't punish you. I just want to talk.

Whatever he said finally convinced me to come down from the stall and eventually open the door.

I walked out and there we were, face to face. I did notice that he had a bit of a smirk while holding my crumpled-up drawing, trying to remain calm and fair about the situation. He was very understanding.

I don't remember his exact words, but after a deep breath he looked at me in as gentle a manner as he could, (smirk) and said something to the effect of, "What you wrote was a very, very bad thing. You just have to promise me that you will never, ever write anything like that again. That was a horrible thing to write about women." I nodded in total agreement and promised him profusely that I'd never write or draw anything like that ever again, so long as I lived.

We came out of that boy's room with a new understanding. He never punished me for what I did. No detention. Nothing. I don't think he ever said anything to Phyllis about it either. Just a quick conversation to point out how important it is to respect women. It stuck. He looked at me squarely afterward, knowing that I got his point. And with that, he sent me outside to play with the other kids, since it was recess by this time.

I ran out, found Ricky Sanborn, who did nothing but stick his tongue out at me while on the swings, laughing at the trouble I got into, all because that bastard ratted me out. But I learned a lesson that day about respecting women that is with me to this day. Granted, I was a fifth-grader, but Mr. Waldier set the record straight. He had class and wisdom and handled a situation that nowadays would've been ended with a suspension. He will always be my favorite teacher that I hold in the highest esteem.

A BLACK EYE AND A TWO-BY-FOUR

I don't remember specifically what I said or what I did, but I'm pretty sure I lied about something that made Philly hit the roof. I'm also sure I was very apologetic, never understanding why I lied as it had become my safety default mode. Regardless, whatever I lied about got me a black eye and a two-by-four to my back.

I do remember what she said, telling me, "You're a piece of shit and you're never going to amount to anything," which was followed by a couple wallops to the face, both sides. Repeatedly. The difference this time was that she put a fist to my face and gave me a black eye. She'd never done that before, and I was shocked, to say the least. I was also cowering by this point, begging her to please stop hitting me. But she didn't. In fact, she upped the ante and even said something like, "You want me to stop? You want me to stop? Oh, I haven't even started" and proceeded to find a healthy two-by-four that was about three feet long, and while I was trying to get back up, covering myself with my arms, she struck me so hard on my back that I fell to the ground. She hit me a couple more times with that damn thing and all I could do was cover my face, hoping she wouldn't hit me there again because the black eye was hurting me enough.

She finally got tired and put the chunk of wood down, walked away for a minute or two, then came back to me, apologizing and trying to hug me. She asked me, "Where do you hurt?" and I pointed to my heart.

That's all I could do to get my point across to her. She hugged me even closer and apologized again. A little late for that now. The last thing I wanted was to be touched by her. The distrust, the fear, and plain disgust I had for her enveloped me in a cocoon of hidden rage that I couldn't express – I just held it in and hoped to God that someday I could get out of the hell I had been forced to live in.

A couple days later, Maureen came back home from a sales trip, her job at the time. She wandered in and out of my life during those years, and I always welcomed her presence. She was a breath of fresh air and light every time I saw her. I always secretly wished that she could take me away from there. When she arrived and hugged me, she looked at my face and saw the black eye and asked me what happened. Then she looked at my arms, seeing more bruising. She instructed me to take off my shirt too, exposing the damage on my back. She didn't need to ask much more; she knew how I got them.

When Philly entered the room, she spoke to her about it, then told her to get into her bedroom where they could speak a little more privately. From just out of earshot, I strained to hear what was happening in there. There was a lot of screaming, what sounded like some slapping, then Maureen saying loudly, "How does that feel?!" followed by more slapping. Maureen was a strong and stout Irish woman who didn't let herself get pushed around. She was so furious at Philly for doing that to me, she couldn't contain her rage and she gave her a little piece of what I'd gotten. It was fairly satisfying to hear Philly pleading for Maureen to stop, which didn't happen. I couldn't help but smile a little, then I walked away to do kid shit, whatever the hell that was, as Maureen continued to give Philly a piece of what she deserved. In my honor.

I was always grateful for that moment. Since Maureen was a strict Catholic and previously a nun, she was ashamed of that moment of weakness she displayed and vowed to never be violent like that again. But she never regretted standing up for me. That event also made her move out for good shortly thereafter, leaving me feeling unprotected and completely exposed to the devices of an abusive foster mom. And that's how my life would feel for the next few years – exposed and unprotected. Afraid.

SUICIDE BY CRYSTAL DRANO

In the tiny second-floor bathroom, I used to stare at this bottle of Crystal Drano that we kept up there. So many times, I'd been tempted to drink it and end it all. I thought harder about it after that beating. This time, I actually poured some into this plastic drinking cup of mine on the sink. I poured a lot of it into that cup. I looked at that cup half-filled with Crystal Drano and thought about how great it would be to free myself from the pain of living in that house. I even brought that cup to my lips and almost drank. At the last second, with tears in my eyes and the cup to my lips, I heard my mom's voice in my head, saying "What the hell're you doing?! Stop that right now! Don't you know you have to live for me?!" I was so mad at her for telling me that because I just wanted to end the pain. But her voice made me take that cup away from my lips and put it down, while sobbing and heaving. I promised her right then and there that I'd never kill myself and if anything, I'd live for her, because she couldn't live for me, and she knew it. It was a very powerful moment, a moment that forever changed me and made me just a little bit stronger, unwilling to be beaten down any longer, literally or figuratively. From that moment on, I was no longer living for myself, but for my mom.

I poured the Crystal Drano down the drain, rinsed the cup, wiped the tears from my eyes, walked out of that tiny bathroom and shut the light off. To this day, I never told Philly or my sister that I almost killed myself.

SINGING MR ROBOTO AND OTHER TUNES ON MY BICYCLE

My sister and I listened religiously to the Top 40 Countdown with Casey Casum on WBLM 102.9FM. Popular radio was where most of our music was coming from when I was ten to thirteen years old and she was fourteen to eighteen, which would bring us up to around 1981-1984. We were still using four-track players, which I couldn't stand because they'd start fading out in the middle of a song.

So stupid. I didn't miss them one bit when tapes took over. However, I do reminisce over my *Styx, Paradise Theater* and *The Cars, Greatest Hits* four-tracks. I played those until they started getting wrecked.

My sister and I would sing along to countless songs that came on the radio. We'd record songs we liked onto blank tapes so we could bring them to school and play them on the bus when the bus driver was in the mood - being older now, I completely understand why blaring music at 7:30AM is no bueno for the mind, or share it with our friends. We'd get the Maxell or Memorex 90-minute tapes and record the Countdown when it reached the top twenty or the top ten.

In this era, there were many different kinds of bands and music getting played, so pop music was so much more versatile than it is nowadays. You could hear Stevie Wonder, Cyndi Lauper, Madonna, Men at Work, The Police, the Talking Heads, David Bowie, Duran Duran, Berlin, Blondie, Hall & Oates, Motley Crue, Tom Petty, Van Halen, Twisted Sister, Def Leppard, The Go-Gos, Joan Jett, Journey, Culture Club, Simple Minds, and so many British bands or One Hit Wonder bands, like Dexy's Midnight Runners ("Come On Eileen"), Nena ("99 Red Ballons"), Midnight Oil ("Beds Are Burning"), or Madness ("Our House") in one place. The list went on and on, and most of the music was excellent and well-produced, and most of it influenced me.

There were countless moments during the summer where I'd be riding my bike into town and singing songs at the top of my lungs. There really wasn't anybody around, so it was a perfect time to "practice", if you will. I certainly didn't know I was practicing, I was just trying to perfect how certain songs were being sung, like "Mr. Roboto" and *Paradise Theatre* by Styx. I can't believe how much I sang "Mr. Roboto." I was obsessed with that song, singing it night and day for over a month.

Another song was "Man Eater" by Hall & Oates. Hysterical, I know, but I'll tell you, that vocal track was so badass, I just had to sing it like Daryl Hall. I mean, that intro line, "She'll only come out at night, the lean and hungry type." For a twelve-year-old, that is BAD ASS.

I also loved their older song "Sara Smile" – so pretty. Another tune I sang a lot was "Part-Time Lover" by Stevie Wonder. It was really catchy and I loved the melody. "Come on Eileen" and "Our House" were other songs I just loved to sing. Such fun and catchy tunes!

Even before these years, my sister and I would practice dance moves together during the late 70's disco craze. We practiced that shit for a long time. She loved singing along to "Last Dance" and boy, could my sister sing! Hell, she could dance too! She was a little badass. She even won a talent contest that was being held at the Cracked Platter in Harrison, dancing to "Sir Duke." She danced the shit out of that song. I wasn't surprised in the least when she won that year. I wonder if she kept that blue ribbon? Anyway, we did lots of dancing and singing together through that special window of time. My sister also sang in talent shows at her high school and even dabbled in pursuing a career as a singer, but soon realized it was going to require a lot of sacrifice, and it wasn't all that glamorous behind the scenes. She had, and still does have, a very sweet and pretty voice and naturally good pitch, but her desire to pursue it full-time just wasn't there.

However, I'll never forget those years of getting all excited with her, listening to the Top 40 on Sunday mornings, singing along to songs and dancing around, just having a fun time of it, and singing along to them while riding my bike into town for years.

Little did I know I was training my voice to be a singer as an adult. Ha! Little Son Vo just loved singing. I still do, and I attribute it all to Mr. Roboto.

CHRIS OLMSTED, MY FIRST TRUE BEST FRIEND

I remember the day I met Chris Olmsted, the new kid in school. He came to Waterford Elementary halfway into the fifth-grade year. He ended up sitting beside me on his first day of school. He had really blonde hair, cut short, was a little chunky with silver square-framed glasses and had these super blue eyes. He asked me a question about what we were reading and I answered him. He seemed to be a nice kid and we immediately connected. We were basically nerds who instantly bonded. I was the semi-Asian version of him, with 80s-style feathered dark brown hair, parted to the side, square plastic-rimmed glasses and brown eyes. I quickly found out that Chris skipped a grade, so that officially put him in the nerd column. He also didn't have any friends.

As time went on, we hung out a lot and talked about much of our frustration with life during recess. We'd walk in the woods and plot escapes from our parents. We would obsess over details of what we would pack, when we would leave, and where we would go.

We both ultimately knew we'd never have the nerve to follow through, but those therapeutic conversations got us through our fifth and sixth grade angst.

His parents owned Bear Pond Campground in Waterford, Maine. I had many sleepovers there on Friday or Saturday nights. His dad was the chief of police for a town nearby and his mom ran the campground. She was a warm and kind person. She let us roam the property freely, so long as we didn't bother the campers. The main house was fairly large, nestled beside the woods and overlooking the pond, which was actually a small lake. They had a little store right as you walked in, and the living quarters were tucked behind that. The bedrooms were on the second floor. There was a cottage-sized house to the right of their home where the pinball machine lived. We spent a lot of time there.

This was during the time when the Atari 2600 came out, and Chris's parents were one of the first amongst the kids I knew to buy it, so that was extra incentive to spend the night over there. The Atari was in his parent's room, where the large TV was, and we'd sit on the edge of their waterbed during many hot summer afternoons, playing Space Invaders instead of playing outside. We were completely addicted, me moreso than Chris, admittedly.

We would also listen to Casey Kasem's Top 40 radio and record our favorite songs on Chris's tape recorder, then try to decipher the lyrics. "Maneater" by Hall & Oates was a song we had a hard time with. "Mr. Roboto" was also pretty tricky. But man, it was fun. Chris also loved playing his live tape of Chuck Berry performing "My Ding A Ling." I never took to the song but looking back, I think it's absolute gold that we listened to that song way more than I ever wanted. And I did think Chuck Berry was masterful at leading his audience to sing it along with him.

They also had paddle boats that they rented out, and we went on a couple excursions with them. We had a fun time together because we talked on the same wavelength. We were always processing our emotions with one another, although it's interesting that I never told him about the abuse I would endure at home. For some reason, that was conveniently left out in our conversations, but I still felt like I could talk to him about things I couldn't with anyone else.

DRINKING LIQUOR AND GETTING CAUGHT BY CHRIS'S DAD

I have one memory that secured the disdain from Chris's dad, a Vietnam vet who already had a rough time just looking at me. One night, Chris's whole family went to visit some of his parent's friends.

While there, with the parents in another room, we were hanging out in the living room, where I was dared to drink some alcohol. So, I did. I drank some peppermint schnapps and some whiskey. When we drove back home to their campground, the dad said that he smelled alcohol. It was quickly determined that I was the culprit. I'll never forget the red-hot face looking back at me on that drive. If I had been his kid, he would've stopped the car and given me a good whoopin' right then and there! But he didn't, of course. He just drove, stewing with anger, and rightfully so. He never liked me anyway, but that stunt supplanted his dislike until the end of time.

In the summer after sixth grade, he told me that his family was moving to Pennsylvania. His dad had been hired as the police chief of the town they were moving to. That crushed me on many levels. It was as if the innocence of my youth was also moving away with him, and I was forced to push forward without my best friend to confide my secrets and fears. He was also very sad about this. We at least got to spend a whole weekend together right before he left. First, I went to his place, then he spent the night at my place. His mom Judy also got along really well with Phyllis, and they had great conversation while Chris and I fooled around, waiting for the moment when he finally had to leave.

There's just something about those years, before you're a teenager, where the innocence of childhood is still intact and friendships are pure. I knew once he moved, even though I couldn't explain it at the time, the innocence would leave and my world would enter an unknown chapter, one without my best friend.

PHILLY'S ICE CREAM SHOP IN HARRISON

Philly opened up an ice cream store in Harrison, Maine, right beside the Village Tie-Up, and called it Philly's Dari-Frost. Or maybe it was Philly's Dairy Frost? I forget. Anyway, it was the summer after fifth grade and I was pretty excited. My sister and I worked there a few days a week. The prices were stupid cheap for our soft serve ice cream: ten cents for a small, twenty-five cents for a medium, and fifty-five cents for our large, which was very large. Our scooped ice creams were maybe fifty cents per scoop? It took a little time to learn how to make a perfect soft-serve swirl. It was basically vanilla, chocolate, or half-'n-half. Let's just say that it was a very fun summer.

I became friends with the Worster boys, the two younger ones, whose dad owned the marina down the street. We'd hang out a lot and play Space Invader's at The Cracked Platter or ride our BMXs around town, up to Crystal Lake and through the paths behind it.

Tom Kostevik was also part of the crew. He was the only one who knew how to use a skateboard. He looked like he should've lived in Venice, CA and would've fit right into Dogtown. He had Vans sneakers before anybody knew what they were, the California tan, with straight dirty-blonde surfer's hair and just a vibe that was anything but Harrison. He was also really good at street hockey.

Harrison had summer sports events at Crytal Lake's recreation center to keep the kids busy. We played a lot of street hockey on the basketball court. I was almost good but just didn't have the dexterity. Some of these kids would do whatever they could to bend their hockey sticks at just the right angles, just for street hockey! They were dedicated. I still had fun. The competitiveness was fun.

The second year of owning the ice cream shop, Maureen and Philly decided to have an occasional Chinese Food Saturday Night to boost up some business. I know, that's a pretty ridiculous combination – an ice cream shop that sells Chinese food. But we did, for about a month.

It was actually too successful and created long lines that became unmanageable. I remember the first time they decided to do it. I drove to the Wok Inn with Maureen in Portland, Maine. We picked up large tins of chow mein, fried rice, sweet and sour chicken, and Szechuan beef, then drove back to the ice cream shop. We placed them on warmers until we were ready to handle the masses of eagerly awaiting Chinese food-eaters. Within an hour, a long line of customers formed, and they just kept serving them until the food was gone. There was never enough food to meet the demand, which created impatience, frustration and even fighting in the line. They tried to adapt to the demand, but it never seemed to work out, arguments were increasing amongst customers, and after a few more attempts, they decided it was time to stop serving Chinese food in at the ice cream shop.

SUMMERS IN HARRISON, MAINE

Summertime in the early eighties Harrison, Maine was consistently memorable. I spent a lot of time in the town itself, due to Philly owning the ice cream shop. I biked around on my Sears Huffy BMX with a few guys I previously mentioned; the Worster brothers and Tom Kostovik, as well as Ricky Sanborn. There was also Scotty and Charlie, who would occasionally bike with us around town. There were bike paths we used behind Crystal Lake which traveled behind the Cracked Platter and Market Basket and ran past a damn, looping back onto a road and onto Main St., where we'd either head to the arcade, my ice cream shop, or the marina on Long Lake. We'd spend our days collecting cans to raise money for video games or hope one of us had enough money to spot us all some quarters.

We played Space Invaders at the Cracked Platter, a sit-down version, which I loved and was obsessed with, or games in a new arcade at the very end of the Main St. Building basement. Our summer needs were simple: gather enough cans for video games, soda, and candy bars. We'd go to the Village Tie-Up and have them count our cans, then they'd give us our money and we'd be off to our next adventure.

FIRST TIME SEEING PORN MAGS

One day, while hanging out at Crystal Lake, Scotty asked us if we wanted to see something. There was something mischievous in his delivery. We either said "What was it?" or "Yes" and he said to follow him. So, we biked through the back paths beside Crystal Lake until we reached an empty summer cottage a few minutes later. He went underneath the front stairs of the cottage and brought out a pile of nudie magazines. We were obviously all intrigued.

I had never seen a porn magazine, especially the kind he had brought. There were of course the standard Penthouse and Playboy, but he also brought ones called High Society, and Juggs, which is the one that grabbed my attention.

I hadn't been exposed to many porn magazines at this age, except for the liberal female book *Our Bodies, Ourselves*, which only had illustrations of the female reproductive region.

We each grabbed a magazine and looked through them, showing each other pictures that clearly had share-potential. I had never seen a picture of an actual vagina, let alone one so close! I'd also never seen "juggs" so huge in my life, much less boobs that may not have been as large but, were exposed and simply looked awesome in every way! It was a goldmine of pre-teen sexual exposure and we stayed there looking at those magazines for quite a long while.

Mind you, we were still under thirteen years old, so our sexual drives weren't yet full-bore, but this experience opened up a whole new window to what women looked like for me. We never saw those photos of nude women as being exploitative, our fascination came from a much more innocent place than that. We were discovering a new world that we hadn't known existed, and we now yearned for more, as that window had been opened up.

We swapped turns bringing them home for a week or two at a time, then brought them back to share with the next one in line. However, I got caught with them. I hid them underneath some clothes, but poorly, and Maryanne was horrified when she found them. She slapped me, showed them to Phyllis, and insisted I get rid of them. Thankfully, Phyllis wasn't nearly as shocked about them as Maryanne.

She was much more comfortable with the subject of nude women, whether that was appropriate or not. She softened the blow of Maryanne's response, and I immediately brought them back for the other guys to do as they pleased with them.

I was never able to unsee what I saw after looking at those magazines. Those nudie mags forever changed how I saw women, at least when I imagined seeing them naked. It truly wasn't from some perverted perspective. I finally got to see the most private parts that I could possibly see, before I probably should have seen them, and it only made me more curious about women.

Yes, the magazines were obviously pornography, but when you're a naïve preteen, you don't comprehend the industry behind the machine. You come from a much more innocent place, one of wonderment and fantasy and thinking that you were able to see what wasn't allowed in proper society, but also feeling like you were granted some kind of secret knowledge. Nude magazines were just a part of the growing-up experience.

SOCCER AND BASEBALL MEMORIES

Baseball was a game that I was just good enough at. I had a good arm, so I was always put into the outfield. I never understood that logic as a kid, though. I figured the kids who weren't quite good enough were placed in the outfield, so I always thought I wasn't quite good enough to play the infield positions. Then again, I also liked having a lot of time daydreaming until an important hit would come, which I would catch only half the time, tops. The outfield was boring, but you could also do a lot of nothing out there and still be part of the team.

One day, Walter noticed that I was left-handed and I could pitch fast and accurately, *and* could pitch a natural curveball. He taught me how to hold the baseball in-between the seams, and when to release to throw a truly devastating curveball – for a twelve-year-old skinny-ass pitcher.

He helped me see baseball as more than just baseball. He made me want to become a pitcher. I had a natural sixty-five-mile-an-hour pitch. He thought that was good. I had no idea. He wanted to train me to become better. At the time, I remember I didn't understand why somebody I hardly knew would want to spend their time to make me better. But I knew that I trusted him, and that he knew baseball, and that he believed in me.

We'd go out to the Harrison baseball field and he'd make me throw dozens of pitches at him, for about thirty minutes or until my arm got tired. He was able to get me into the little league team as one of the starting pitchers.

Our team was pretty darn good. There were a few truly talented players, then there were others who put in the effort and were just good enough. I was part of that second tier. Wade Day and Tom Kostovik were the really talented players. We would play against towns all around us – Sebago Lake, Sanford, Oxford. I don't remember that we ever won a title, but we came close and we got to the finals once.

There was one particularly memorable home game. I forget who we were playing, but it was a storybook moment. It was the ninth inning, we had one out and were behind by at least one run. I was next to hit. I swung on the first pitch. Strike. I looked at the second pitch. Strike. I looked at the third pitch. Ball. I swung at the fourth pitch. Tick ball. Phew. Then I took a breath, slowed down, looked at the pitcher, and looked at the ball as it came in. Everything was in slow motion, just a tiny bit, as that ball came in. I gave it my all, hit that ball dead center on the bat, and it flew into deep center field, right up into the bottom of the fence. The center-fielder had a hard time grabbing it. By that time, I was on second base and everyone was yelling at me to keep running, so I ran to third. They told me to keep running to home because they wouldn't be able to make the throw in time, so I kept running. The whole place was hooting and hollering in hysterics as I ran in while the entire team massed at home plate, jumping up and down and patting me on my helmet. It was one of the greatest team moments I've ever experienced and I will never forget it. We went on to win that game, of course, because of my in-field home run. Ha! Skinny little Asian kid, me, hero of the day. Somehow, I dug in deep and the rest is history.

I also played soccer as a kid. I enjoyed the sport but, again, I was only adequate, not talented. I had to work at it but I didn't want to practice enough. It's a sport that requires a lot of foot skills and finesse, things I had no desire to work on. I was decent enough to play the wing positions, and apparently, I could naturally kick a long way, so they'd put me out on the wing. You don't get as much action there as in the center, so it was a better bet to keep me where I didn't have to have the foot skills.

The town of Harrison had arranged for our team to play against a team in Montreal, Canada. It was broken down into three age levels: the youths, the intermediates, and the teens. We'd host their players when they came into Harrison, and the following year, they'd host us. It was my first exposure to the French language, or at least a dialect of it. It was cool to hear.

But I could also tell when they were making fun of us in their language, then look at us and laugh it off, which left a little edge. There was definitely some of that we're-from-a-city-and-more-refined-than-you-town-folk vibe, which created a little rivalry, at least among the kids. The adults had no idea this dynamic existed. Just as well. It was motivation for us to play as well as we could. And it balanced out over the years. Some years we'd beat them, the next they'd beat us; it was a healthy competition.

There was one year that stuck out more than others. It was the year we traveled up to Montreal to play on their turf. I stayed with a very kind family. They spoke a lot of French Canadian in the house. It was also the first time I was exposed to cable television and I was amazed at the options it had. Harrison was too small of a town to have cable TV, so I basked in it while I was there!

On the day of the games, I was pretty pumped up and ready to play for some reason. I really wanted to kick their asses on their home turf, so I played more aggressively than I ever had. Somehow, despite playing wing, I was close to the net, and the ball came right to me, without anybody around me. It was just me and the goalie, who was wearing that 'Oh-shit' look, while I unloaded on the ball and kicked it into the net. Goal!!!!

Later down the line, as we continued playing, I found myself in the position to kick the ball, and *hard*. I had a little running head start to kick the ball, then suddenly, the ball was replaced with this kid in front of me, and instead of kicking the ball as hard as I could, I kicked him in his ribs as hard as I could. I couldn't stop the force of my kick so he got the brunt of it, and boy, did he ever get kicked hard. I heard a scream, he went down, and he and didn't move. I just stood there feeling terrible. The game stopped and they brought in a stretcher to lug him off the field.

A few minutes later, an ambulance screeched in to take him away. Apparently, he'd broken a couple of ribs. They thought it was wise to take me out of the game at that time. Fine with me. I was wracked with guilt even though I didn't mean to hurt him. *Or did I?* That's the kind of question that creeps in after an event like that. We won the game, but under a cloud of suspicion, thanks to me. However, though not much of a consolation, I did find myself with a new reputation of somebody to look out for. A new enforcer, if you will. Little, skinny, Asian me: The Enforcer. Hilarious.

This was also the trip where Philly decided to give me a satchel full of candy for the bus ride to Montreal. It was meant to be eaten during the duration of the trip, not in one fell swoop, which is what I did. The irony is that when we were returning to Harrison, though most of the candy intended for the bus ride back had already been eaten, I ended up puking. Badly. The coach called me a glutton.

Funny thing is, I had shared all of my candy with everybody, so what he saw didn't encompass the full picture. He just saw a kid start out with a satchel of candy and end up puking on the ride home. But I hadn't eaten any candy on the ride home, regardless of how it looked when the boy-with-all-the candy puked. A lot. Irony can play its own tricks. It only added to the cloud hanging over what should've felt like a winning weekend. I was ultimately fine with the outcome. We won, I scored a goal, and I looked tougher.

In sixth grade, I also went to University of Southern Maine soccer program to try to improve my game. I practiced and practiced and learned some fundamentals that were never taught to me before, but by now, regardless of how much I practiced, I never seemed to improve. I only had so much talent and willingness to practice, and I always preferred to use my time reading or drawing. Soccer wasn't a passion; it was just something to do.

TWO BLACK EYES AT THE OUTHOUSE

Our contractor from the house-building-party, John Gray, was getting married on his property, in maybe Sweden, Maine? I don't remember. Anyway, one week prior to this wedding, I had been hanging out with Ricky Sanborn, a friend I've mentioned before, from Waterford, Maine. I somehow got a black eye while we were playing. You know, boy stuff, roughhousing – who knows. Fast forward a week later.

Philly, my sister, and I arrive at the wedding celebration. There's an outhouse on the property away from the crowd, which I had to use. Down the hill from it, about fifty feet away, were Ricky Sanborn and John Gray's kids, Danny and Joel.

While I was inside the outhouse, they decided that it would be a great time to hurl rocks at it for target practice, just to see if they could hit it. Well, they were hitting it quite fine from my perspective. From inside, I was yelling for them to stop throwing the rocks, and, of course, they were either conveniently deaf or fucking with me, because the amount and velocity of rocks being thrown increased! It was driving me nuts, and I stepped out of the outhouse. Just as I opened the door, a fat-sized rock hit my left eye and man, did it sting. Holy shit, I was pissed at them. I screamed, "Hey you fuckin' assholes, I *told* you *not* to throw rocks at the outhouse!" They finally *did* stop but they continued to walk towards me, giggling under their breath. I couldn't pinpoint who threw the rock that nailed my eye, all I know is that I was fuming and in acute pain. They just looked at me and my eye for a little while, then walked away to find something else to do, and I just stood waiting until the pain subsided. Dickheads. Oh well, boys will be boys. So, I walked around school for the next week with not one black eye, but two. What are the chances of that happening?

OLD HOME DAYS IN HARRISON 1980'S

"Old Home Days" was a Harrison tradition since I was a little kid, about nine years old. It was a mixture of a small fair and a circus at the same time. There were rides, animals: baboons, lions, and leopards, - I'd feel terrible for them if I saw them now, but as a kid from the '70s and '80s, I didn't know any better. Plus, an arcade and live entertainment.

The highlight of it all was the Flatland Cloggers, I believe they were from Texas, at least that's what one of the pretty blonde cloggers told the audience. I loved watching them dance in unison. Fast, loud, and in sync. And the music! Well, it was fast fiddle work was all I could remember. And it would change rhythm and tempo. I couldn't figure out how they did it, but I knew they were pretty, smiling, and dancing in ways I could never dance.

One year that they brought wild animals to the fair, we were looking at the baboons through the bars of their large pen, and Philly told us to never put your arm in the cage as they might grab onto your arm and pull on it. So, what does Philly do? She puts her arm into the cage as an example, and what did a baboon do? It immediately came down, grabbed her arm and started yanking on it with a lot of force, enough to scare the shit out of all of us.

Luckily for her, the baboon let go, having gotten bored of tugging. As we leave, she says, "See? That's what can happen if you put your arm in the cage." Point clearly made, although I'm pretty sure she didn't expect the animals to actually follow through. I thought she was pretty goddamn stupid for doing that.

EDDIE ROLF AND THE DUNKING BOOTH

There was a dunking booth where citizens of notoriety in Harrison would occasionally volunteer to sit in for a potential dunking. Eddie Rolfe was one of those volunteers, a highly respected citizen. I pitched for the Harrison Little League team that year – 1983? Anyway, I walked by the dunking booth and he's sitting in it, egging me on to throw a pitch at him. Phyllis was also there and encouraged me to throw a few balls. Why not? So, I did. Eddie was full of bravado and did everything he could to discourage me and my throwing arm from hitting that bull's eye. I missed on the first throw. Then I noticed a crowd gathering. This was actually starting to feel like a big deal if I could dunk him. I concentrated hard on the target, threw the baseball as accurately as I could, and BLAM!

DUNK! Eddie fell into the tank of water and all I heard were cheers and laughter. Eddie got dunked by a skinny little 12-year-old kid! It was a glorious moment, and I felt like I was in a movie. He got back up and said something like, "I hear your mommy calling you, kid!" which drew more fits of laughter.

There were other events that weren't so feel-good. I decided to order large fries with vinegar and salt, and eat them before I got on the Tilt-A-Whirl, a ride that basically does what its name says – it tilts you, then it whirls you about, over and over again. And again. In my case, I was feeling sicker and sicker thanks to the vinegar on the French Fries. Luckily, I made it through the ride. I might've even asked the operator to stop it because I was getting sick. Once the ride finally ended, it took a good hour to walk it off. I needed time to stop feeling dizzy and sick to my stomach. I never puked, though.

There was another event that I'm not too proud of, but the reaction of the ride operator would've gotten him either fired or sued nowadays. The ride only held four people at a time. It was really tall and would transport you up, then drop you down really quickly. It would do this a few times.

When it reached the highest point, the operator would leave you hanging for about ten seconds. Well, I had the brilliant idea to spit out over the side of the ride, thinking it was really fun. I did it a few times and, and my friend and I were laughing.

When the ride was finished, the ride operator asked if we were spitting. I admitted to doing it. Almost immediately, the guy's face got red, he picked me up, then used my back as a mop to clean my fallen spit from the platform. He said something to the effect of "There, I don't think you'll ever be doing that again. Now get the hell outta here! I don't ever want to see your face again!" I was shocked and mortified, to say the least. I looked at all the faces looking at me. Everybody seemed flabbergasted but didn't know what to do about it. I ran off, completely embarrassed, hiding myself in the arcade tent. I'm sure I had spit on him, but I paid for it with my wounded pride, less intact then when I'd arrived at the fair. Other than that, though, Old Home Days was one of the greatest parts of my childhood.

LINWOOD NASON AND FREEING HIS CHAINED DOG IN THE BARN

Linwood Nason was the local drunk of the town. He was an Army Sergeant who fought in World War II and hung his uniform in his breezeway wall, just on the other side of where he'd sit in his kitchen. It was dusty from being exposed to the elements but still hung there neatly, with *its* pride still intact. I'd look at it every time I brought in the firewood, wondering what kind of stories that uniform held.

Linwood owned a respectable farmhouse, which was now in disarray but held a rich history. However, most of it was shut off since he no longer moved beyond his chair in the kitchen, drinking pints of Jack Daniels and cans of Budweiser from the break of dawn until the dusk of night, when he'd finally pass out. I was told to never peep around the house, to just stay in the kitchen area and the barn. I would occasionally peak my head into the living room, where it looked like a completely different house, almost as if a woman's touch had once transformed this house into a home.

Philly and I would go there occasionally to help him out. He was a crotchety old man who seemed to make just enough sense in the mornings, before the liquor got to him, that Philly convinced him to hire me to come a few days a week in the early morning to help with chores before I went to school. I'd tend to his geese, ducks, chickens, and dog, an Australian sheepdog who was chained and locked up in his barn. I would, of course, be paid, even if it was meager wages. Six dollars a week for thirty minutes of work, I think? I forget, it was so long ago.

I'd wake up around 6AM a few days a week, ride my bike from Maple Ridge Road to Carsley Road, take a right on Edes Fall Road, bike for about a mile until it met Linwood's farmhouse on the corner of Edes Fall Road and Town Farm Road. Some mornings were very cold. One half downhill, the other half uphill. Biking back was a bit more uphill, which was complete drudgery at 7AM.

Luckily, I agreed to this arrangement during early spring and into early summer. My chores were simple: I'd bring chopped firewood from his barn into his kitchen, fill up his stove and leave a pile of wood behind for refills. I'd feed the chickens, ducks, and the geese, who slightly terrified me. Geese are very large when standing next to an eleven-year-old, and they hiss without hesitation.

I also had the task of flushing down the feces from the pail Linwood kept beside his chair, as he was often too drunk to walk to the bathroom. This was a once-a-week activity, and obviously the most heinous, and one you should never ask any child to do. He had a toilet in his breezeway, where I would dispose of this filth, then return the pail to the side of his chair where he sat all day. I didn't reveal this to my foster mom until my last week of working there. She was horrified. I was too embarrassed to reveal such a shitty situation, literally. My job ended soon thereafter.

This is also where the dog part of this story begins. This poor dog. When I began my stint there, I would first feed the geese, ducks, and chicken, then bring in Linwood's wood, grab his pan of shit and flush it down the barn's bathroom, which was actually cleaner than the one in Linwood's house, then head to the barn where I would hear incessant barking.

He was locked up in a horse stall. He was a very intelligent dog. I would open up the stall door and see the poor thing chained up, maniacally barking at me, hungry and thirsty as could be. He'd quiet down and warm up to me after about a minute, and I would fill up his food and water bowls. He'd gobble up his food in seconds. I would come closer to pet him as he would hunger for some love and affection, which I gave him. After a few minutes of petting him, I'd leave heartbroken and angry at Linwood for confining such an innocent, good dog alone in a barn, chained up to go stir-crazy. I promised that dog that someday, I would set him free.

After a couple months of this foolishness, I had decided that I was to free him, even if it meant he had no home. This wasn't the way to treat a dog, chained and alone. The weather outside was getting warmer, as by now it was April.

On the final day of working for Linwood, I went through the motions, and after I fed that good doggie, I unleashed him, opened the barn door, and set him free. For a split second, he was shocked, but he quickly realized his new reality. It was a fine spring morning, and he ran out of that horse stall like a liberated prisoner, which he was. All I could hear was him barking as he ran throughout the property. I imagine that for the first time in his life, he actually had freedom and felt happiness.

My eleven-year-old heart knew that was the best thing I could've done for him. I had no backup plan; I just knew he couldn't be trapped any longer. I left satisfied, muttering to myself "Fuck you, Linwood" with a little smirk, but also shaking a little from the adrenaline. Once I got home and told Phyllis what I had done, she just stood there in slight disbelief and chuckled, "Well, hot damn." She knew I had done the right thing.

To add insult to injury, Linwood Nason bitched about how much he was supposed to pay me for that month. Sixteen whole dollars. He couldn't figure out how the hell his dog got loose, but he didn't care enough to get it back, thank goodness! Ultimately, that dog, from what I heard, spent a few days in the woods, then was taken in by a family in the area. Before I heard that, I had wondered what had happened to that dog. The last image I had was of it running in and out of the brush and the woods, happy as can be. I sure hope he did indeed find a good home.

MY SHRINK, DR. AARONSON

Dr. Aaronson came into my life a couple years after my mom passed away. He was my psychologist for a time. He actually looked a little like Bill Bixby with glasses, the guy who played The Incredible Hulk (in that 70's TV series) *before* he became the creature. He was a very good man and was very patient with me. I don't know if he felt like he was helping me.

I'm sure he thought I was holding back information about my home life from him, which I was. I was deathly afraid of telling him that I was being physically and mentally abused by Phyllis. She had threatened me on numerous occasions that if I ever told anybody, she'd hit me even more. Since I preferred to not get hit, I withheld information about my abuse from him. It really sucked as a kid to go through this. I felt cornered, like I was playing games with him which I didn't want to do, but had to do out of self-preservation. The first couple years I went to his office, and then his practice moved into his home on Summit Hill Road in Harrison, so I went there for the last year. He even hired me to mow his lawn that summer, maybe to get closer to me?

One time, when he wanted Phyllis to come along, we were sitting out in the waiting area, and the wildest thing happened. Philly and I decided to start looking for four-leaf clovers. As we began searching, we started finding them. Then we found five-leaf clovers, then six-leaf and seven-leaf clovers! It was the uncanniest thing. I must've saved a dozen of them and pressed them when I got home.

Looking back, I sometimes thought maybe he planted those there to give people hope. Highly unlikely. I'm pretty sure it was just an anomaly, but an incredible one.

The reason why he had wanted Phyllis to attend that one session was because of a false story I told him in the previous session about my mom's ashes at my stepfather's home. I told him that they were up in a closet and that I wanted them to be buried. I apparently elaborated on that story to the point it bothered him enough to include Phyllis the following week. When we both went in, I repeated the story to her.

Of course, she had never heard this before and was horrified. After that visit she contacted my stepfather, who denied that my mom's ashes were in the closet. They were actually on his mantle shelf, along with a little shrine he had created.

When word got back that I had constructed this lie, Dr. Aaronson had a hard time believing me. I had fabricated this story because I was not only upset at my stepfather for not having buried my mom, but I was also upset that Dr. Aaronson couldn't really do anything to help me, so I figured making up something crazy might finally get me out of going to therapy. Well, it worked. I felt bad that I had tarnished our relationship, but I was also relieved to no longer go back.

Since I could never really express to him the abuse I was still receiving from Phyllis, I also couldn't justify how he could ever help me, ever. Suffice to say that I also never mowed his lawn again.

I was sent to another shrink from another town far away with this huge beard and an overly friendly manner, who asked the same stupid questions that got me nowhere. I think I only lasted a month with him.

My stepfather actually took my lie pretty well. I think he figured out the real reason behind it all – I wanted him to bury my mom and give her a place to rest, vs. a creepy shrine in his bedroom. He buried her a couple years later, after it had become obvious that he had to move on from her death. Looking back, if that's what it took to get my mom's ashes out of his bedroom and into a respectable grave, I'd do it all over again.

BRAIN SCAN

Right around seventh grade, I told Phyllis that I felt like I was getting dizzy and leaving my body. I'm pretty sure I even used those exact words. Since my mom died of a brain tumor, there was cause for concern, so I was taken to get brain scans. They wanted to eliminate epilepsy as well as tumors. I think the scans were a month apart, maybe more. They never did find anything wrong with my brain, which was a relief.

I don't really know what answers I was looking for. I think I was literally explaining to Phyllis that I was having out-of-the-body experiences, and I would be looking down at myself from the ceiling, then I'd come back into my body. It was a very surreal time and I was feeling very sensitive about my surroundings at that age.

 I was also feeling sort of a ghostly presence during that time that I couldn't explain. I always felt it out in the hallway of my room and hung a cross over my doorway, hoping that would help for the spirit or entity to not enter. I had a picture of Jesus Christ that I clung onto when I became afraid. His photo always seemed to help. As time went on, I stopped having those out-of-the-body experiences, but still felt a presence in that home. Interestingly enough, a friend of mine, Dawn Wells, came over to our place after school one day and we were hanging out in my room for a little while. Suddenly, I see her looking out the doorway and trying to tell me that she's seeing a ghost while pointing at it. I look just in time to see this black figure in the hallway. It's there for quite a few seconds, enough time for us to look at each other, then back at the figure, until it disappeared into thin air. Let's just say we quickly ran downstairs and didn't hang out in that room anymore. I don't think Dawn and I ever spoke of that moment afterwards.

This was also a time when I was listening to Dr. Demento every Sunday night, 9-12PM. I would hide the radio under the sheets and plug in one earphone, staying up late to hear his top ten. I loved Dr. Demento immensely. It was as if I had grown up a little bit and was listening to songs that were silly and irreverent, not the same Top 40.

I felt like I had found this hidden club for misfits who didn't have another place to hear off-the-wall music, or even comedy. I'd hear Cheech and Chong records, Fish Heads, "Existential Blues" by T-Bone Stankus, my personal favorite, along with "Dead Puppies", "Think I Had a Wet Dream", "Homecoming Queen's Got a Gun", and many other off-the-wall songs. I was in heaven! It fit the bill for a young teenager.

This show helped open up my mind to a world I never knew existed. I truly thought there was only Top 40, country, and classical radio stations, along with the records we owned. Thankfully, that was not the case. Thank you, Dr. Demento and all the artists you exposed me to!

"WHERE IS LOVE?" (MY FIRST VOCAL SOLO)

It was toward the end of sixth grade when my teacher Mrs. Gretchen told our class that she was having auditions for the end-of-year talent show to sing the song from *Oliver!*, "Where Is Love?" A couple of girls auditioned, as well as myself. I was actually egged on by some of them because I was singing along to it and I could hit all the high notes. One of the girls was Allison Smart, who was a really good singer and who I thought was going to get the part.

The auditions were held in the cafeteria/library/activity room of Waterford Elementary School. I was a little nervous but I had heard the song before and knew the melody well. When it was my turn, Mrs. Gretchen began playing the piano and I started singing. I'm pretty sure I hit every note pitch perfect; if not, real damn close. Mrs. Gretchen thought I did well but maintained a poker face. The next day, she told the class that she had chosen the student to sing the song. That student was me. I think secretly inside, Mrs. Gretchen wanted it to be a boy who sang it since after all, Oliver Twist was a boy. I was a little surprised, but I'd been hoping to be chosen.

When it came to rehearsing the song the following week, I hadn't practiced it at all. Mrs. Gretchen was a little disappointed in me for that. Despite this fact, we went through the song 3 times, flawlessly, which I could tell annoyed Mrs. Gretchen even more. She at least wanted to hear one bad note, which I didn't give her.

The next night was the talent show. I actually played Beethoven's Fifth (a condensed version) on piano as well, right after another girl who played the piano much better than myself, so I was a little intimidated. And I also hadn't practiced playing as much as I should've. And it sounded like it. I messed up a part. I was lucky it was only one part. But I digress.

Other acts were performed and then it was my turn! Wow! I was so nervous. There was a stage where plays were held at the school. I was sitting on the front step of the stage, pretending to whittle a piece of wood which was really a number two pencil. I had such stage fright, then remembered Mrs. Gretchen telling me to look at one point in the room if I couldn't handle all the eyes on me. I locked eyes on the EXIT sign in the back of the room above a door frame. Some kid in the front began looking at the EXIT sign, too, because I was staring at it so hard. I couldn't look at anybody in the room.

Mrs. Gretchen began the piano intro, then I began singing. And I kept singing, hitting each note pitch perfect like a church choir boy. I didn't forget any lyrics and just stared at that damn EXIT sign until the very last note left the piano. When I finished, there was this brief moment of silence. I looked over at Mrs. Gretchen, who smiled and nodded at me approvingly, then I heard this wave of clapping and whistling from the crowd, some of them even giving me a standing ovation.

Phyllis was so proud of me. She had no idea I could sing at this level, nor did I, so this was even more shocking to her. Her partner Maryanne had brought her boombox to tape the event, so there's a recording of my very first vocal solo out there. I would love to get my hands on that. After that, Mrs. Gretchen had a newfound respect for me. She kept tabs on my singing during my junior high school years. It was a moment that further cemented my career as a musician before I even knew I would become one.

LEATHER NIKES AND FOOD STAMPS

We were poor, simple as that. For many years, during late fall, winter, and the early spring months, we had to rely on food stamps. It didn't matter that much when I was younger, but as a preteen it did, especially when standing in line watching friends and neighbors see us pay for groceries with unique bills, obviously food stamps. I was humiliated. I tried to erase those memories from my head. It was about survival, not because you *wanted* to be one of the food stamp families. Who the hell aspires to relying on food stamps? Nobody that I knew. The only thing that kept my perspective in check was that I knew so many other families around us who were poorer.

We weren't alone. But it didn't help when I had friends who were middle and upper-middle class. Some level of dignity and pride was erased, replaced with shame.

So, when my sister and I each got our first pair of white leather Nike sneakers with the classic red Nike stripes, it meant a lot. When the other kids saw my Nikes, I was certain they wouldn't think of me as such a poor kid, and I could rest assured at least I wouldn't be ostracized for that. It was tough enough to be the only Asian kid in junior high school among a thousand other kids, so to lessen the pain with a simple pair of Nikes was a Godsend.

My sister and I were over the moon. It helped more than Philly could've ever known. Granted, they didn't last more than six months before coming apart. For such expensive shoes - sixty dollars, back in the day, they sure didn't last long. Alas.

"SAY THANK YOU" WITH A RIFLE TO MY HEAD

I was part of Ranger Rick's book club and would receive a couple books throughout the year. I must've been twelve years old during the last round of Ranger Rick books. One book I remember clearly was *Popeye* with Robin Williams and Shelley Duval on the cover, with his cartoonish forearm and anchor tattoo prominently in front.

When Phyllis handed me the books, I apparently didn't show enough gratitude for them, so she got angry at me, slapped me really hard, and demanded that I say thank you, walking away in disgust. I thought it was over since I said I was sorry and thank you. That wasn't the case. As I stood on our screened-in porch, she came back out with a rifle in her hand. She cocks the gun, aiming it straight at me, and says, "Now, say 'Thank You.'" I was in a state of shock and quite afraid, so I of course said thank you to her repeatedly, out of sheer instinct, just to make sure I didn't get shot.

It apparently worked, as she lifted the rifle away from my head, replacing it with sentences that expressed how "disappointed" she was at how "unappreciative" I was for what it took for her to get me all those books. Unappreciative enough to get a cocked rifle to the head?!

After that scene, I ran into the woods. There was a pine tree that I liked to climb up about twenty feet and hang out. I could still see the house but I was also hidden. I stayed there for a while, trying to process a full range of emotions. I was also running through different scenarios of how I could kill her. As I sat up there, I grew angrier and felt completely confused as well as losing all trust in her. How could such a little thing as not thanking Phyllis for some books make her want to point a loaded and cocked rifle to my head?

After that incident, it was never the same for me with her. I had to find a way out of there. I was seething with anger, vengeance, and confusion. I couldn't live with a person who pointed a loaded gun at me and cocked it. She was ready to use it on me! I still wonder to this day what the hell she was thinking. It was insanity, and if I had been thinking more clearly, I could've told my social worker about this event and left there. But I didn't; I endured another couple years with her.

Sitting in the tree, I heard her calling for me. My stomach knotted. I knew I eventually had to go back into that house. I waited five more minutes just to fuck with her. Then I climbed back down the tree and slowly walked back to the house, not knowing what to expect. I just held in the anger and vengeance I felt towards her. She said some other shit I don't remember, but I know it had nothing to do with apologizing for pointing a cocked rifle at me.

That event was never mentioned again. Obviously. I never told a soul about that. My sister was the only witness, but she couldn't do a damn thing about it. My distrust of Philly grew, and it never left. My singular goal from that day forward was to find a way out from under her. She took away what little childhood I had left that day and filled it with rage. She's lucky it didn't turn into revenge.

Oh, how many countless days and hours I spent imagining ways to kill or torture her, but common sense always kicked in, and images of the Juvenile Facility in South Portland ensured I didn't do anything stupid to destroy my future. So, I just seethed inside until I could find a way out of there.

JUNIOR HIGH SCHOOL

Most of seventh grade was a blur, except for the memory of my homeroom teacher, who began the year with us, left suddenly for a couple months, then returned.

I believe she was on some heavy-duty anti-depressants. She always seemed spaced out. During quiet moments in homeroom, I would see her rocking back and forth in her chair, eyes completely glazed over. I'd get quite concerned at times, but then after a few minutes she'd snap back. This rocking back-and-forth behavior would get longer over the months, until eventually I'd see her full-on swinging, essentially unaware of her surroundings. A few of us were bewildered and confused, not sure if we should be concerned. It was obviously abnormal behavior.

One day she was unceremoniously replaced with Mr. Foster, a local Harrison figure who loved to jog and was a health nut. However, in the classroom, it was clear he didn't really enjoy the role of substitute teacher.

He would get irrationally angry at us, and one time I called him on it. I think it shocked him a bit, because it was coming from me, a really mellow kid, but I also knew him to be much friendlier, and felt like I wasn't getting that friendly person I knew. And he *knew* that somehow. He toned down his anger after I spoke up to him. I don't know what I said, I just know that whatever it was, it shifted him and he seemed to soften for the rest of the year.

MY FIRST JUNIOR HIGH GIRLFRIEND

During the first half of eighth grade, I noticed this really cute, short girl with a great smile, walking the halls of our junior high school. Her name was Stephanie. We didn't share any of the same classes. We just smiled at each other between classes in the halls and talked during lunch when we could. She stood out to me as a warm person. I started writing these little letters that you'd fold up into triangles to hand off to her in the hallway as we passed in-between classes. She'd hand me her own folded triangular notes. The anticipation of getting a note was excitement enough. It meant she liked me.

She had these bright blue eyes and an underbite that I found so attractive, because it accentuated her smile. She even agreed to meet me at Old Homes Day in Harrison and we spent time together going on rides, playing video games, and walking around innocently holding hands, knowing that we just really liked each other. It was my first experience giving a girl the attention she deserved. However, we never kissed, and that I'll always regret. She was so worthy of kissing and I missed out on that opportunity.

Ironically, I lost interest in her in the middle of eighth grade when I became interested in her best friend, Terri Tripp, who was asking about me and which sparked my interest in her. Ahhh, tales of an eighth-grade romance! I broke Stephanie's heart for about a week, but she was definitely a sport for letting her ex-boyfriend pursue her best friend!

What's funny is that I saw Stephanie at a Grateful Dead show in 1988 at Oxford Plains Speedway, in a hippy dress and all smitten over a guy she had obviously come to the show with. I was high as a kite at the time and almost approached her, but I didn't have the heart to interrupt her experience, which seemed to be going well. I was glad to see her happy and on the right path – after all, she was at a Dead show!

EIGHTH GRADE AND DAVID LACOMBE

The school year was still young. During science class, I noticed there was a quirky new kid with a bowl haircut sitting next to me. I soon learned that he had just transferred to public school from Hebron Academy. He obviously did something to get himself kicked out. It was a very prestigious school. So here he was, sitting beside me, already more outspoken than the average kid. I, of course, introduced myself and he did as well. His name was David Lacombe. We immediately got along and became friends. I liked his quirkiness and sense of humor. We also sat across from each other in homeroom.

I began to go over to his home in South Paris after school, a traditional New England farmhouse, large but cozy, with many happy cows nestled about a couple hundred acres of mostly pastures. He had two brothers (one was a stepbrother) and an older sister who had already graduated from high school.

His dad, David Lacombe, was a doctor who practiced in Norway, Maine, as was his stepmother, Ingrid. I saw how he got along with his brothers and that their banter was more mature, filled with cynicism and chummy ribbing. This was where I was introduced to *Star Trek* and *Monty Python's Flying Circus*, as well as *Inspector Gadget*, which we watched every time I came over.

We didn't have cable in Harrison, so late afternoons and early evenings with these programs was completely new and eye-opening to me. It opened up a new world, making me feel a little more cultured.

GINNY THE GOAT & SMOKING HASH IN THE BARN

One day, David decided that it was a great idea to bring out his hash bong, which was something I had never seen or even known existed until this moment, and go out to the goat barn to smoke some hash. I just followed him. We got to the barn and David introduced me to his goat, Ginny. He had this brilliant idea of creating a noose-like knot to tie around her neck so she wouldn't get away.

This turned out to be a terrible idea. Once he put the noose-like knot around Ginny's neck, she began to pull and pull and bleat, then panic and pull against the noose-like knot even more, until we clearly determined she was choking.

By this time, I was literally screaming at David to cut her loose. Luckily, he had a pocket knife with him and we eventually cut her free, but not without being shaken by the incident. I gave him a lot of shit for that event.

Once we calmed down, David brought out his hash bong. As he was putting his ball of hash onto the pin of the bong, he dropped the ball of hash!

You have to understand, we were attempting to smoke hash in a goat barn, where goat poop pellets were littering the floor. The hash ball had fallen onto the floor of similar-sized goat poop pellets. Both of us frantically tried to find this ball of hash. After a minute, I screamed out, "I found it!" We picked up the ball and placed it on the pin. We put a lighter to it and I took a deep toke on it. Then I immediately exhaled and coughed, screaming, "That's not hash, that's goat shit!" David was laughing in fits, barely able to get a breath. I think I eventually laughed once I got the taste of goat shit out of my mouth. It was a day to remember. We never did find that ball of hash.

NOTE TO HASH SMOKERS: Never smoke hash in a goat barn.

TEACHING MYSELF THE DRUMS

Around February of eighth grade, Marianne had gotten a drum set for her birthday. Marianne had begun living with us the year before. She and Philly met a couple years prior and after being in a very abusive relationship, Philly asked my sister and I if we were okay with Marianne moving in with us. We liked her a lot so we had no problem with that.

Fast forward to a year later. Marianne took to the drum set quite well, but for the most part, they stayed unplayed in my old bedroom, so I would often ask her if I could play them, to which she would obligingly say yes. Being that it seemed like such an extravagant instrument to have, it was always exciting to sit behind the set.

There were drum instruction books that I read through. I was surprisingly methodical in teaching myself, starting from scratch and looking at the illustrations of how to hold the sticks, going through the basics of reading the music, starting from page one. Since I'd been playing piano for 7 years, reading basic snare drum music wasn't difficult. I plowed through the first instruction book fairly quickly then moved on to the drum set instructions, which were a little more difficult. I just kept it slow and taught myself simple beats. I definitely felt a connection with them and a sense that I wanted to go another level by getting drum lessons someday. This was my first taste of passion for an instrument, one that wouldn't leave me. I just had to wait another year for it to be fully realized.

BREAK-DANCING AND WINNING TICKETS TO THE 8TH GRADE PROM

In the last week of school, there was a pep rally to talk about the final dance of the year. Our gym teacher, who was also the teacher for a new program that included a break-dancing class, was speaking to the entire class and proposed a dance contest to win two tickets to the final dance of the year. My hand went up immediately. I wanted those tickets bad, because I had a girlfriend, *and* I had been practicing my break-dance moves, in and out of school. Mind you, this was the entire class of students – jocks, popular kids, stoners, nerds, wannabe valley girls, you name it, and there were no other challengers. It was just me. I requested they play the song "Axel F" on the boom box, which the gym teacher happened to have. You have to understand that during this time, I was a complete Michael Jackson and break-dancing fanatic. I mostly liked practicing poppin' and lockin', as well as the moonwalk – forwards, backwards, and sideways. I wasn't as good with the floor spins, but I sure as hell tried.

The entire school body was on full alert now. Unchallenged, I walked to the middle of the dance space that they'd created for me. I am, of course, wearing my black parachute pants with the zipped-down red stripes on the sides from Chess King. The play button gets hit and "Axel F" begins to play.

From this moment on, I go on auto pilot, doing everything I can remember in the break dance world, starting off with the robot, then poppin' and lockin', and doing the moonwalk, which started the cheers in the crowd. That's when I decided, fuck it, and began doing haphazard floor-moves, ending with a back spin, which *actually* almost worked, but *definitely* worked for *this* crowd, because I basically shocked the shit out of them. The music stopped, there was a moment of silence, and there was a roar of clapping and whistling from the whole damn student body. Even the jocks and popular kids clapped and whistled wildly for me. They couldn't believe this quiet little Asian guy basically had the balls to improvise dance moves in front of the entire student body, just to win a pair of tickets to a dance.

What was even more awesome was our gym teacher asking everybody if I had won the contest. The collective roar of approval sealed the deal. He officially congratulated me, then announced that I had won those dance tickets. My motivation was to give my girlfriend, Terri Tripp, the winning ticket, which I did.

Now it's very interesting to observe, when writing about moments like this, that I had this inherent ability to step up to the plate, to do whatever it took to get what I wanted, despite the attention and potential humiliation it could've generated. In fact, the attention was somewhat a subliminal motivation factor.

I seemed to have the ability at a young age to overcome any fears I had and to perform well, because I seemed to have an inherent self-confidence in my abilities.

PUNCHING PHILLY IN THE GUT

I arrived home late one day toward the end of eighth grade to find Phyllis was in my room, and she was pretty upset. I couldn't imagine what she was so upset about. I had done nothing wrong. It escalated to the point where she smacked me hard, and I instinctively punched her in the gut. I was completely shocked by my reaction, as was she. She looked back at me, knowing at once that I was no longer a little kid she could smack around, but also angry and a little bit afraid. I gave her a look that she was sure to remember – one that stopped any thoughts of smacking me again. I remember looking down at my clenched fists as she was walking out of the room, knowing the tide had changed. Smacking and hitting me was no longer an option, not without physical retaliation.

FRIEND OR FOE?

Toward the very end of eighth grade, Chucky (I've changed his name) would sometimes ask me questions about my home life on the school bus before we drove home. More specifically, he asked me if my foster mom was a lesbian. As a self-conscious teenager during the mid 80's, this was like a dagger to the heart.

I never succumbed to him, but I'll also never forget when he asked me the question, with this piece-of-shit, smug smirk on his asshole face, knowing it was mortifying to me, "is she a lesbian?" and I replied, "fuck you." It didn't erase his shitty smirk. In fact, it made him more motivated to keep asking me over and over again, "She's a lesbian, isn't she? Isn't she?" – his shit-hole smile never leaving, until I finally concluded it was best to just ignore him. Admitting to it could've began an endless windfall of taunting from so many others, and the fear of the ridicule was overwhelming.

That pencil-neck, bowl-cut-hair little fucker tried to egg me on but I refused to play along. I needed to respect the privacy of my home life, which he had no respect for. He was immature, lacking confidence himself, and just wanted to embarrass me. I refused to let that happen from some skinny piece of shit hick with a shitty asshole drunkard dad. Granted, his dad was a Vietnam vet, and rightfully never liked seeing me when I came to visit him – I'm sure I reminded his dad of things he was trying to forget.

And what the hell was up with that bowl-cut hair of his?! It looked like his mom saw a photo of Dorothy Hamill in a magazine, plunked him down on a chair and started cutting away. I should've come right back at him and given him shit about that, but I wasn't quick enough on my feet.

Alas! It was hard to be an Asian kid in a school, a *town* filled with mostly white people, then add to that dynamic a foster mom who was considered 'not straight.' We all tried to keep it under the radar. It was the kind of stuff that small towns know, but don't talk about. But junior high and high school kids are different; they can be cruel.

I hated hiding something that I personally thought was just about loving who you love, but tell that to kids who've been taught all their young lives that being homosexual or bisexual is evil and against the teachings of Christ. Funny thing is, Jesus wouldn't have given two shits. But that was the secret that my sister and I had to tamp down every day. It was hard to do. I hated feeling ashamed about something nobody should ever feel ashamed about. We did it though, while holding our breaths, and hoping nothing terrible would happen to us if anything ever got revealed to the wrong people.

THE NIGHT MY WORLD CHANGED AGAIN

Now that I had graduated eighth grade, I decided that it would be a great idea to vandalize the town of Harrison. On the last day of school, Chucky and I talked about going around town with toilet paper and doing stupid shit late at night.

We made plans for me to bike to his home, which was right on Route 35, half a block from the town square, and we'd go out together from there. Well, he didn't take me seriously, so when I showed up at his place around midnight he was surprised, to say the least. He quickly dressed and met me outside. We were both very quiet, since the whole town was quiet as well. I had packed a bottle of shaving cream, a dozen eggs, and a couple rolls of toilet paper. I figured that'd do the trick. But we were respectable, conscientious vandals! We used the eggs only on select truck tires, since we knew that eggs would destroy paintjobs, and we only used shaving cream on the windshields of a couple cars. We made sure we didn't do too much harm to any property. We only wanted to make playful pranks around the town.

We walked down a quiet street and tossed toilet paper up into a few trees. Then we walked to a dock and changed words on some signs, morphing them into words like "shit" or "fart." We snickered at our own cleverness and moved along.

We finally ended up at the Harrison Post Office, ready to separate, BUT... along came the only police officer in town! He took a left off Main Street onto Route 35, made an immediate right into the parking lot, and shined the brightest light I'd ever seen in my life straight in our faces as we plastered ourselves against the brick wall of the post office. Chucky and I looked at each other and either started crying or froze in place, knowing we were both fucked.

By this time, it was about two in the morning. I could not have cared less about Chucky; I was only thinking about myself. The officer was kind enough to put my bike into his trunk as he drove me back home. He had already called Phillis, so I knew this was going to be a big deal.

When we arrived, he took out my bike, talked to her for a spell, then I talked to her, knowing this was the deepest level crap I had pulled so far and not knowing how to explain myself. I could only plead that it was the last day of Junior High School and I just wanted to have some fun.

I somehow managed to fall asleep. When I woke up, I was driven back into town by the same policeman to clean the shaving cream off the truck I had vandalized. The owner of the truck was none too pleased but also relieved that I was respectful enough to keep the eggs off his paint job. Once I had finished cleaning up, I was driven back home.

When I arrived, I noticed my social worker Roger was at the kitchen table, talking to Phyllis. I was a little confused, but soon found out that Philly had decided that the best thing to do was to send me off for a couple weeks to what was called a "Big Brother's Shelter", so she could have a little time to process what had just happened. This, of course, devastated me at the time. I cried for a while, not knowing if I was ever coming back. I was told to pack up a suitcase full of clothes, which I did, between sobs.

I hugged Philly and said goodbye. Somewhere in the back of my mind, I understood that she didn't know what to do with me, pulling such a brazen stunt made her look disreputable in the eyes of the town. She had a troublemaker kid. I totally got it. But I still felt betrayed and confused. Surely what I did wasn't so terrible that she couldn't handle me?! Apparently, she thought differently.

BIG BROTHER'S SHELTER

The Big Brother's Shelter was a program created by the Department of Human Services to help troubled teenage boys from all sorts of situations. They didn't accept violent or mentally unstable boys, just ones who needed a little help to get over a hump in their lives.

Packing up my suitcase and driving over there with my social worker felt like the longest hour. The shelter was located in South Portland, about a quarter mile from the Maine Mall, a very popular place in its day. My social worker, Roger, had my best intentions in mind, and sending me to this place was something he actually suggested to Philly. Once we arrived and I had been processed, there was a little meeting room where he summarized what my options were. He basically told me I didn't necessarily have to go back to live with Philly and that he could find me another place to stay.

The shelter was actually a house, with a dozen teenagers, two per room bunking together. There were two counselors on board at all times taking shifts. On the first morning, after breakfast, the counselors went through the rules. Pretty basic: don't get into fights, don't do stupid dangerous shit, wake up and go to bed at a certain time. Everyone got an hour of counseling a week. No biggie, I was fine with all of it. They also gave us five dollars a week allowance, if I remember correctly, which we'd take to the Maine Mall and spend on video games and an Orange Julius or snacks.

I was around fourteen years old. There were a couple "hard core" sixteen-year-olds who had gotten out of Juvenile Detention, but after hearing them talk, they weren't all that tough. They just played tough, but really, they were just as uncertain as the rest of us. We all watched a lot of MTV, read car magazines and comic books, and played basketball on the court out front. I became pretty good at going around them and putting in lay-ups.

My friend, David Lacombe, got wind that I was there. He had called me in Harrison but Philly told him I wasn't living there at the moment, so he asked where I was then came flying down to visit me, along with his dad and older brother. They appeared pretty shocked when they arrived, not believing that I had somehow gotten to this point. I did not know until years later that his dad was ready to adopt me right then and there.

Boy, my life would've been completely different had that happened. I would've been going to a private school and possibly to college, living with incredibly wonderful people. David's dad was a doctor, and one of the best men I knew growing up. Anyway, we all went to the Maine Mall and hung out for a little while, then they brought me back, and they left with me essentially not getting the hint that I could've gone back with them.

Who knows, maybe in my heart I didn't really want to live the life they had – I wanted something completely different, a big change, a seismic shift. That's exactly what I got.

FINALLY ADMITTING TO ABUSE

After a week of being at the shelter, my social worker Roger came by to visit me again. By this time, I had acclimated to being there and had thought about what he had said about not having to go back to live with Phyllis.

He thought that there had been abuse while living there, but I had never admitted to it because I was too afraid of the ramifications – such as even more abuse if she found that I had ratted her out. At least that's how a threatened child's mind works.

So, we had our meeting. I don't remember if he came right out and asked me if I had considered what he had said to me about not living with Phillis anymore, or if I just blurted out to him that I no longer wanted to go back there. I just remember the weight lifting off my shoulders when I told him I wasn't going back, and the look of shock and relief that came over his face when he heard those words come out of my mouth. We shared a moment. I think he truly felt that he had finally made a difference in my life for the better and that his job finally gave something back to his spirit.

A weight fell off his shoulders that morning as well. I could tell he was relieved that he didn't need to bring a child back to a home that was abusive and could've escalated to a dangerous level.

He told me he'd research some options of families I could live with that were emotionally stable and could foster my growth without fear of further abuse.

A few days later, he came back and told me he had found a family open to bringing me into their home. They were very interesting: a musical family, vegetarians, didn't own a TV, had two daughters, and didn't live too far away. He described them a little bit more and I liked what I heard, so he arranged a meeting with them.

A few days later, we drove over for a first meeting. They lived in a very nice Victorian home on Cottage Road in South Portland, Maine (I found out later that the first mayor of Portland, Maine had lived in this house – impressive!) As they gave me a quick tour of the house, I remember thinking how tall the rooms were, looking up at the decorative aluminum ceilings, twelve feet high.

The parents were Henry (Dick) Wagener and Judith Plano. Dick had the Abe Lincoln look going on, so he stood out amongst the crowd. Judy was dark-haired, had a lot of it in fact, and was warm towards me. She taught piano and violin there, as well as played viola in a chamber orchestra and sang in a choir.

She was incredibly musical. Henry was very philosophical. I remember being very impressed by the books they had: *Seth Speaks*, *Bhagavita*, books by Alan Watts and Carlos Casteneda and many other amazing minds. Their daughters were Jael and Kyla (eleven and nine years old). They were very sweet girls. Jael was a little more outgoing while Kyla was shy but inquisitive. I liked them all very much and after the meeting I wanted to be a part of their family. The feeling was mutual, and they wanted to bring me into their home. It was set! We decided that I was going to be a part of their family and live there! I was very excited and a little scared. I was also going to be transferring into a new school where I didn't know a single soul, nor did I know the town, which was much larger than Harrison.

Now the tough part – telling Phyllis that I wasn't going to be coming back and that I was going to be taking all my stuff to my new home. This was where my social worker Roger really manned up and made tough decisions. We first went back and told Phyllis the news, which took her completely by surprise. She thought that my being at the shelter was just a temporary stay so she could gather her thoughts. I thought differently, and had used my time there to gather my own thoughts, deciding that this was the one opportunity I had to finally leave an abusive home. I had been holding it in for so many years and I finally had been handed a get-out-of-jail-free card.

This devastated Phyllis. She thought of me as her son, she had raised me for *nine years*. She didn't expect this outcome. She cried and pleaded for me to stay. When we left, I felt so free, freer than I had ever felt in my life. I thanked God for my social worker.

However, I was going to miss Corky, my retriever mutt dog. He had been sitting at the door and looking out through its window for weeks, waiting for me to come home. Leaving him was the toughest part of leaving that house, actually. I loved that dog and was going to really miss him. After I'd left for good, he apparently still sat in front of that door every day, waiting for me to come back, until he passed away. That was heartbreaking to hear. I keep a photo of him and me by my computer so I can look at it frequently and remember the joy he brought me as a child.

He'll always be the best dog I've ever known. He'd whine and squeal, and his entire body would wag when I got home from school. He just loved me so much. I still miss and cherish him.

The toughest part was yet to come, logistically, which was getting my stuff out of Harrison and into my new home, since I had officially moved there.

Roger did his final duty, which was to drive me back to Harrison so we could pack up his Ford Escort wagon to the hilt, then drive back to South Portland and unload the car with me. I look back at this feat and consider it one of the most heroic things that any social worker could do.

He went WAY above his duties because he sincerely cared about me. I'll always have admiration for him and gratitude for the second chance in life that he gave me. I wish I could find him and thank him in person.

CHAPTER 4

MY NEW FAMILY IN SOUTH PORTLAND, MAINE

Everything was so new and different. I remember walking around feeling relieved but also nervous, because I didn't know anybody. I met some neighborhood kids that I would be going to high school with and who were also going to be ninth graders. One kid lived across the street from me who I found to be very nice. There was another kid who was nice enough to me, but we didn't really connect and become pals. They were both really just being polite and good neighbors. Our next-door neighbor would let us shoot hoops in his driveway that first summer I arrived. I think the kid across the street was Jewish and the other guy was Italian. He even talked like somebody from Brooklyn or the Bronx, which I kind of liked. I'd never met an Italian kid like that, so it was fun to hear his accent. There was actually a fairly large Italian population in South Portland. I loved walking up the street to DiPietro's Market and getting Italian sandwiches or a pizza. They couldn't beat Amato's Italians but hey, nobody can to this day.

I spent a lot of time alone that first summer, walking up to the basketball court on the corner of Cottage Road and Pillsbury Street (now called DiPietro's Park) and shooting hoops. I had no real friends and no real direction, being too shy to venture out past my neighborhood.

I did spend some time at Willard Beach. It was a new thing for me to have an ocean beach accessible to me, and I loved it. I'd walk out to the lighthouse that sat atop a path of huge rectangular granite piles. It was a small beach but nonetheless did the trick for a bored, lonely kid in the summertime. Preble Beach melded into Fort Preble, which was also the campus of South Portland Community College, and it was a great place to walk and explore. Fort Preble was built during the Civil War, and there were a few cement bunkers you could investigate. It was fascinating and fun for a teenage boy.

TROY PETERSON, MY FIRST FRIEND IN SOUTH PORTLAND

It was getting closer to school reopening, and I was biking around the neighborhood when I came across this funny-looking kid wearing geeky, square metal-rimmed glasses, like myself, mowing his back lawn (on Thompson Street, although his house was on Kittredge Road) and very obviously not enjoying himself. He ran out of gas or something and I asked if he needed any help. He said no, but it sparked a conversation.

His name was Troy Peterson and we soon discovered that we were in the same grade. We started hanging out a little bit, but not really too often until the summer of tenth grade.

I think the majority of what we did from the summer before tenth grade into the summer of eleventh grade was walk around and talk about how we wanted to score weed. He had a friend called J.P. who would sell us joints. "Three bucks a bone, two for five - fuckinnnn..." and listened to nothing but Iron Maiden, so when we went over there to score some joints, we endured Iron Maiden (cranked way up) while waiting for the weed to arrive, which didn't even happen most of the time. It was *torturous.* We just *talked about* scoring it throughout many of our walks around his neighborhood, and honestly, this was almost as much fun as actually scoring it. I credit Troy for introducing me to Led Zeppelin. When becoming a drummer, it really changed my entire perspective of how good I had to be if I was to be a great rock drummer. But that's another story.

MUSIC LESSONS REQUIRED

After a couple weeks of settling into my new home, one night after dinner, Judy gave a speech about music lessons, although the speech was actually directed towards me.

She told me how they (her and Dick) felt it was very important for their kids to learn a musical instrument, so they wanted me to choose an instrument to learn as well. I asked her, "Any instrument?" She said, "Yes, any instrument." A lightbulb flashed in my head, I got a little excited, and in response, I asked her, "Well...Can I learn the drums?" I was doubtful that this could be a viable option. There was a long pause followed by a polite smile, and knowing she couldn't take back what she'd just stated, she replied, "Yes, you can." I asked her again, because I wasn't too convinced, knowing how loud the drums can be, "Are you sure?" She nodded and said, "Yes, we are." I actually couldn't believe that they'd said yes, and a huge smile lit up my face. I promised her that I would practice diligently and become really good. This was the first chapter in really dedicating my time to an instrument, and the true beginning of my path toward being a musician.

DRUM LESSONS WITH BILL TIMMS

Dick heard about a drum teacher by the name of Bill Timms. This is who I began learning drums from, a master jazz drummer whose biggest influences were Buddy Rich and Louie Bellson. He was the first snare player for the West Point Drum Corp and he taught me to read snare drum music from the very same books he had studied, as well as drum set music once I advanced.

I read from the snare drum book for the first couple months before even delving into the drum set books, practicing the rudiments diligently. It was difficult but I was determined to not just learn the drums, but to be *great* on the drums. I practiced for hours at home after school and even more during summer break, sometimes eight hours or more, whatever I could get in. I was obsessed, completely in love with playing drums.

The first breakthrough I had was learning the double-stroke, something that required my wrists to relax until I felt the sticks bounce back up, then alternate hands. It was a huge accomplishment and made me even more determined to progress. I dug even deeper into learning more drum rudiments.

I was given a drum pad set for the first six months, which didn't make as much noise. They also didn't want to invest in a drum set in case I decided that I didn't actually like them. The drum pad set taught me accuracy since the heads were much smaller than a drum set. I practiced playing efficient motions from the snare to the toms and floor tom, while also practicing my reading skills.

Bill taught me that fluid, efficient motions from the toms to the snare were essential to being accurate and having dynamic control as a player.

He would sometimes demonstrate these motions as well (there were two drum sets in the room.) I would watch him move around from the toms, floor tom, and snare, completely mesmerized because he was able to pull off Buddy Rich licks. He even looked a little bit like Buddy Rich. To me, there was no better drummer than my drum teacher. I wanted to emulate all the things he could do, which also kept me motivated. I knew damn well that it would take me years to get to that level, if ever, but I did feel like I had it in me, and he thought the same. He told me that I was his best student and favorite one to teach.

He got excited when I came for my lessons because he knew I would practice. His face would light up, his energy seemed to become buoyant. After about a year and a half of lessons, he started teaching me Latin beats (Samba, Cha Cha, Bossa Nova, etc.) and would quicken the tempo to see if I could keep up, which I eventually could. It was a real challenge to read Latin drum set charts, but I was determined. I had to start all of the rhythms slow as a turtle, then build up to speed. It was all about syncopation and mastering independent limb control. Some of these beats took me weeks, if not a full month, to learn.

But I was a sponge, absorbing everything he threw at me, and I wouldn't stop until I had become proficient with all of the Latin beats. Once I reached a level that he was satisfied with, he then had me reverse the roles of each hand and play the beats. Man, that was another level, but I practiced diligently until I could do all the Latin beats reversed. It taught me a lot about syncopation and muscle control. It does something to your brain, being able to cut time up and reverse roles like that. Very empowering to the spirit. Becoming ambidextrous on the drums was a great achievement, thanks to Bill Timms.

One day when I came in for my lesson, he announced that he was going to retire. My heart just sank hearing that news. He saw that I was unhappy, but looked proudly at me, telling me and Dick that I was his favorite student and he had been honored to give me drum lessons for the last couple years. At my last drum lesson, he decided to gift me his favorite and most beloved Ludwig Speed King bass pedal, as well as his coveted all chrome LP cowbell. He felt kind of bad that he would no longer be teaching me, so he wanted to make sure to send me off with tokens of appreciation and memorabilia, believing in his heart that I had the potential to become a great a drummer. I was blown away by the gifts and held them very dear. I used that kick drum for many years and it helped me to build a very strong and fast kick drum foot. I could do triplets like nobody's business, especially for being only fifteen years old.

It was a hard final drum lesson to get through. I was going to miss him a lot. He was my hero. But he left believing in me, which felt really good. I took that belief to heart and kept on practicing.

At the end of that last lesson, he recommended a new drum teacher, whom I soon found out was just as much of a bad ass in his own way. His name was Phil Verill. I took lessons with him for another year and a half. Phil steered me towards contemporary beats and higher-level Latin beats.

He taught me how to play the ghost notes on the snare, something I wasn't accustomed to doing, as well as nuances of the snare and hi-hat relationship. I started getting into odd-time signatures, but I wasn't the best at them. I didn't practice them enough. And to be honest, things at home would quickly change and I was soon unable to practice drums anymore at all.

What kills me is to this day, I try searching online for Bill Timms' name, and nothing comes up. Absolutely nothing. Here's the most amazing drummer, who should've been mentioned alongside Krupa, Buddy Rich, and Louie Bellson – but nothing! It's as if he just vanished and never existed. He was, to this day, one of the top three drummers I've ever had the pleasure of watching play drums. The only two above him, in my opinion, were Buddy Rich and Chad Wackerman. Argue all you want, that's my list. Bill decided to settle down, and give up the musician lifestyle, so he became forgotten, ignored – a ghost. But I know what I saw and I know what he taught me and I'll be surprised if I ever see that level of skill and talent again. I'll never forget him showing me the one-handed drum roll. I didn't know it could be done, until he did it. Sure, other great drummers can do it, but I saw it first-hand, alongside other amazing feats. All the Latin beats he could play effortlessly, the super-fast crossovers from toms to floor tom to snare – just incredible ideas, and lightning-quick. Here's to you, Bill! I'll never forget what you taught me, and I'll never forget that I gave you some sense of hope when you were feeling down, that yes, there are students out there who want to learn, who can learn, and who have loads of passion.

GETTING STONED AND WALKING ON THE MOON

Troy Peterson and I had finally scored a gram of weed. It was shake, but nonetheless, it was weed, and we were excited. We were finally going to be able to roll a joint, smoke a bone, and get high!

There was this little wooded section off Preble Street in South Portland that stoners apparently used as a perfect stoner hideaway to smoke their joints, so that's where we went, of course. We had been dreaming of this moment for longer than we'd like to admit. So, we walked into this semi-wooded area and after coming into a place we thought was safe from capture, we took out our fat joint and inhaled a few tokes. After a few hits, I started feeling the effects from the weed. Granted, I'd smoked pot a few times before, but it never took. But this time, it did. And boy, did it ever!

We walked out of there, and Troy said, "Man, I'm feeling' pretty fuckin' fucked up, maaan" with his shit-eating grin. "That was some pretty good shit, man. Like, wow, I'm pretty fucked uuup." At least that's what I think he said, or pretty damn close. All I know is that I was feeling the effects of it as well, and lemme tell ya, it was glorious. It was as if everything instantly felt like I was in a cartoon. The problem was, I had to talk, and in order to do that, I had to look at other human beings, but now, they appeared to be cartoon characters. That became quite the conundrum because at this point, everything I was looking at was a giggle-fest. We began laughing at everything. We couldn't even look at each other without laughing. It's what I consider the "chasing the dragon" moment for pot smokers that they'll never find again. You only get that first giggle-fest moment, then it's gone forever. But man, that moment is never lost.

On this most momentous day, I had my Sony Walkman clipped to my waist with the tape of *Regatta de Blanc* by The Police in it. As I walked out of the woods, I put my headphones on, pressed play, and I have to say, it changed my world. From the very first notes of Andy Summers and Sting, with his guitars panning left to right, to Stewart Copeland's reggae-like beat, the tone was set just right.

The magic of the moment was seared into my memory, making that first high not just a funny experience, but also an incredible musical sensory experience, the likes of which I've never been able to replicate in depth.

I sauntered along to the song for a little while, smiling and blown away at how *good* music could sound. I heard every detail of the song.

When the song finished, I clicked the tape off and decided that I wanted to buy a pack of Marlboros. So, Troy and I walked over to Al's Market, not even a hundred yards from where we were. Al was this short, older Italian guy who was a mix of Picasso and Mr. Roper from *Three's Company*. He had lived in the neighborhood for decades, along with his wife.

Once Troy and I got to the market, we had to stand out in front and get our giggles out of the way. I was cry-laughing, unable to contain myself. I was also trying to build up the courage to walk in and ask for a pack of smokes, something I'd never done. Troy couldn't do it because Al knew him and he was afraid his mom would find out, or something like that.

Anyway, I walked into the little market, went to the counter, looked at Al, tried not to giggle, and asked for a pack of Marlboro Reds, thinking the Reds part was a pretty smart thing to add to make me sound all mature and shit. Then he asked me, "Box or soft?" and I immediately panicked. I'm asking myself, "What the fuck is soft or box?!" but I just said, "What?" Al repeated his question "Box or soft?" and sounding a little short with me now, so I just quickly said, "Box" hoping that was the right answer.

He turned around, got a pack, which was apparently the box type, placed it on the counter, and rang me up. I gave him the money, he gave me the change, I turned around with a smile and walked out, not believing that I had just gotten away with buying a pack of Marlboro Reds as a minor, while stoned as shit!

Troy saw me walking out, giggling uncontrollably, and said, "Well, did you … do it?!" Troy couldn't believe I had done it. Nor could I. We just stood there for a moment, first packing down the cigarettes, then walking off and smoking them and getting a whole different kind of high. I think I even had to go back in to ask for a pack of matches! After that we proceeded to walk around the neighborhood, giggling like the stupid high teenagers we were. Man, oh man, that was one of the best days of my life, bar none. Thank you, Troy, Al, and *The Police*!

I'LL KICK YOU IN THE FACE OVER BEATLES PHOTOS

Funny enough, this was my only friendship that was cultivated from a threat I made to kick someone in the face. Matt was friends with Brent and Kelly. They all lived in the same neighborhood, on or close to Preble Street in South Portland. Matt was one of only two black guys in the high school. I was only one of three Asians in the same school. He was overweight but always confident and looked a lot like Rerun from the TV show *What's Happening*, even moreso since he wore a red beret.

One morning at school, while Brent and I were at Kelly's locker, Matt came by and I was introduced to him for the first time. I thought he was kind of shifty, like a car salesman but charismatic. He brought out some photos he had of the Beatles that he wanted to sell for five dollars per photo. They were the headshots that came inside The Beatles White Album, but I didn't know this at the time. I thought they were great, so I bought the photos of John and Ringo, paying him ten dollars.

Weeks later, once I found out that they were essentially free photos, I was pissed. I confronted him about this and he admitted that they were in fact free, but I had already paid him, so I couldn't get my money back. This made me even more pissed off, so I told him he had to pay me back at least half the money. He kind of blew me off for a couple weeks.

Finally, one afternoon as he was about to get off the bus, I told him, "You better give me my money back or I'll kick you in the face." He tried not to laugh, but after a brief pause, he did just that, not able to contain his composure. "I mean it, man. I'll kick you in the fuckin' face."

He said, "OK, OK, I'll get you your money back, dude" as he walked off the bus, not concerned in the least about my five dollars.

I never got my money back from him, but I did earn his respect and we ended up hanging out more. So began my long friendship with Matt Beal. To this day, we're still friends.

A DOZEN ROSES TO MY SECRET CRUSH

I didn't have any girlfriends in high-school. Zilch. Nada. I had no game, nor did I have the social skills to talk to any girls who showed any interest. I was a geek, at least from ninth to tenth grade. I played Hackey Sack obsessively in my driveway alone after school, and eventually found some guys to play with during lunchtime – they were also geeks. But we weren't the classic brainiac geeks. We didn't fit into any mold. We were just creative-minded, if you will, although we certainly didn't classify ourselves as that; we were just trying to get through the day. Mind you, we weren't harassed, but we were easily overlooked.

Once tenth grade hit, I slipped into the tweed-overcoat and growing-my-hair-long phase. Bono was making that look popular, and I happened to like that look. Not that I was a big fan of U2, I just liked having a look that made me feel cool, and even if I was still a geek, I was trying to break that mold. I went so far as to break my plastic-lens glasses so as I could get a pair of round, metal-rimmed frames that resembled John Lennon, who I was obsessed with at this time.

I'm quite certain that Dick and Judy didn't believe my story of how I tripped in the basement, and my glasses suddenly fell to the floor, my foot landing on a lens and breaking it to pieces. Those lenses were considered unbreakable. Judy gave me a quizzical look, but couldn't do anything about it but replace my glasses. It was well worth the scheme, for the sake of fashion.

I got a pair of metal-rimmed glasses that were similar to John Lennon and was no longer embarrassed. I finally felt like I had an identity; any hurtful words would bounce off like I was made of Teflon. Some jocks would even say, "Hey Bono" to me as I walked down the hall, like it was an insult. I'd just snicker at them and move along. It was laughable.

BTW, that tweed overcoat also came in handy during Chemistry class when I wanted to sneak out glass beakers and parts to make custom bongs. The teacher eventually became suspicious of me and started checking my pockets, but it was too late – I had already smuggled all the parts I needed.

When late spring arrived during tenth grade, I mowed lawns to make some money. After a few weeks, I had gathered enough funds to buy a dozen roses for my secret crush, Alicia. She was a ballerina, in my same grade, quiet, but also somebody I knew was actually going for it as an artist, and would actually take time to pursue it at such a young age. I was inspired by her drive and focus. Plus, she was so pretty. She was Italian and didn't speak much, like myself. She was mellow, and I liked looking at her walk down the halls of the school with her feet out like Charlie Chaplin, always ready to be in a ballet position.

Her family also knew Dick and Judy, and babysat Jael and Kyla when they lived in a house close by on Sawyer Street. One Saturday morning I walked into the only flower shop on Cottage Road, bought a dozen red roses, and asked them to be delivered - from a secret admirer.

A couple days later at school, I knew that she had gotten them after overhearing her cousin talking about it. Nobody knew who had sent them. I smiled. My secret was safe, even though I really wanted her to know, but I would've been too embarrassed had it gotten out.

Summertime came, and I apparently felt bold enough to write her a letter, fully exposing my crush. It was the most important letter I'd ever written at the time, knowing my chances of "being with her" were slim to none. But she had to know how I felt about her.

Boy, was I bold. I even told her what music I listened to. That's crucial information – if you can't connect musically, you probably won't connect mentally. I mailed my tell-all letter to her, then never followed through. Life events shrouded any hopes of a future together.

Jump forward about twenty years. I looked her up on Facebook on a whim, wrote some quick thing about the past, and she responded the next day, saying she remembered me. Mind you, I'm happily married now, just curious about people in my past, and she responded. We talked on the phone for a bit, reconnected, and it was so wonderful to get her perspective of me as a geeky teenager who had the balls to expose my heart to her, despite knowing it would never lead anywhere. It was about being brave with my feelings, hoping it would touch her in some way.

A couple years later, she sent me a PDF of the letter I wrote to her. First, I couldn't believe that she had kept it. It meant the world to me – the innocence and timeliness of the questions I asked her, but also the brazenness I revealed of myself. I wasn't afraid to express myself, even at that early an age, despite the potential for ridicule. I consider her a good friend to this day.

DISHWASHER AT THE BLUE MOON

My second official job was at a restaurant named The Blue Moon on Fore Street in the Old Port of Portland, Maine. It was right around the corner from The Record Exchange, beside the garage building. I was hired as a dishwasher, making $4.75 an hour. Matt Beal got me this job. He was the prep cook. Funny enough, within a couple weeks of my getting a job there, Matt quit. I stayed on, of course. The crew was fun. The owner David was very kind and cool-headed, a dark-haired handsome Italian guy (more Italians! What's goin' on?! Ha!). For months I had no idea he was gay and was an important figure in the Portland gay scene. Since I wasn't in that scene, it never occurred to me. I just knew he was a really nice guy, treated everybody well, everybody treated him well, and he had a nice restaurant.

Peter was the sous chef, this tall and scraggle beard nerd of a guy with nerd glasses and big teeth. He looked a lot like David Bromberg and was the one to turn me on to Steely Dan; their album *Gaucho*, specifically. He played that album there a lot, then I bought it at The Record Exchange, on tape, and played it a lot at home, Man, did that album open up my ears.

Then there was Adam Powers, the prep cook, who was twenty-four years old but looked like he was eighteen. He was a quiet but very friendly, positive and inquisitive soul. He loved Led Zeppelin, so we got along just great. We nerded out on all things Zeppelin. He was recording this demo tape at the time and starting a new band called Twisted Roots, which I thought was a great name.

Frank was the late-night chef, a fun, gregarious kind of guy. He was in his early twenties, but seemed much older than Adam who, again, looked like he was eighteen. This guy liked to party but it never affected his ability to work. He worked a few days a week.

Aesop was a newer hire, a cool black dude who had just come out of chef's school. He got hired part-time, but quickly came to take over the kitchen due to some issue that occurred with Peter. I was gonna miss Peter but I certainly didn't mind working with Aesop, who quickly revealed that he was pretty damn funny and entertaining. So long as I worked hard and fast, which I did, we'd get along just fine and the jokes would keep rolling in.

During down times in the kitchen, Aesop would teach me a lot about cooking: how to make sauces, soup stocks, how to cook steaks versus different kinds of fish or chicken, how to cut vegetables certain ways to get the best flavor from them, how to sauté, fry, broil, and many other skills.

It was basically like going to school. I'm sure I learned a couple years' worth of skills while working with him. And he shared his skills openly with me, knowing I was receptive. He also wanted to see me elevate beyond being the dishwasher, as he clearly saw I had the potential to learn beyond those basic skills.

The sad thing was I only stayed at The Blue Moon for about a year before I decided to leave and work Denny's night shift as a cook. Aesop laughed out loud when I told him, rightfully so. Funnier thing is I only lasted two nights working at Denny's, utterly depressed at the end of those shifts, knowing it was a huge mistake to have ever left The Blue Moon. I always look back at those times fondly and wonder if I would've ended up becoming a sous chef had I stayed.

DISCOVERING THE BEATLES AND OTHER MUSIC

That record store at the bottom of Exchange and Fore Street called "Record Exchange" was the hippest and only record store around unless you went to the Maine Mall in South Portland. This one had all the alternative bands, though.

I was beginning to get curious about The Talking Heads, The Police, and The Beatles, as well as David Bowie. I ended up buying *Little Creatures* and *Hunky Dory* for my first albums, then I got tapes of *Outlandos D'Amour*, *Rubber Soul*, and *Zeppelin I and II*.

Most of these were bought between ninth and tenth grade. I was getting sick of playing hacky sack in the driveway alone and decided I needed to get more into music.

I believe *Rubber Soul* started my journey. Once I put that Beatles tape into my Walkman, wrapped my headphones around my ears and pressed play, there was an instant sophistication that I felt and heard in their songwriting and singing that I had never experienced with any other band, ever, and I immediately fell in love with them. I listened to that tape over and over, learning the lyrics and singing along to them. This was before I was writing music, but during the time when I was actively learning the drums.

Then came *Little Creatures* by The Talking Heads. I loved their song, "And She Was" which, to this day, has the best sounding kick drum recorded of all time, and that spurned me on to buy the album. We had a really nice Harmon Kardon sound system at home, which I utilized often. Dick was very proud of it, but also cautioned me to never touch the EQs on it as the settings were perfect for the room.

When Dick and Judy would go out occasionally and leave me alone in the house, I'd bring the drum set down into the living room from the attic so I could play along to their songs.

I'd crank the volume up and have a blast. I also did this with *Hunky Dory*. By this time, I was hanging out with Michelle Sanborn and Zibah Williams, who were complete Bowie and Cure fans. I didn't dig The Cure, but I definitely dug Bowie.

He was alternative and hip, something I hadn't heard before. He had a similar songwriting sophistication as The Beatles had which I was immediately drawn to. I loved his melodies and concepts.

Next up, The Police. I'd heard "Roxanne" and that was it. The beat was so unique. It had that semi-reggae vibe meets funky rock beat. It was addictive to listen to, and I had to figure out how to play the hi-hats like Stewart Copeland. I'd put on their tapes, *Outlandos D'Amour* and *Regatta de Blanc*, and play along to them obsessively.

Then came Led Zeppelin. My first experience with their music was after coming home late one night and having taken some old LSD. It wasn't really hitting me that hard, just enough to affect the music and my senses when I closed my eyes. I had bought *Zeppelin I* on tape and played it on my Walkman as I was going to sleep, and it just brought me into this other state of being. The drumming was on a level that I had never heard before. They were the perfect rock band as far as I was concerned.

Besides learning about Buddy Rich, Louie Bellson, and other jazz greats, these artists formed the foundation of my musical influences. Pink Floyd and their album *Animals* was soon to follow and become my favorite album of all time, even to this day.

What's funny is that despite my dislike of how far back the cymbals were recorded, and how dry and flat the snare and toms sounded, it's still my favorite album, in both concept and its overall vibe. It even beats out *Abbey Road*.

TAOISM AND NATIVE AMERICAN TEACHINGS

By the time I was halfway through eleventh grade, I was connecting with Taoism and reading up on Native American culture. Taoism seemed to fit how I wanted to think. It "checked all the boxes" if you will: it wasn't a religion, but it felt very spiritually fulfilling. It answered questions I had about life with questions, which seemed very clever the more I reflected on those questions; and it explained perception in a very balanced manner, at once spiritual and logical, without emotional attachment, while feeling immediately connected in its answers.

For every action, there is an equal and opposite reaction. How can that not resonate with a curious young mind? But add the mystical aspects to it, and you have something that stimulates an unquenchable thirst to keep seeking more knowledge from it.

I also began taking out library books on Native Americans, specifically books on the Sioux and Cherokee nations. I was fascinated by them. I also was obsessed with photos that depicted Native Americans throughout the United States, and I read quotes from the chiefs of many nations. Reading about them made me realize that high school hadn't taught me the real history of America, and how we had basically demolished entire cultures in order to gain power over their land, which represented economic resources. It was very sad and very sobering. America wasn't founded on good faith; it was founded on contracts filled with false promises and on the destruction of a people who had lived peacefully for thousands of years, until their peace was decimated by disease and deception. I was horrified. Welcome to the real world, where promises don't mean shit, and survival means out-tricking your adversary.

So, I wrote a paper on Taoism instead of on the Native Americans. Taoism was much easier to wrap my mystically curious head around. And hey, I got an A- on my report. I was quite proud of that report. A couple months later, I quit high school.

RUNNING AWAY TO PHYLLIS

An incident occurred when I came home late one night at 11PM and was confronted by Judy at the door, holding a corncob pipe with aluminum foil on top of it and pin needle holes poked through it. She asked me what it was for. I told her I was smoking tobacco with it. She didn't believe me and smacked me really hard. Ironically, I had done that to smoke weed, but I could never score any weed to smoke through it, so I smoked tobacco instead with it. She told me to go up to my room and we'd talk about it in the morning.

This began the odyssey of teenage friction between me and Judy and Dick. Judy came from a place of constant worry. She also didn't believe me about anything, which began the cycle of distrust that I was trying to leave behind with Phyllis. It made me really sad that she now didn't believe me, but hey, it doesn't look that good when you own a corncob pipe with a piece of aluminum as your screen. She was afraid I was becoming a druggie. Granted, I was beginning to change at this age, becoming influenced by the hippy ideologies of the 60's and music of the 60's-70's, and wanting to change my look by growing my hair, wearing a tweed overcoat at school and wanting round glasses like John Lennon.

I also rummaged through Dick's closet and found a couple of his hippy shirts, which I loved wearing. So yes, she had reason for concern, but it went overboard. It actually caused me to call Phyllis, collect, at the Cumberland Farms payphone up the street and ask her to pick me up, which she did. I was feeling very confused and regretful that I had ever left her. All I had was a backpack of clothes. I'm sure Dick and Judy were worried when I didn't call them until the next morning. It was Saturday morning and I agreed to come back on Sunday. I got to spend some quality time with Phyllis. We reminisced and did some healing. She understood I had to go back the next morning and drove me there.

Once I got back, we all had a family meeting. It was tense. They still didn't trust me but at least I aired out my grievances. I was grounded for a month, if not the summer, only allowed to go to work and come back home.

BECOMING ADOPTED THEN RUNNING AWAY

Dick and Judy adopted me in May of 1987. We were still patching things up from my running away, so it was kind of ironic that the formality of my adoption came shortly after that event. I had mixed feelings about getting adopted at that time even though I certainly wasn't opposed to it. I still cared for them greatly, as well as for Jael and Kyla, my sisters.

What should've been a very momentous occasion felt more anti-climactic, given that I had just recently run away and was also grounded for some ungodly amount of time. Imagine that – grounding a teenager for months, after they've run away, without any therapy or outside help and influence, thinking that this was the formula to encourage my sticking around with my newly adopted parents. To their credit, they were in a bind with me. I couldn't go unpunished, but I had certainly stopped listening to them.

Only a month after being adopted, I hastily packed my bags and ran away again.

Since the corncob pipe incident secured a level of suspicion and paranoia about my drug use (in their minds), the next incident was only a natural escalation in securing a paranoid belief that I was a complete stoner and addict. They noticed that I had begun to burn incense in my bedroom, which is something that only people who smoke pot do.

Ironically, I wasn't smoking pot in my room, nor had I ever. It was brought to my attention by Dick one morning when I was on my way to work, in his stern way, eyebrows twitching and all, that since I was burning incense in the house, unattended, for the second time, I was "a fire hazard to the household", and I was "to be fined seventy-five dollars".

He went on further to stipulate that if I didn't like the rules, I could leave. Well, little did he know that the leaving option really stuck in my head. After finishing his incense speech, I silently nodded in agreement, then went back upstairs, seething.

They were already taking half of my paycheck to "help the household" and this was adding insult to injury, since I'd never smoked weed in our home, ever. I decided right then and there that I was done with this bullshit. I went into my bedroom, grabbed my bag, packed a few days' worth of clothes and waved goodbye to them as I came downstairs to leave for work. I was done with their rules. To be grounded was one thing. To be fined and labeled a fire hazard to the household was another level. I was so angry, insulted, and hurt. I could not, with my teenage brain, believe this was a healthy environment for me to live in any longer.

I'll never forget the last interaction we had before I walked out the door. I looked at them as I came down those stairs, backpack full of clothes unbeknownst to them, and smiled as if nothing was wrong. I acted as if I was going to be complacent and follow their rules, looked at their smiles one last time, knowing I was never going to live there again, and left.

It was at once a feeling of liberation mixed with deep internal anger. I was so sick and tired of adults not believing me when I was actually telling the truth. It was, again, the cycle that I had endured with Philly, only to be revisited with Dick and Judy. And look at where it got me – in the same emotional place, of not trusting those who were supposed to believe in you.

I could say in hindsight that this moment was emotionally pivotal, but it was also coming from a confused sixteen-year-old mind with major trust issues, to say the least. Regardless, walking out that door gave me a huge sense of freedom, even if it meant I had to go it alone. At least I wouldn't have to deal with adults who didn't trust me. It was painful to deal with the guilt of leaving behind the stability and support they had given me. But I was sacrificing all that in order to regain and build some sense of dignity, and an identity other than that of a walking liar.

So, I took the city bus and went to my job at The Blue Moon. The next time they saw me was a month later when I came to pack up the rest of my belongings.

CHAPTER 5

INDEPENDENCE IN PORTLAND, MAINE

LEAVING DICK AND JUDY, BEING HOMELESS, FINDING MAUREEN

When I officially ran away from Dick and Judy's, I initially had no plan. I felt free as a bird, so long as I had a job. I told Michelle and Zibah what I had done but they could only let me crash at their homes for a couple nights at most. Once I had exhausted my nights sleeping at their homes, I began walking around late nights on the Western Promenade, overlooking the West Side of Portland. It was quiet at nights, but I could never get much sleep because the silhouettes of other homeless people would freak me out. I'd be thinking that they were staring at me in the dark, so I'd move along so nobody could watch me while I was resting.

I didn't get much sleep for the first few days of officially being homeless. For a couple mornings, I'd crash inside parked cars that were enclosed in the garage beside The Blue Moon, where I worked. I became pretty adept at sneaking under the gate since I was so skinny. Once I was in, I'd walk around and test the handles of car doors. Most were closed. Sometimes I'd get lucky, like one night, when I tested a Porsche 911 door handle, and lo and behold, it opened up. I snuck in, grateful to be out of the cold and have a seat where I could rest for even an hour. I had to watch it because it was about 5-6am, and the security guard was driving around, so I had to duck down in order to not be seen. He passed. Phew. I opened the glove compartment and found nothing but some paper napkins and registration papers. I opened up the middle compartment, where I found some change and a little coke spoon. It's a Porsche, of course there's a coke spoon. No coke, of course, but I wouldn't have known what it was if I saw it back then. I put the $1.50 of change into my pocket then hunkered down into the seat and closed my eyes.

About an hour later, I woke up and heard the city waking up, so I decided it was time for me to move on. I snuck back out from under the gate and began my morning journey.

I walked up Exchange Street with my backpack, waiting for my lunch shift at work and hoping I wouldn't become another homeless teenage statistic. The reality of where I was at began to sink in quickly. I went to Green Mountain and grabbed a cup of coffee, sat on one of their benches, and thought about my predicament, hoping this wasn't going to be my new normal.

In a few hours, I walked back down Exhange St., took a right on Fore Street and walked into work. The familiar bantering with the cooks was refreshing, and getting some food in my belly, as well as a warm place to be, was all a welcome distraction from what awaited me once my shift ended and nightfall came.

I went back out and walked around, slowly and aimlessly. I walked over to the Western Promenade again but didn't dare stay there. I just climbed that tree beside Maine Medical Hospital, smoking cigarettes and looking down on the western side of Portland where Danforth Ave crawls out to the I-95 and Forest Ave slides perpendicular to it. I spent a lot of time up in that tree, or so it felt. Then I'd climb back down and walk towards the cemetery where Zibah, Michelle, and the gang would hang on the weekends. I thought of sleeping there, but that seemed a little too creepy. So, I'd just walk the streets again, not quite knowing what was safe and what wasn't, and tired from lack of sleep.

The next morning, back at Green Mountain, sipping coffee on one of their benches again, enduring the morning chill, I'd had enough and decided I had to figure something out quickly. I swore to myself that I'd never be homeless again after this nonsense. It wasn't worth the hardship, but I also refused to go back to live with Dick and Judy.

I did the only thing I knew to do, which was to call Philly. I think I even called her collect. She picked up the phone and we had a good conversation. I told her my predicament, and she mentioned that Maureen, or "Momo" as I liked to call her, was living in Portland, and that I should call her. My heart lit up with this information, so I asked Philly for Momo's phone number. She gave it to me, we talked a little longer and then I thanked her, hung up the phone, and immediately called Maureen. When she answered the phone, I shyly told her who it was. She was delighted to hear from me, but was also very surprised as we hadn't been in touch since I was twelve years old when she'd lived with us in Harrison. I loved her dearly and missed her, hoping we could reconnect. We'd had a deep and loving connection. She was always worried about me when she went off to work, leaving me alone with Phyllis, concerned about my welfare since she couldn't live with her either. But here we were, talking on the phone finally.

I told her a little bit about my predicament. She told me she was living with Terri, a woman I had met years ago, and I really liked her as well. Terri had a two-year-old son, Nicholas. I asked if I could visit them. She said of course I could and gave me their address. They lived in a 3-bedroom apartment up on Munjoy Hill on Lawrence Avenue, barely a mile away. I hung up the phone and excitedly walked there.

Fifteen minutes later, I arrived and knocked on their door. Maureen opened it, smiled her Irish cherub smile, chuckled loudly and gave me a huge hug. I was so happy to see her as I had missed her so much. I felt such relief knowing that she was actually still alive, and better yet, right in front of me! Terri was right behind her and welcomed me with open arms and a huge smile, and most likely had a Newport Lights Menthol 100's cigarette in her left hand. She was a warm and good woman, as well as a professional concert violinist. I walked in and sat down on a chair in their kitchen, and we talked for quite some time.

Now that I had the time, I told them my situation at length. They told me they had a spare bedroom where I could spend the night. I was very grateful. I'm sure they asked me if I was hungry. I'm sure I said I was. A little while later, I was introduced to Terri's son, Nicholas, who was playing in his bedroom. He was a little shy at first, but once he warmed up to me, we were good. He was a little hyper, like most boys are, and very bright. His father wasn't a part of his life, so I had some empathy for him. I could sense a little need for a father figure, or at least a male role model to be around for him. He wasn't as aware of that, but he was happy to have me around. We played for a little while and he showed me what he liked, which were Teenage Mutant Ninja Turtles and Nintendo. He got bored after about ten minutes, so we went back to the kitchen where us grown-ups talked a little more. I'm pretty sure Terri and I smoked a joint to christen the moment. Yes, they were very open-minded. Stoned and content, I went into their guest bedroom and slept for what seemed like a very long time.

When I woke up, Terri and Maureen had apparently talked it over and decided to ask me if I wanted to stay with them, at least for the time being. It was music to my morning ears. I would pay rent and give them some money for groceries. I was secretly hoping that they'd suggest this when I woke up. It felt like a dream come true. Little did they know how much anxiety they quelled when asking that question. They became family.

COLLECTING MY BELONGINGS FROM DICK AND JUDY

Once I had settled in after a couple weeks, the intense and unfortunate reality of getting the rest of my belongings from Dick and Judy loomed over me. It had to be done, and a phone call had to be made.

I gave them a ring and luckily, Dick picked up the phone. Judy was too distraught over the whole situation, and rightfully so. I told him that I was living with Terri and Maureen and that I needed to retrieve my stuff. Dick acquiesced and arranged for us to come over.

Terri was kind enough to offer to drive me there and help me pack her car up with my belongings. My stomach was in knots once we arrived. Judy showed her face briefly, saying something that came from a place of pain and anger, then went back into hiding. Dick was trying to be as gentlemanly as he could be while trying not to reveal the guilt and pain he was feeling with every handful of belongings I brought out to Terri's car. He even helped carry stuff out, despite being in a state of shock. He admitted to me years later that he felt like he had failed me as a father. I felt terrible for Jael and Kyla, my sisters. They were so young, and for them to have to go through such a traumatic event haunted me for years.

We finally packed the last load into the car; I said goodbye to Dick, and as we drove away, I watched his shoulders and head slump forward in sadness. As difficult as it was to leave them in this way, a huge emotional weight lifted from me. I had survived my decision to leave them. It could've turned into a much worse situation that involved homelessness and other unknown events, but that wasn't the case.

I was very fortunate and grateful to have essentially been saved by Terri and Maureen, welcomed into another new family, but one with Maureen, a person whom I'd known and trusted since I was a kid. I must've thanked Terri half a dozen times on our way back to my new home. She smiled at me, rolled down her window, and lit a much-needed Newport Menthol cigarette.

I was still processing what just happened, happy that I was brave enough to enter that house again, but regretful that I had left so much sorrow behind. I didn't want it to be that way, but I knew I couldn't live with them. I could only look ahead and hope that the decision I made was the right one. It sure felt right.

QUITTING HIGH SCHOOL

As I got settled into living with Terri and Maureen, I continued to go to South Portland High School while working five nights a week at The Blue Moon and juggling homework. It was very challenging. I was exhausted all the time. I tried to transfer to Portland High School, but Judy was too angry at me to sign the transfer papers. It was quite disheartening as I wanted to continue my studies, but biking to South Portland in the winter, or taking the city bus there, then walking a mile to the school five days a week, took its toll.

One night after coming back from school, I broke down to Terri and Maureen, telling them I just couldn't do it anymore. Terri actually gave me advice that resonated, stating that it wasn't such a big deal if I quit. She just said, "So, quit." and shrugged her shoulders, a practical expression on her face. I knew that I could always get my GED later. She made me feel that it was OK to decide to do that, and not ashamed. It was a huge revelation in my life, and it didn't take long to mull over the option of quitting once she said that. So, after a few more minutes of talking to them and wiping the tears from my face, I decided that I was going to write my guidance counselor a letter explaining my decision, bike to school in the morning for the very last time, and end the suffering.

For the first time, she showed me that I actually didn't *have* to go to school, that there were options, and that I could obtain my GED later. She showed me that I had the power to make changes that benefitted me, even if it wasn't the best or typical path for everyone.

I wrote a letter to my guidance counselor about my difficulties managing school and work, as well as not living with my adoptive parents, and that not being able to transfer to Portland High School made my decision to quit all but final.

Morning arrived; it was really sunny and the snow was melting. It was mid-March and I'd decided to bike to school for the last time. Once I got there, I asked the front desk secretary to put my letter into my guidance counselor's mailbox, which she did. The funny thing is that after she did that, she also handed me my driver's license, which somehow had gotten lost, found, and handed in without my being aware of it. That felt like a sign, validating that my decision was a good one, for me.

After I handed that letter over, I walked outside, got on my bike, and experienced one of the best feelings of joy in my life. To join in the celebration, the clouds parted and the sun came out, shining down and warming the air.

I got back on the road, and by now the snow was really melting, and I was feeling elated, light as a feather, and fully in control of my future. I rode back into Portland, Maine while a huge weight fell off my shoulders, and was replaced with a huge smile of relief. I felt like my life was, at last, my own, even if it didn't seem like a rational decision. It made complete sense to me, and I knew I could get my GED later. A diploma from a school I felt disconnected to didn't hold any emotional weight.

I returned to my new home, looked at Terri, and when she asked, "Did you do it?" and I answered, "Yes," she gave me a big hug and smiled a mother's smile, followed by another big hug from Maureen.

They made it clear they were proud of me, knowing I did what was best for myself. They showed me what it felt like to take control of my life at a young age and it empowered me, teaching me to feel confident in making decisions that benefitted my mental health.

From that day on, I felt more in charge of my destiny, because I realized life was about figuring out what you needed to do for yourself, doing it, and accepting responsibility. It was a powerful shift at a very impressionable time. I wouldn't change that decision if given a second chance.

From that day forth, my new life began without Dick and Judy. I felt like Terri and Maureen became my true parents – open-minded, open-hearted, and able to provide me with a fresh beginning.

The next morning, I woke up to my friends, Matt and Brendan, pushing a pot-filled pipe to my mouth, with Matt saying, "Wake and bake, dude." I took a hit, coughed a lung out, and immediately got high. Welcome to my new life. Ha!

GREEN MOUNTAIN COFFEE ROASTERS AND THE OLD PORT

In 1987, I began hanging out at this coffee shop in Portland, Maine called Green Mountain Coffee Roasters, located on Temple Street, right beside Nickelodeon Movie Theaters and below a parking garage. There were park benches in front, three on each side facing each other, and grassy areas where you could sit and hang out.

Previously, I would drive by on my bicycle and see an array of different characters – kids with mohawks, all black clothes, army jackets with Dead Kennedys logos stitched on the back, leather-jacket-wearing punk rockers, goths, patchouli-wearing hippies, writers, you name it, and I would wish I could be a part of that scene. It was so electrifying to me that I just had to hang out there, too.

One day, I finally did. I began meeting the very people I had been watching from afar. The first one was Terryle, a very short girl who had a semi-mohawk and a skateboard. She was very sweet and talked fast. She introduced me to Zibah Williams and Michelle Sanborn, two artsy goth girls whom I quickly became friends with. Zibah tried to be aloof but she was too sweet to pull it off. Michelle was a little rougher around the edges, but still, sweet as can be. They were obsessed with The Cure and Morrissey, obviously. Of course, we all smoked cigarettes as we would hang out, talking about wanting to smoke weed or trying to score some weed. We drank coffee just as an excuse to hang out.

Zibah Williams and Michelle Sanborn also talked a lot about their friend named Regis, who I apparently just had to meet. They thought we'd hit it off since he was a singer, guitarist, and songwriter. From the way they talked him up, and how much I trusted their judgement, I assumed he had to be a pretty cool guy. He was obsessed with The Beatles and Pink Floyd, which was right up my alley.

MEETING REGIS McNICHOLAS

The time finally came when Regis and I met. Zibah, Michelle, and I were at Green Mountain. It was late early evening, and he came walking across the street with a huge head of wavy black hair and wearing this thick, pale-green Army overcoat with a huge collar. We were introduced to each other, and because of all the hype that surrounded our meeting, we pretty much knew were going to be best friends right away. He had a really gentle demeanor, yet a wacky sense of humor, which I noticed and appreciated. We immediately started talking Beatles, then our dreams to start a band. The conversation was effortless, imaginative, and full of enthusiasm that had merit, because we were actually talented musicians with goals. Ours was a friendship that eased the pain of our abusive, younger years and created an emotional foundation from which we could build. We wanted to be rock stars, and we felt we were good enough to be just that, even at such a young age.

Regis got me listening to more Pink Floyd, which was a good thing. I hadn't delved much into their music at the time. I was such a Beatles fanatic; other bands were pushed to the wayside. But after listening to "Wish You Were Here" and the album *Animals*, I was convinced they were just as legit as The Beatles – in their own way, of course.

From that initial meeting on, we were the best of friends, inseparable and dreaming our loftiest of dreams together. It was the first friendship in which we shared horror stories from our childhoods, connecting in an emotional way that at once felt cathartic, creative, and healthy. We were revealing the darkest moments of our past to each other, and it felt good. Seconds later, we'd talk about getting a band together, writing music, or breaking down Beatles songs, or just cracking up at the darkest jokes we could muster, usually very Monty-Python-based humor. Our friendship came at the most important time of our lives. I don't think Regis would disagree that our lives would've been less significant had we never met. Our souls at that time were committed to making music together. I'll forever cherish those days.

Besides Zibah, Michelle, and Terryle, there was Scott, a big and burly self-confessed "art fag", as he proudly called himself, who liked to change his hair color and styles frequently. The skinheads never messed with him – they respected his girth and height too much for that. Terryle, the stout little Irish skate punk was always around. Then of course, there was Regis and myself, who were the Beatles-and-Pink-Floyd-loving hippies of the clan. There would occasionally be others that would come into our circle, but they didn't stay for long. Bruce was one of them. He started as a skate punk, then left and became a skinhead. He was nice enough but had a short fuse, so Regis and I kept our distance.

TAKING PSYCHEDELICS FOR THE FIRST TIME

I was getting curious about psychedelics like mushrooms, peyote, and LSD. I had read numerous Carlos Casteneda books by now and had hung out with like-minded kids who had already tried LSD and touted its mind-expanding powers, so long as you don't abuse it. Step one was getting the LSD, so we went to the one guy we knew (whose name I won't mention out of respect for privacy) who had his own trustworthy connection.

He had this really clean acid called Zen, and he also had Four-Way Window Pane, which we didn't get because it was too powerful (four hits of acid in one tab) for a first experience. So, we went with the Zen. I mean, the name instills instant trust and implies a guarantee of no bad trips. It cost five dollars a tab. We got four tabs for Zibah, Michelle, Scott, and myself.

The next morning around 11am, I think we met at Michelle's apartment. She lived on Sheridan Street on Munjoy Hill, Zibah lived literally a stone's throw away from her on Monument Street, and I lived two blocks away from them on Sherbrooke Avenue. Scott lived further away on the Western Promenade but was there as well. I don't know who decided on the Eastern Cemetery at the foot of Munjoy Hill, but that's where we ultimately headed to begin our journey.

I was a rookie, so I had to be told to put the tab on my tongue and let it dissolve, which I did alongside the others. We hung out for about 30 minutes, and nothing. I was getting a little impatient but one of them told me it can take up to an hour or more to hit you. We were sitting on the South side wall of the cemetery, dangling our feet and looking to our right at the humble Portland skyline toward a couple tall cranes beside some building structures.

Then the cranes started moving a little bit, and clearly the Zen acid had begun to kick in. I couldn't tell if they were actually moving or if I was imagining it, but the cranes started looking like giraffe necks and heads, moving quietly about at a distance. I must've stared at them for a good fifteen minutes, amazed at their graceful mobility. I looked up at the sky as it was a perfect summer day – the clouds high, the air clear, while the sun would peek out as a gentle wind occasionally whispered around us. It was perfectly serene. The cemetery behind us felt at peace, and the clouds were creating shapes that clouds don't normally create.

By this time, I was officially starting to trip balls. I looked at Zibah and Michelle, and their expressions looked animated, making me giggle, and also making it hard to look at them. They were giggling, too, at whatever was tripping them out. I decided to get a cigarette out and smoke it. This turned into an incredible vivid observation, and the most physical experience I've ever had. As I took a drag, I felt the smoke envelop my lungs and watched the red and orange embers go down behind the ashes, entranced by the whole experience. I never knew smoking a cigarette could feel intimately perceived.

After over an hour hanging at the cemetery, we decided to walk to the Old Port, going up and down Exchange Street, tripping our gourds out, and then we decided to go to Andy Emory's house. I'd never met him. He worked at the comic book store on Exchange St., Moonshadow's. It was a classic geek headquarters. Andy looked like a character right out of an R. Crumb comic book. He was thin as a rail, wore square metal-rimmed glasses with lenses that were always smudged, had long, straight, greasy black hair, and always wore jeans and black boots up to his knees, with a t-shirt sporting some comic book character or quirky saying. He was their weed connection and old enough to buy beer and liquor for us.

He had an interesting way of talking. He liked telling stories and had a little smirk in his eyes when he began to tell one, which was often and he'd spout off intellectual concepts, facts, or whatever came to his mind – he always sounded smart but cynical. I quickly grew to like and appreciate him. He rounded out our cast of characters nicely and completely.

We told him that we were tripping our balls off and he gave us sanctuary while we were coming down from it. It was in his apartment that I had this epiphany that the entire universe is connected by the same energy source like an endless spiderweb. Any information you wanted could be had, so long as you stayed connected.

Time was irrelevant since it was all one and the same. It was an incredible moment to feel in my body, mind, and soul. I had felt like I'd figured out the meaning of life. Not that I'd figured out why I was here on this planet and why I was living, just the simplest form of what existence was. It was a revelation that's stayed but was strongest at that moment. I smiled, feeling very satisfied, and watched the end of my cigarettes burn down as I inhaled, amazed at how they looked, staring into a mini alternate environment. I highly approved of that LSD experience.

We visited Andy often or would just run into him while walking around town. I became friends with him as time went on, and we hung out, but not nearly enough.

Since this was before the world of cellphones, the four of us would tell each other our schedules the day before, meet up at Green Mountain in the late morning, then reconvene there in the evening to walk around Exhange Street, Fore Street, Market Street, up Congress Street, and return to the Old Port and the surrounding area. There was a bank on Fore Street with upper parking on the roof where we'd go a lot to hang out late at night and smoke cigarettes, desperately wishing we could get beers and get drunk. We spent a lot of time talking about how to get beer. We succeeded a few times, waiting out in front of 7-11 for a person who looked like they'd be cool with doing that for us. Ahh, the trials and tribulations of being underage.

FRANK ZAPPA, MY FIRST CONCERT

By this time, I was pretty damn serious about my drums. I was just about to turn eighteen and practiced as often as I could, which was a challenge. I still managed however, even if it meant doing paradiddles and double-strokes on a pillow.

One early spring day, I ran into Andy Emory, and he told me he was going to see Frank Zappa at Cumberland County Civic Center. He had just moved out of his place in the Old Port on the corner of Market and Fore Street, a killer little pad on the second floor, and now lived on Spring Street, literally a block away from the Civic Center. He asked me if I knew much about Zappa, and I had to admit that I didn't. He was thrilled to hear that, because he had an extra ticket for the show, so who better to ask but a complete virgin to the Zappa experience?! He explained to me about the high-level pedigree of the band members, specifically talking about Chad Wackerman and Ed Mann, the drummer and percussionist. He was a big fan of Zappa's music and was more than happy to share his enthusiasm.

A few days later, I went over to his apartment. We cleaned his bong of resin and smoked a few tokes, then walked the short block down to the Civic Center to watch Zappa and his band.

The first thing I noticed was how much older the crowd was. These people were actually in their thirties and forties! Ha! This made quite the impression on me. I also noticed the familiar scent of weed floating about, as well as joints being liberally passed around as the night went on. The band started a little late, but damn, once they started, they immediately blew my mind on every level. I never knew music could be at once so complex and display such deprecating humor. I was sold.

The IQ level of this band was through the roof. The odd timings they played were so complex at times that I just couldn't keep up.

I had no idea, for example, one section could play in 7/4 time, while they'd have another section play in 3/4 time, then another one in 4/4, etc., and they'd all "meet up" on the 12th measure, 21st measure, or 28th measure, then do it all over again. The level of complexity in their playing, whether due to how long they'd been together or because they were such pros, blasted my mind open.

Chad Wackerman's drumming simply blew me away. My eyes could not be peeled from his playing. I listened to his ideas; schooled, fluid, complex - just how could he absorb so much information and execute it on the fly? It was beyond my skills at that time.

Emotionally, I turned into a complete fucking invalid watching the band perform. I rode a rollercoaster of desire to throw my drumsticks away while listening to them, then determined to become as good as them, and back to sinking into a corner in the fetal position, rocking in dark isolation with all confidence stripped away. That's how much this band affected me. It was the highest level of music I'd ever heard before, let alone in live performance!

During this tour, Frank had hired a six-piece horn section, so they were able to play more horn-heavy tunes (maybe from the *Grand Wazoo*?) as well as performing this crazy medley of Beatles tunes and "Stairway to Heaven" (with the horn section playing the guitar solo) to end the night. Of course, the lyrics for the Beatles tunes had been altered and adulterated. There was "Norwegian Jim", "Louisiana Hooker with Herpes", "Lucy in the Sky with Diamonds", "What Kind of Girl", and maybe another Beatles tune. It was at once theatrical, farcical, and fucking incredible. The fact that Frank admitted to the crowd that they were playing pretty loose that night and making mistakes only added insult to my personal emotional injury. I didn't notice shit but them being musical wizards.

It was the first time I ever equated music to alchemy, and Zappa was the one who wielded this power to join such great musicians, not only using music as a vehicle to mock virtually everything worth mocking, but being so skilled at arranging, he could literally get away with playing and saying *anything*! It revealed the freedom of music's potential to the spirit and mind. Again, I was sold. This is how shit's done, and if you don't like it, well, why would you ever give a shit when you're this good and surrounded by literal geniuses of instruments and voice?!

And that was my first concert! Think about that – Frank Zappa was my first concert. Did it ruin all concerts afterwards? Pretty much. No other band ever compared, even Yes, or even their offshoot of Anderson, Bruford, Wakeman and Howe. I mean, I saw Santana live, The Grateful Dead quite a few times, The Who, and so many others - none of them even touched how I felt with Zappa.

The closest band that impressed me was Little Feat, when they toured with the Grateful Dead that same year in the summer of 1988 at Oxford Plains Speedway. I think the tour was called Dead Feat – brilliant. They blew me away. I was literally about twenty-five feet from the stage. They forced the Dead to play their asses off that night – enough that they ended the night with 'Hey Jude' and had the entire crowd singing along. Little Feat was still better than them, in my opinion.

Besides them, Zappa will always be king of any live band performance, ever. Sure, I've had many lovey-dovey moments at shows, but as far as highest-level musicianship, showmanship, deprecation, and humor all wrapped into one in an arena setting? Yeah, Zappa ruined all concerts for me afterwards. And that's just fine. I should refine that statement and say that Zappa gave me perspective, and from that point on, I used his concert as the measuring stick of greatness. Oh, the second and only other show that impressed me at such a level was this amazing quartet jazz band I saw perform at Café No, a venue that had great bands perform there as well. I never got their name.

After the concert, I must've thanked Andy more than a dozen times while walking back to his apartment, absolutely lost in a fog of amazement. I needed time to digest what my senses just absorbed. It was like going to a few years of music school over a one-night concert. I'm sure Andy was pleased with how it got into me.

We even saw each other a week later, and talked about the show again, grinning ear to ear about it. Yeah, thank you Andy – little did you know how much that concert actually paved my path, and "straightened my ears" if you will, to really enhance the way I'd hear music to another level, particularly regarding music arrangement.

You brought me to the realization that music doesn't have to be so damn serious. You can have your cake and eat it too, so long as you bust your ass learning how to bake the best damn cake you can.

THE BIRTH OF LOW TOLERANCE

Gregory came over to our apartment with Regis after school and told us about a band competition that was happening against other schools. He really wanted to sign up for it. So did Regis. Gregory was this super-skinny extrovert with a big nose, big eyes, and full of unwarranted confidence. He could sing just enough, but his confidence fed the illusion to everybody who didn't know him that he was better than he really was. Since Regis and I didn't want to be the front men, that was fine with us to have him be the lead singer. Over the course of the next few days, he'd come over and we realized we needed a bassist, and even more importantly, a band name! As we were hanging out drinking beers while thinking up stupid names that became Monty-Python-level stupid names, Gregory exclaimed, "Man, I have low tolerance!" as the beer was getting to his head. Then his eyes it up and he said, "That's it! Low Tolerance! That's our band name!" We all thought about it for a little bit and agreed. It was a good rock band name. The band Low Tolerance was born.

Soon thereafter, we began practicing at Gregory's house on Peak's Island. This meant lugging our gear to the ferry, which was no small feat. Thankfully, the house had a drum set there already, so I was spared. I'd help Regis walk his seventy-five-pound Peavey combo amp nearly a mile to the port to catch the ferry. We were in a rush and almost missed it. Luckily, youth was on our side, but damn, that amp was heavy. We did the classic lifting it with the right hand for a hundred feet, then switching over to the left hand for the next hundred feet, until – a mile later and arms melting into the ground – we finally arrived at the ferry station. The ride to the island was beautiful and peaceful. We were, of course, very excited. By now, we had recruited this very reluctant shy kid named Josh to play the bass, an instrument he had never played before, though he *had* played acoustic guitar. He also had stage fright, which sure came into play later.

Once we arrived on the island, it was another third of a mile trek to get to Gregory's house. More painful lugging of the heavy-ass Peavey amp. Phew! We finally arrived and set up our stuff. I admired the 1967 four-piece Ludwig set that looked exactly like Ringo Starr's. It was beautiful, with a chrome Roger's snare. It was my favorite snare to this day.

I sat on the drum throne and started practicing my rudiments until everyone got their stuff set up. Gregory had a crude Peavey PA system – those tall, skinny towers with just enough power for one vocal mic. And we rehearsed. We probably rehearsed a couple more times before the competition, even though Josh was only available for one more rehearsal. We played two originals and one cover. "Sympathy for the Devil." We also got to meet Gregory's older brother Sean Kinney, who played bass quite well, but he was too old to fill in as the bassist for the competition. Darn.

PORTLAND ROCK OFF '88 AND FIRST RECORDING SESSION

The day came and we arrived early morning at Deering Elementary School, the location of Rock-Off 88'. The other bands were there as well, mingling about in anticipation. In our minds, the only competition we had was the band The Trade, a group of rich kids that had a three-piece horn section, sounding all sophisticated and shit. We laughed at them because we were rock 'n roll, and they were light rock trying to hip and funky. But they had that horn section. Hard to beat that.

There was also a band called The Baked Potatoes from Cape Elizabeth. They were a hippie jam band before that genre name was popularized. I liked them but their songs weren't as strong as ours. They played their three tunes, then we were up. What happened next was nothing short of a classic movie moment. Josh, the bassist, got extreme stage fright, so it took us a couple minutes behind the curtains to convince him to play. He almost walked off the stage and we had to get him back on. Regis or Gregory convinced him to just play with either his back turned to the audience or to look down through the entire set. He did both, starting with his back to the audience.

We played our first super catchy song, "You", written by Regis. It went over great. We'd rehearsed it and nailed it. The second song was "Down", a very psychedelic song that was ethereal and Pink Floydish. This is where I was able to shine. A few minutes into the song, the drum solo came in, and I just went into auto pilot. Apparently, it went over well because the crowd was ecstatic over my solo. Then the band came back in and the song came to a huge and awesome crescendo, ending with huge applause and a standing ovation. Josh by now had turned around and was able to start looking at the audience. I'm sure the applause helped. We ended our set with "Sympathy for the Devil" with Gregory riling up the crowd, getting everybody to sing along to the "hoo hoo" part. We got a standing ovation.

Then the fucking horn-section rich-kids band came on and tore it up, sounding like a bunch of well-polished douchebags itching to ruin our chances of winning the competition. We already knew they had it in the bag because of the horns, but we also knew our songs were more original and straight-up better.

The winner was announced: The Trade, of course. But we placed second and we were very happy with that. For the record, Lois Phillipe, the one who put it all together, actually liked us the best. He also knew The Trade would win but thought we were the band with better songs and more natural talent. Second place earned us two songs on a compilation record of winners. It would be the first record I'd ever recorded, and my first time ever recording in a professional recording studio.

It was a huge learning experience. The studio engineer suggested we play to a click track to make punch ins and multiple takes easier to mix. I had never played along to a click track before, so I had to adapt quickly. I had practiced for years with a metronome, so it wasn't that far off to play along to a click track, but for a first-time experience, it definitely took the life and spontaneity out of the recordings. I understood it had to be done, but it also left me less than enthused about click tracks. Of course, that's all I do nowadays, but for a seventeen-year-old, that was a new world.

Gregory had some trouble with his vocal parts, and insisted on singing lead for Regis' song. I forget how it turned out. I think Regis eventually got to sing his song and Gregory did the backups, but it was all a slog and took so much longer than it needed to. At the very end, I actually ended up adding a high harmony. One take. Ha! They were just surprised that the quiet drummer could even sing. Surprise! The record was released a couple months later. I sure wish I had a copy of that.

FIRST OFFICIAL LOW TOLERANCE GIG

A month after Low Tolerance finished recording for the Rock Off 88' Album at Reindeer Records, Louis Philippe (the owner) offered us a gig to open up for his band, The Cuddly Kittens. I know, terrible name, but if you'd met Louis, you'd understand within seconds. We were Louise's favorite band of the bunch, and he thought we had the potential to kick some ass, so he gave us a chance. He also kind of had a little crush on Regis, which helped to secure the gig. Beggars can't be choosers, right? So, of course we accepted and frankly, we were pretty excited about it.

The gig was sometime in the late summer at a VFW Hall in Buxton, Maine. We rehearsed quite a bit and got a full hour of music together to perform. It wasn't glamorous, by any stretch of the imagination. You can't consider a gig at any VFW hall to be glamourous and have rock-star-level accommodations. Nevertheless, it was a gig and we were ready to rock. We lugged our gear in and set it up with the exception of myself. I just used the main act's drum set and brought in my prized Rogers snare. When it was time to play, we killed it. It was a tremendous first gig. There's nothing like an entire room cheering and whooping it up with the energy smashing through the roof. I thought to myself, *I could get used to this*. That first gig definitely had me hooked. I was in this for life.

The only sad spot was losing my prized Rogers snare drum at that gig. Somebody either accidentally grabbed it at the end of our performance, or somebody stole it. I was incredibly bummed about this. It's still the best sounding snare drum I've ever owned. It was the 1970's Dynasonic "Script Badge" (a chrome script, not the black lettering badge) 14" x 5" Custom Built model. I could always get another one now on eBay, but back in the day, there wasn't an eBay. It was lost forever. I guess there was a lesson in there somewhere, which is to always keep your eye on your gear, especially when it's the only piece of gear you brought in.

MY FIRST APARTMENT WITH REGIS

In 1987, Terry and Maureen told me that a musician named Bill, who lived in the apartment above theirs, had a couple rooms about to open up, so Regis and I decided this would be perfect for us. This was at 3 Sherbrooke Street. There was a huge back bedroom, which I took, since it seemed the perfect place to have the drum set. Regis took the other room - we found out a month into living there that somebody had hung themselves in its closet. Great …

Bill was a funny-looking kinda dude, straight back from the 70's. Forty years old, long black hair, a mustache and no upper teeth, but he wore dentures. He was also a vegetarian and had odd hours – I found out those were "musician hours" - waking up at 4PM and staying up until 5AM. Lord knows what he was doing in his bedroom when he closed that door after a gig, but he played the bass and played it very well. He was into Yes and other prog rock bands as well as hard and classic rock and played in cover bands for money.

There was also another musician who lived there for the first couple months named Rick. I really liked him. He was more of a classic rock guy who looked a lot like Clapton. He had a light beard and slightly long hair and he played a Strat.

We used to smoke pot and talk about the Beatles late into the night. He'd have squabbles with Bill, which is what eventually made him move out. They had one too many fights, which was obviously an unhealthy relationship. Rick also stopped playing in his band. After about half a year, they both moved out and it was Regis' and my place. We were stoked.

Regis had graduated from Portland High School that summer, and since there were vacancies, we invited a couple guys to move in with us from his school. One was kind of preppy and the other was my friend, Matt. It was a fun time for a few months, until September arrived and we realized that Matt hadn't paid the rent, instead buying a CD player, a hundred dollars' worth of CDs, and an ounce of weed.

How we found out was when our landlord knocked on our door asking for the rent. We were totally confused until we put it together – we'd handed Matt our rent money and he had never handed it to our landlord. Needless to say, we confronted Matt, and the summer party quickly ended in a cloud of weed and CD's bought from our rent money. A couple weeks later, we had all moved out. Matt went back to his home in South Portland, Regis and I moved to Peak's Island to live with Sean and Gregory Kinney. The other roommate went back home as well, or off to college. I was pretty upset with Matt for pulling that stunt and didn't contact him for about a year. A kick to his face would've been well deserved. Alas, I was not the violent type, so we just temporarily parted ways.

MEETING DRUMMER NEIL CARROLL

This story is almost embarrassing as it shows an arrogant side of me that I didn't realize I had at such a young age. I guess you could also interpret it as having a high level of self-confidence in my drumming abilities.

I was practicing some kind of jazz beat; maybe a fairly complex syncopated beat. I look up and see this guy that I've never met with a lot of fuzzy hair standing in the doorway of my bedroom. I stop playing and he nods at me amicably, and says "That was some good shit, man." Defensive, I spat out a retort. "Well, I wouldn't exactly call that shit." He quickly tries to backpedal, rethinking his choice of words as I'm throwing him a snobby vibe. "I mean, that was really great stuff you played, dude." Poor guy. Looking back, it was an asshole thing to say to someone I've never met who was trying to give me an off-hand compliment. I got down off my drum throne and since he wasn't offended enough to leave the room, we introduced ourselves.

To this day, I feel like such an asshole for that first impression I gave. I wasn't even that awesome yet as a drummer, and regardless of talent, nothing warrants that level of dismissiveness. Luckily, Neil was a very good-natured guy and years later we became dear friends. Ironically, he later became the drummer for the band Tao Jones.

SOUTHERN COMFORT AND CAPE ELIZABETH COPS

Matt Beal and Brendan Hayes encapsulated a piece of my time from ages seventeen to eighteen. We were misfits and the stoned Three Stooges combined. Once we got together, we were inseparable. Brendan was from Cape Elizabeth. He lived in this modern style house with pool and a brown lab named Shilo, and we'd go over there to hang out quite often before we were of age. We'd get drunk and smoke weed in Brendan's dark-blue 1976 Chevrolet step side, which he constantly maintaining. Trucks like that always need work.. They'll take care of you if you take care of them. And he did.

Brendan was a wandering soul who was seeking to branch out before going off to college, and we were his compadres. We were very good friends and had many moments that I hold close to my heart to this day. They stand out because he was one of my rare friends who actually wasn't a musician, but he appreciated music, and appreciated the same bands I appreciated. He was a good man.

His step side was our trusty horse, the one we'd get high in before most any activity, or the horse we'd wait in until we scored our weed. That truck was legendary. I loved that fucking truck. It was privy to our every adventure, and misadventure.

Granted, this was Cape Elizabeth, South Portland, and Portland, Maine, so it wasn't like cruising Sunset Boulevard, but the cruising we did was to beautiful locations, like Portland Head Light and Two Lights State Park.

We never got bothered by the cops there, and we'd just go out to the craggily coast at night to get high, watching the moonlit waves crash against the silhouette of the rocky coast. It was pretty awesome. And of course, once you've taken a couple puffs, the sound of the waves would start changing, churning around us like we were spinning about, when we were actually sitting still.

One night, while Brendan's parents were away, we planned to get a pint of Southern Comfort for each of us, then walk from his home to Crescent Beach State Park. It was about a mile away by foot. The moon was almost full, so it lit up the night enough that we were not walking blindly as we cut through yards and fields. We didn't even need flashlights. I was pretty new to Southern Comfort, so I guzzled about half of the bottle before we even made it to the beach. Once Brendan and I reached it, we sat on this bench that was nestled back and hidden by beach grass that grew about a foot tall. We were having a laugh for about fifteen minutes, then we decided to get up and walk on the beach.

That's when the SoCo hit me hard. I started getting dizzy and said, "Oh man, I don't think I feel so good." The dizziness increased substantially, and I bent forward and puked my guts out. Finally, I could hurl no more, but I just couldn't stop feeling dizzily sick. I told Brendan to go on without me and leave me to lay in the beach grass for a while.

I must've been there for half an hour before the Cape Elizabeth cops arrived. They were doing their routine check to make sure there wasn't any riffraff around or funny stuff going on. I was still feeling sick as shit and I was definitely not moving. As they approached, their flashlights caught a glimpse of me in the beach grass. Once they were standing right over me, I heard one of them say, "Is he alive?" That's when I forced out some kind of noise, and mustered up enough strength to lift my head and pleaded with them, "Help me, please. I don't feel good." They asked me if I'd been drinking, and I told them that yes, I'd been drinking Southern Comfort.

They didn't even confiscate the bottle, nor did they did try to help me up, advising, "Try to get up and walk it off. You'll feel better in a little while." Then they walked away, chatting about something else, and left me to suffer my Southern Comfort fate.

After a few minutes, I mustered up enough energy to pull myself up on my two feet, wobbling and dry heaving for the first fifty feet. I kept trying to put one foot in front of the other, knowing that I couldn't sleep on the beach. It was getting cold and I had to get back to Brendan's house. Of course, I couldn't find Brendan at this point, so I tried to remember how to get back to his home. I walked through the fields, and some landmarks I remembered. That's when I ran into Matt, and we somehow found our way back to Brendan's home, just sitting in his living room recliner and chuckling at us. I was feeling a little better by now, but my desire to keep on partying ended out on that beach.

To this day, I'll never drink a hundred proof Southern Comfort ever again. Ever. Again. Just the smell makes me want to puke. And who says there aren't good cops? They exist in sleepy town Cape Elizabeth.

LOW TOLERANCE ON PEAK'S ISLAND

After being evicted from our first apartment on Sherbrooke Street, Regis convinced me to move out to Peak's Island and live with our band, Low Tolerance. It didn't take much convincing. It was around September, two of the bandmembers were brothers whose parents owned the house, and there was a Beatles-style Ludwig drumkit set up in the living room. I was in!

I had all these visions of grandeur. We'd rehearse all the time and become bad-ass rock stars, start playing out, then recording our music and get signed. That was the plan. But that wasn't the reality that played out. I got settled in, and after a couple weeks, Regis and the lead singer, Gregory Kinney, got jobs picking apples at a hippie orchard in New Hampshire.
The bass player, Sean Kinney (Gregory's brother) and I were the only ones living there. He was a really cool guy, and the oldest of us all. He played in a couple punk rock bands, had a brooding vibe, and worked as a carpenter. He was really skinny and had dark kinky hair like some of those Roman statues. Just take off thirty pounds, add black jeans, a worn-out t-shirt, and a 1976 Fender Precision Bass, sprinkle a dash of mellow pensive Tom Waits vibe, and you've got Sean Kinney, our soulful bassist.

For about a month, I felt kind of lost, abandoned, and confused. Why would my band ask me to move in with them, then have two of the bandmembers take off? To shake off these feelings of melancholy, I would bike around the island, which would take about forty-five minutes. It was a perfect time of the season to do just that. I'd go up to the abandoned fortress outposts and look out into the ocean. It was very peaceful. I read a lot of philosophy books, listened to music, and practiced drums a lot. I was very productive despite feeling lonely.

Then the guys came back from their apple-picking jobs, and the energy came back into the house. This lasted for about a month before everybody decided it was time to disperse. Regis moved to Madison, Wisconsin with his girlfriend, whom he had met at his job. Greg moved back to New Hampshire, and Sean moved back to the mainland to live in Portland. I obviously had to move out as well.

It was a very unfortunate turn of events. The band didn't get much of a chance to move forward. But Regis also couldn't handle Gregory in the band. It wasn't the direction he wanted to go. I could understand. He had the charisma, but his vocal chops weren't quite up to par, and he didn't have the desire to be as disciplined as us to become a true vocalist. It was more of a fun thing for him. I totally got it. We all needed to move on. It was fun while it lasted, even if it didn't last long.

BOB DYLAN TEACHES ME HOW TO WRITE MUSIC IN A DREAM

I would have to say that this is the most profound and important dream that I ever had. I might even classify it as the most important musical experience in my life. What's kind of funny about the dream is that at the time, I didn't really dig Bob Dylan, at all. Until I had this dream. Ever since then, I've had a sublime respect for him. Here's my dream:

I was walking in SoHo, Manhattan, on the left side of the street, and decided to go into a club. I walked down a small flight of stairs and entered this room with shallow ceilings and small round tables. The space felt larger once I was down there. As I walked further into the room, I noticed a small wooden stage, maybe a foot higher than the floor, with an upright piano on the right side.

As I moved closer to the man performing, I recognized the voice and the big hair. It was Bob Dylan singing and playing his acoustic guitar. I caught him at the end of his last song and set. He said his Thank You's and started putting away his guitar.

I figured it was a good time to approach him, so I went up to him and told him he sounded really good. He said, "Thanks, man." I approached closer then asked him, "So, how do you write a song?" He just looked up at me and said in his classic Dylan lilt, "Well, it's easy man."

By this time, we were both sitting on the piano bench and he began showing me piano chords. "First you do this", which was a C major chord, "then you do this", which was another chord that was related to the C major chord. "Then you can do this", which I'm sure was another chord that worked with C. He continued to show me the basics of how chords work and how you can change the key and have it sound the same. He basically told me "How to Write Songs for Dummies" in just a few minutes. I thanked him and he most likely said, "You're welcome, man" in his unforgettable cadence. I walked away and then I woke up, wondering what the hell just happened.

I walked downstairs and made a pot of coffee, poured myself a cup, then walked over to the piano in the music/living room and plunked myself down. I tried to remember what Bob told me (yes, I'm going to call him Bob from now on) and slowed it down even more. I went deeper into all the piano lessons I had as a child as well as when I was fifteen.

I began with middle C. Then I played what is considered a major chord (C E G) and that made sense to me. Then, I asked myself what makes a chord a minor? I fiddled around a bit and realized that if I move the E note down to an Eb, that made it sound like what I was hearing in my head – a minor chord! That was a Eureka moment.

Then I asked myself, "What if I move everything up to the D note and play notes that sounded like C major?" So, I did. I played D, F#, and A. Another Eureka moment. I kept moving up with every note on the piano until I heard every note create a major chord. Then I would move my middle finger down one note to make a minor chord.

The revelation began at that moment. I realized right then and there that with these chords, I had the tools to write songs. I realized that if I started with the E note on the C major scale that I could play the same chord but in a different position. I moved up to the G note of the C major chord and did the same thing. I basically learned the idea of chord positions. The revelations kept on coming. I was beyond ecstatic and immediately began writing a song, if not a couple songs. All because of meeting Bob Dylan in a dream. I'd have one heluva story to tell him if I ever met him. If it wasn't for meeting Bob in a dream, I might've never become a songwriter. Thank you, Bob.

CHAPTER 6

MOVING TO NEW YORK CITY

Right around the end of October, I left Peaks Island. My band Low Tolerance was no more. I moved into this dump above Danforth Market with some more hippies that had no heat or power. That lasted about two months before I decided to migrate to New York City with this scruffy Russian guy who was living with us named Lenny. After buying a Greyhound bus ticket, I had forty dollars in my pocket. He was very charming, and smart, and he convinced me to come with him. When we arrived at his home in Brooklyn, his Russian parents didn't approve of him bringing a stranger (me) into their home. They had baggage to work through with him, due to his dropping out of NYU. They argued in Russian. I tried to make myself a shadow.

We always took the train at the end of his street, Gravesend Neck Road. That street name always stuck with me - it had a good ring to it, and in fact, it became a song title a few months later. I overstayed my welcome at his parents' home for four days, then Lenny talked to his good friend Chris Whiting, who by the grace of God decided I could stay at his apartment. He lived in Jamaica, Queens and worked for Greenpeace, which is how Lenny knew him.

I got a job there as a canvasser after a couple days and things stabilized a bit. For the record, I was terrible at my job. I somehow lasted there for a few months before I got fired. Ironically, the day I was fired was the day that I was the only canvasser in the neighborhood to make quota.

GREENPEACE AND SHERYL-ANNE

It was also the day that I knocked on the door of the most beautiful girl I'd ever seen with a smile as wide as a rainbow. I rang the doorbell, she opened it with her huge smile and bright eyes, I did my Greenpeace opening statement, which she happily listened to and then invited me in. It was February and ten degrees outside, quite chilly. She had a bubbly personality and was full of curiosity. I did my Save-the-Whales speech for a few minutes and we had some good banter, then I figured it was time to leave and bid her a good night.

As I walked away, I was overwhelmed by the need to tell her what I thought of her, so I turned around, rang her doorbell again, and said something to the effect of "I'm sorry, but I have to tell you that I think you're one of the most beautiful women I've ever met." She just smiled even wider at me and asked if I wanted to come back in.

That's when I saw the piano right behind her on the left side of their den. My eyes got big and I asked her if I could play it. She said, "Of course you can!" We both walked to the piano bench and sat down, and she asked me what I wanted to play. I think I began with a Beatles tune, then I asked her if she wanted to hear a song that I wrote. She immediately gleamed and said, "Yes!", and with that open invitation, I sang her a song I wrote, "November Day". She was blown away and I was all smiles. Then she asked me to play another original. Before I knew it, I had sung five songs. A connection was created. It was definitely time for me to go, but not without exchanging numbers. I called her a week later and we ended up going on a date. She came over to where I was living and we talked for hours. I told her my story. She was fascinated, which made me wonder how lucky I was to find somebody so beautiful and engaging at the same time. She was just magical.

TEACHING MYSELF GUITAR IN QUEENS

While living in Chris Whiting's apartment in Queens, he turned me onto a lot of music I would've never heard on my own. He had a versatile collection of music.

He introduced me to The Kinks, Elvis Costello, Charlie Parker, Billie Holiday, and BB King. We of course listened to The Beatles and other rock bands, but those five artists stood out.

Chris had a classical guitar hanging out and I would just stare at it, thinking how I'd never be able to learn how to play it. Once I lost my job with Greenpeace, I had a lot of time on my hands. I'd still go out for interviews, but the jobs were pretty drab. I actually interviewed to work at a button factory, and midway through the process, I walked out. It was like a scene straight out of a Dickens novel. The boss had gotten red-faced, screaming at some poor soul who hardly spoke English for not noticing a two- vs. three-hole button discrepancy. Just nightmarish to witness.

With all that free time on my hands, I decided to teach myself guitar. Chris had a guitar book that had the essential chords to learn on its back cover, which I went through diligently for weeks. I worked on playing those chords to perfection, slowly but surely, for *hours*. If there was anything I took away from drum lessons, it was to start slowly until you could do it well, and *then* speed up. This method worked for the guitar as well.

After a few weeks, I began writing songs on the guitar. I was also singing along to a lot of albums, mostly Beatles and BB King. *The White Album* was my favorite to scream along to – "Why Don't We Do It in The Road" and "Happiness Is a Warm Gun" - basically punishing the poor neighbors.

I must've sounded like a rooster being choked when I aimed for those high notes. Oh well, I didn't care. I just needed to practice until I could sound good.

Chris would come back from work and be shocked at how quickly I was learning. However, not having a job took its toll, and though I was rapidly progressing on the guitar, I had to get a job soon so I could stop borrowing money from Chris.

DIAL-A-PORN CARDS AND A PIG ON A HORSE IN BROOKLYN

I finally found a job sometime in March, walking up and down the city streets placing dial-a-porn cards on car windows. I actually really liked that job for the first month. I got a lot of exercise, and bonus, I got to know the subway system and all the boroughs, except for Staten Island. The job also began early Spring, so the weather was starting to warm up nicely. Into the end of the second month of doing this, I was forced to quit after being accosted by a pig on a horse in a Hasidic Jewish neighborhood of Brooklyn.

The horse-riding cop noticed me and another worker (a young black woman, who obviously stood out as well in this neighborhood) placing cards onto cars and he stopped us. He asked me what we were passing out and insisted I hand a card to him.

I gave him the least offensive one, the one that had the word LACE on it. All the cards either had 1-800-212-WHIP, -LICK, or -BOOB printed on them.

As he studied the card, I watched his face grow red as he fumed with disgust. He looked like one of those cartoon people with smoke billowing out of his train whistle ears. With his horse breathing down my neck, he angrily asked me, "Do you know what this is?! This is SMUT! It's *SMUT*!!" Then he bent down even lower with his face right up against mine to say, "If I ever see you two in this neighborhood again with this *filth*, I'll *arrest* you! Now get the hell outta here!!" Or something to that effect.

I was shaking a little bit after that, and the girl I was working with was trying to help keep me calm. As we walked away, I decided I couldn't do this job anymore, so I sought out a pay phone to call the dial-a-porn office. I got into an argument with one of the owners about the altercation with the cop. He didn't believe it happened and thought I was making the story up, so I said "Fuck you", slammed the phone down and immediately quit.

What's funny is that up until that moment, the girl working with me thought I was a possible snitch, but after hearing me yell at the owner over the phone, then quit, I gained some of her respect.

Minutes later, we both threw our cards into a trash bin and took a subway home. A week later, I collected my final paycheck, and a couple days after that, I left New York City to go back to Portland, Maine.

If I could ever find Chris Whiting, I'd thank him for the all the musical influences he exposed me to, as well as letting me crash on his couch for many months, termites and all. I still owe him some money as well, something I'd love to pay up if I ever ran into him. Thank you, Chris. You opened up my eyes to the Kinks and to Elvis Costello at a level I never would've absorbed without your guidance, as well as Charlie Parker and Billie Holiday. Oh, and by the way, when I'd get high, Billie would sound like Donald Duck singing and I'd start laughing. I just couldn't listen to her after smoking weed, I wouldn't take her seriously. Charlie Parker, on the other hand, was like listening to somebody creating lullabies while watching the sun rise or set. His phrasing was silk. It felt beautiful while wearing but fragile and ready to break at a moment's notice.

BACK IN SOUTH PORTLAND LIVING WITH MATT BEAL

I returned to Maine from my stint in Queens, N.Y., all ready to hunker down and learn the guitar. I reconnected with my friend Matt Beal who lived on Preble Street, just around the corner from Al's Market, and he suggested I move in with him.

Just prior, I'd been living with a couple of old AA guys in a rundown apartment on Sherman Street. Less than a week there, the landlord showed up early one morning with a cop at hand, banging on the door and informing us we were being evicted. I couldn't believe it. I had paid one of the guys sixty bucks to let me stay there, but that sure didn't last long. I was in a bind. The only person I could think of to call was Matt Beal. It was a good call. He invited me over to his mom's place, which is where he was staying, and apparently, she was fine with me staying there, too. So, I took the next bus out to Preble Street in South Portland, my old neck of the woods, and it was old times again with Matt. A nice respite from what I'd just left.

His mom was a warm and loving Irish woman, a social worker for DHS who worked with troubled children, so she was just fine with me staying there. In fact, she had a soft spot for me, and I always felt safe around her. She was sharp as a tack with a great sense of humor, and she didn't miss much, but also didn't interfere with the obvious late-teen-lessons that Matt and I still needed to navigate in order to mature.

They were also Quakers, which didn't seem to interfere with anything. While we're at it, I might as well add the story of the rocking chair that they had that was made by either her grandfather or her husband's grandfather.

When a fire enveloped and burned down almost everything in the grandmother's home, by some miracle this rocking chair survived unscathed. According to legend, the floor all around it was burnt, save the circle around that chair, leaving it untouched by flames. It was also rumored to rock on its own at times. I never got to witness that, but looking at its ornateness, the chair surely had a vibe. It was not to be messed with. I respected that chair.

I consider this time in my life as formative years, learning the guitar ever so diligently and amateurishly writing songs. I was still trying to go from chord to chord without hesitation while also building my chordal vocabulary. I was working to develop my right hand, trying to be more rhythmically sensitive and adept.

Because I didn't have access to charts for scales, i.e., pentatonic major, minor, diatonic major and minor scales, I had to make charts for myself. I created a system that used numbers from the scales, which made things easier to break down while learning all the positions. Because I had already learned piano, I understood what inversions were. I just had to adapt the same language into my guitar-learning process. It wasn't that hard once I created all the charts. I spent at least six hours every day practicing either chords or scales.

Throughout this time, I continued to practice my singing. My tone was terrible and trebly. When I tried singing high notes as loud as I could, I'm sure a few birds died near my vicinity. I had no control of vibrato, and my range wasn't very wide.

But I had ideas, and some of them were very good. So, I carried on. I visualized that I could become a great singer, or at least above average, enough to support my songs and not have them sound terrible. Between practicing singing and learning the fretboard better by the day, I improved.

Matt had also acquired a small Fostex four-track recorder, which I began exploring as well. I recorded a song with it, my first original recording: "Bye, Bye Yesterday" and man, I wish I still had that tape. It was raw, but the song was an Elton John knockoff with harmonies in the verses. For a first crack at recording, it wasn't too bad. I could *hear* my first song recorded and I could that it sounded like a *good* song. It pressed me to want more.

TAKING ADAM'S LES PAUL

This was not my proudest moment. It was, and still is, the stupidest thing I've ever done. Let me backtrack a little bit.

Months previous, when I was living on Peak's Island and still playing drums every day, I had auditioned to be in a band called Twisted Roots.

Adam was the songwriter and Scott was the bassist. They came over to our house and had me play a few tunes. Then they did one that went in and out of 5/4 timing, which I had a little difficulty with, but I impressed them enough in learning the beat that they were psyched about my skills and by the end of the audition, I was in the band! We were all ecstatic! They had a rehearsal space in Portland where there was a drum set, so I could go in and practice when I pleased. Adam had just gotten this amazing black Les Paul Standard that I admired. I'd go back home and obsess about it.

One morning, I had the brilliant idea of taking it and bringing it back home with me. I literally walked in the cold, across the bridge into Portland and back to South Portland, and there it stayed, in my little room in the basement. I didn't even know what I wanted to do with it, I just knew I wanted it. It was as if I was possessed and had completely lost my mind. Rational thinking temporarily deserted me, until I got a call the next day from Adam, frantically asking me if I knew where his guitar was. He and the bandmembers had been driving around asking all their friends about it. I told him the truth, that I had taken it and brought it home with me. I couldn't give them a reason why I took it, any more than I could come up with one myself. I wanted it and I had to have it, even if it was just for a few days.

Ten minutes later they'd arrived and made their way down to my room. I was ready to get my ass kicked, and I knew I deserved nothing less. Adam's eyes were full of deep disappointment and complete loss of trust. I felt horrid to the core. Instead of getting an ass-kicking, they took my acoustic and slammed it a few times against the wall, then onto the floor, smashing it to pieces. They ran out whooping at the top of their lungs and sped away in their van. I just sat there feeling miserable. Obviously, I was out of the band. It took me decades to forgive myself for this stunt. It was only Adam's sincere and heartfelt pardon that allowed me move forward without shame.

MOVING TO MADISON, WISCONSIN

It was around that same time, as summer marched towards fall, that I decided to reach out to Regis, who was living in Madison, Wisconsin. My lifelong goal at that time was to play music with him, forming a band together, and he convinced me to move out there to live with him and his girlfriend. Matt was saddened by this news, but he understood that I had to follow my dreams. Our fun summer was coming to a close. Regis and I were going to be rock stars. *Madison, Wisconsin, here I come!*

Late September, I hopped a Greyhound bus to Wisconsin, and moved into the house Regis was renting with his girlfriend, along with another female tenant named Denise. She was very sweet and open-minded. She let me sleep in her bed the first night I arrived.

It didn't take me long to acclimate to Madison, Wisconsin. Where we were located was pretty much a hippy town with a food co-op, a friendly soup-kitchen, a few liberal-minded book stores, and basically a vibe that welcomed a liberal-thinking population. After all, it was a large college town.

I got a job at a recycling company called Earth Care that sold recycled paper products. That lasted for about half a year, until I got into a discussion about LSD with a young girl that devolved into an uncomfortable debate. I didn't even start it, but I was blamed for it, and sent down to work as a packer with these ex-gangbangers who sabotaged my packing orders to get me fired, which worked without fail. On my way out, I stole their small coffee-maker as retaliation. I did make some friends while there, Erik Ness and one very cool girl, but we never stayed in touch. We did commiserate over a few beers to mark my firing, though.

There was a period of about a month when I found myself jobless. I called my adoptive dad Dick Wagener, knowing that he had a savings account the DHS had created for me, in case a time came when I needed it. Well, I needed it.

He was kind enough to mail me a check for sixteen hundred dollars, which I immediately spent on a drum set and to finance a money scheme that failed, miserably.

I was also growing better at the guitar, writing some great songs, one of which was "Life Is Illusion." The winter in Madison was harsh, so we dug in for the long haul. For ten days in January, it dipped down to minus ten degrees, and with the windchill factor, it went down to minus fifty-five degrees, the coldest it had been in decades. We wore multiple layers just to go outside for twenty minutes. Fear of frostbite was a reality.

I soon got a job as a dry cleaner about half a mile from where I lived, and that lasted a few months. I did well there, but I didn't see myself staying. The manager liked me, plus there was a cute blonde girl that made the time easier, but it was tedious and redundant; it got to me and I left in the middle of April. I realized I didn't have the stamina nor desire to stay in Madison any longer, even to start a band with Regis. It just didn't feel right. The experiment had failed. There was a very depressed vibe to the entire town and I couldn't shake it off. Once April arrived, I told Regis that I had to leave. He let me stay in his room the last week before my hitchhiking journey back to Maine. Now *that* was an adventure that I didn't plan out too well.

HITCHHIKING BACK TO MAINE

On the third week of April, I left Madison, put my thumb out, and hitchhiked back to Maine. My first ride was from a psychology student learning about Freud, so that's what was on the speakers. He dropped me off in Notre Dame. The next ride was with a pervert who wanted me to either jerk him off or give him oral excitement, which I didn't do, but it made me quite scared.

That was the most awkward two-hour ride ever. He dropped me off at a major truck stop in Indiana and ended it by saying, "It's too bad we couldn't have taken care of the monotony of the drive." I just ignored that and thanked him, then walked into the diner to figure out what I needed to do. I called my dear friends, Terri and Maureen, collect, because I was scared. They just told me to get back to Portland and that everything was going to be O.K. It was still very cold outside, so I stayed at the truck stop overnight, watching a movie in their theater room, even taking a little nap, then waking up and eating at the diner. I finally walked out at around 7AM toward the freeway and got picked up by a female trucker with her little Shepherd dog. She was very kind and was going all the way to Massachusetts, which meant I got a twenty-four-hour pickup. Score! I learned that she loved clipper ships, and I'm pretty sure we shared our entire histories within a day's time. It was a godsend.

I wish I could remember her name. She saved me from an experience born of one of the worst decisions I'd ever made, hitchhiking back to Maine. Luckily, she saw an innocent kid who needed a lift and some serious help on a very cold day.She ended dropping me off in Worcester, Massachusetts, where I decided to visit Sheryl-Anne, the beautiful young woman I'd met while working for Greenpeace when I lived in Queens the previous year. I somehow found her number, called her, and told her I was in town. She was a little surprised to hear from me but let me visit and stay with her for a few days. It was a great time to catch up and hang out with her. By the end of the week, it seemed time for me to leave, so I had her drop me off at a highway entrance, where I continued my hitchhiking expedition back to Maine. With a peck on the cheek, she wished me good luck as I got out of her car, then she drove off. Alas, I never saw again.

I soon put my thumb out for a ride and got picked up by some older English guy in a VW Rabbit. Luckily, he was going all the way up to Maine and past Portland, so I got my final ride back home. An angel was looking out for me.

BACK IN PORTLAND, MAINE - VOLKSWAGON ALLEY AND DOW STREET

"Volkswagen Alley" was the stuff of legends. I consider this summer to be an impressionable and unforgettable benchmark of my youth. It was a perfect fusion of freedom and innocence, blended into a world of late-80's hippies having the best times of their lives. Simply put, it was an epic fucking summer, especially for this nineteen-year-old kid.

It began with Tony Fralliciardi, who was about to graduate from Portland High School, wanting to get an apartment with "like-minded" people.

He was a Grateful Dead fan and moreso a Jerry Garcia fanatic, something I didn't quite understand at the time, but I liked his quirkiness and dedication to learning guitar and music theory. We hit it off immediately. He asked me if I wanted to rent an apartment with him. I said yes, of course, so long as I could set up my drum set, which was coming from Wisconsin, in the living room. With a shit-eating grin he enthusiastically agreed. Of course, we hadn't yet asked our neighbors how they might feel about it. The apartment was on the third floor of 25 Dow Street in the West End of Portland, in this hideously bright baby-blue building.

The current tenant was a guy named Tim who was a dead-ringer for David Letterman, space between his front teeth and all. Looked just like him, and he played Saxophone just adequately enough to get our attention. He also provided beer for us, since he was the only one who was over twenty-one and he also worked at a local convenience store a block away. We could either buy beer there or at Cumberland Farms, literally a couple hundred feet from Dow Street, on the corner of Brackett and Pine Street. We'd get a case of Busch bar bottles wicked cheap a few times a week. We'd all scrounge up a couple dollars and make a night of it. Well, many nights of it, actually.

So, it was Tony, me, and Tim, and then we got a few other colorful characters into the mix. There was Adam, a real-deal Deadhead; Tom Jacques, another young hippy with curly blonde hair, but possessed an air of responsibility; and Whit Horn, who came for a whole month. There was also an older guy named Del. He was a Vietnam vet who could play the shit out of the harmonica and was a friend of Tom's. He and I connected immediately. I really liked him. He was a gentle giant, if you will, kind of burly, but he had stories glinting in his eyes. He had a sweet little black lab to round out the mix.

During this period, even though I still considered myself a drummer, I was practicing guitar pretty heavily, teaching myself scales and all their positions, trying to memorize the fretboard. Since I couldn't find any guitar books that had scales written in numeric format, which I thought was the most logical way to memorize scales, I created my own scale charts. I broke them down into inversions, starting with one and going up to eight. I created charts for all the basics: diatonic, major and minor pentatonic, natural and melodic minor, augmented and diminished scales, as well as the whole-tone scale. I practiced these scales diligently every chance I got. Sometimes it was just an hour, other times I had half the day to hunker down. I was also writing songs as they came along and singing as much as I could without trying to bother the neighbors with my horrible tone when hitting high notes.

A couple blocks away on Congress Street, there was a music store named Buckdancer's Choice, where I purchased this groovy fifty-watt Guild three-by-ten-inch guitar amp, something I wish I had kept. It sounded great and was very unique. I also bought a white Guild fretless bass. For the life of me, I don't know why I bought that bass, but I was drawn to it and I felt like I should've known how to play a fretless bass.

I also wish I had kept that bass.

Apparently, Guild had my attention that summer. I actually practiced that bass a good amount, enough to understand that I had to acquire muscle memory in order to hit concert pitch correctly on that instrument and in order to sound halfway decent. I gained newfound respect for fretless bass players.

But back to Del. He would ask me to sing this song I had just written for my newest friend/girlfriend. It was titled "Gentle Woman" and he would ask me to sing it over and over again. He'd just close his eyes and listen, and sometimes tear up. Then he'd open his eyes, sigh deeply, and tell me how beautiful he thought that song was. He really felt music. It was one of those three-minute tunes that came from outer space right into my mind that I knocked off and made something out of. It was a stepping stone song, if you will, having all the elements of a perfect love ballad while also retaining a sense of my identity. I knew I was becoming a better songwriter after that song came to fruition. I was motivated to keep writing.

There were other characters that came into the picture and we all hung out with each other a lot. It was a family of young hippies who loved music. Most of my roommates owned VW's, which is how "Volkswagen Alley" came to be. There were a couple VW busses, including a '67 Moon bus, and three VW bugs – one from the 50's with a split rear window, a red convertible owned by a roommate's girlfriend, a classic beat-up '76 owned by Tony, and the one we used to drive to concerts.

I even put money down on a VW Thing but opted out at the last minute. It was only four hundred dollars, which made me suspicious. I still kind of regret that I never followed through with that. I think I just wanted to add to Volkswagen Alley, moreso than wanting to own the VW, foreseeing that it would be a constant maintenance headache.

There were many late-night parties and jam sessions. I'm sure our neighbors loved us! *Sarcasm.* We just dug hanging out together, singing, smoking shit tons of weed, drinking Busch bar bottles, talking music, and jamming. We also attended many concerts together. We all went to a couple Dead concerts down in Foxboro, Massachusetts. Adam actually snuck in by scaling over a fence. We had no idea it was him until we heard some commotion as we walked in, then saw somebody falling from high up with his backpack. He turned around and we were like, "Adam! Dude!" and he was like, "Hey dudes!" with a shit-eating grin. We all proceeded to walk in together. Very funny.

We also saw Santana, Anderson, Bruford, Wakeman and Howe, and a couple other bands. While we were heading down to one of those shows, it was raining a little bit, so the highway was a little slippery. On the other side, we saw an eighteen-wheeler put on its brakes as it started to jack-knife right towards us. There was only a small guardrail between us. It would've been no match. Our screams escalated as it approached, looking like we were in imminent danger and feeling like a B horror movie.

At the last millisecond, the driver corrected himself and the big rig only drove into the grassy section as we sped forward, looking behind us at what was a close call. It truly made us appreciate the concert all that much more.

CAP'N NEWICK'S LOBSTER HOUSE

I was working at this seafood restaurant named Cap'n Newick's Lobster House. It was just across the bridge in South Portland, Maine on Broadway Street. It catered to bus tours of seniors and tourists. A summer lunch crowd could be six buses, sometimes more, sometimes less. Our lunch rush consisted of hundreds of people for a few hours of non-stop mayhem behind the line.

There were at least a dozen fryers and a broil cook. Most of the meals were fried clams, fried fish, and French fries. We'd toss a row of thick paper plates on the table every few minutes to fulfill the orders, put them on the rack for the waitresses to pick up, then slam down another row of plates and keep on truckin' until every ticket was taken off the order wheel and delivered to their table. The adrenaline rush was at once electrifying but also highly stressful. The temperature back there was usually in the high nineties, despite the massive fans pulling the heat from the fryolators.

I was initially trained by this cantankerous guy named Tom Brown, who happened to be the uncle of a bassist I'd be playing with in future years. He'd come to work hungover and get grouchy if I wasn't working up to the speed he wanted. His mood changed from day to day, so what was O.K. one day wasn't the next. I was possibly the only person who talked back to him after he kept on my ass about not going fast enough setting up plates for orders, when I had enough and finally pushed back, "You know, I could just walk out on you right now." Well, he got a good laugh from that. But I was genuinely pissed and sick of his moody bullshit. I was ready to storm out right then and there. He actually laughed out loud and said to some of the other guys that worked there, "Hey, did you hear that? Son just said he could walk out right now!" It was busy as shit, but they were still able to get in a little chuckle from that. I looked at him, steaming with exasperation, ready to ditch the job, when he looked at me, smiled a little bit, calmed down, and said something like, "O.K., let's get back to work." His energy changed and I have to believe that I gained some respect from him that day because I stood up to his bullshit. Apparently, most everybody working my job actually did walk out on him. I just had the balls to threaten him and he respected that. From that point on, we became closer. We actually had some really good conversations. I learned that he was a big blues fan and he was excited to learn that I was a musician who loved the blues. He liked it even more that I could sing. I remember when Tom Petty's "Free Falling" came on the radio, and he told me to sing along to the chorus, which I did. I apparently sung it well enough to impress him. More respect.

There were a pair of brothers who also worked there that loved Buddy Guy. They knew the blues quite well and genuinely loved them. They also loved Stevie Ray Vaughn. I can only remember the older brother, Terry, who worked the broiler. He was only thirty years old, but I thought he was so much older. Looking back at it now, it's so funny how young the thirties actually are and how perspective distorts how you view age.

I had a lot of fun times there. My friend Brendan Hayes was working there and suggested I apply for a permanent kitchen position. So, I did.

MY FIRST PANIC ATTACK

It was around September; I was still living on Dow Street. After having a crazy dream, I awoke to the horrific sound of someone kicking a dog down the stairs of our apartment building. I felt like I was outside of my body; out of control. The feeling was simply terrifying, like dropping into an abyss and waiting to land, but never landing, so that the fear has no end point.

It was dusk, and when I came to, trying to manage this uncontrollable fear, I walked out to the living room and saw that Tim had literally kicked Del's dog down the stairs.

I looked down at those stairs and saw a confused and injured dog, whining helplessly, wondering why it got kicked down the stairs. Then I looked at Del, who clearly wanted to punch Tim in the face but felt defeated since he knew he wasn't an actual tenant in our apartment. He looked at me one last time with the saddest eyes ever before slinking down the stairs, picking up his dog and leaving the apartment for good.

I was absorbing this most abusive event while in the midst of a panic attack. I only figured out that it was a panic attack later on. It was so disturbing. Of course, I now saw Tim in a completely different light, having watched him, emotionless and smirking because he finally got his way. It took away his humanity, and I was disgusted. Tony and I left about a week after this event.

What also stuck with me was this new vibe that I'd never dealt with before. I felt disconnected, like I couldn't control my emotions, like I wasn't in my body. I didn't know when another panic attack would come, so I existed in a constant bubble of anxiety, waiting for that dreadful feeling to crash in at any moment. A full-on attack rarely came, but living with the anxiety of its potential was pure torture that haunted me for the next couple years. I could never sleep without a light or radio on.

They helped me to feel like I was still on planet earth when I closed my eyes; otherwise, I'd fall into this black hole where I could not find solid ground.

It began to affect my sleeping habits as well, and it eventually made me quit working at Cap'n Newicks' because I had a panic attack once right as I was clocking in. The walls were caving in like an LSD experience as I was walking down into the kitchen. I just couldn't handle it, so I left right then and there, never to return.

STAYING AT TONY'S HOME AND GETTING MY GED

Shortly after my quitting Cap'n Newick's, all of us left 25 Dow Street. It was around late September and Tony offered to let me stay at his mom's house temporarily. I don't think his mom was too pleased with the arrangement. Granted, she was kind and respectful toward me, but she dropped clever hints to be sure I was making plans to leave and not staying long term.

Tony and I slept in a spare bedroom for about a week, during which time I noticed there was a school across from his home that offered GED courses. I walked in one morning and asked if I could take my GED. She recommended I take a pre-test, which I did, and I passed with a B+, so I decided to take the official test afterwards.

This time, I didn't pass with such a high mark, but I didn't really care, so long as I passed. It was algebra that killed my score. Everything else I excelled at. That's always been the case with math and me. Ironically, *this* Asian is *not* good with math. Nevertheless, I passed the test and a couple months later, I got a GED certificate and an invitation to join a GED graduation celebration, which I declined. I was so relieved to at least have gotten my high-school equivalency diploma. It would make applying for jobs and colleges much easier. That was a huge weight off my back, and it was all accomplished in one afternoon while staying at Tony's mom's home for ten days.

Early one morning, Tony's mom woke us up and basically said I could no longer stay there; it was time for me to pack up and find a place to live. Even though I knew this day was coming, I was kind of shocked that it came so quickly, and so early in the morning. I immediately called Terry and Maureen, and asked them if I could stay with them for the time being, just until I got myself together again. They were really instrumental in helping me during this era; I was suffering pretty badly with those panic attacks and had a hard time just going out, let alone applying for jobs. They were a godsend.

WALNUT STREET WITH TERRY AND MAUREEN

Terri came and picked me up. I loaded her car up with my belongings, thanked Tony and Tony's mother, who thanked Terri, and off we drove to Terri-and-Maureen's humble little house on Walnut Street.

It was so nice to reconnect with Maureen. Terri's son, Nicholas, was eight years old and very bright. It felt like the right place to be. I continued to suffer through panic attacks, or, should I say, the constant anticipation of panic attacks. I had no control over the random symptoms that would come without warning, seemingly stretching buildings in and out as I was walked by, or feeling like I was only an observer of my own body.

It was like a bad acid trip that went on for years. Thankfully, I had Terri and Maureen at my side. They helped me through the discontent, even though we never spoke about it while I was living there.

When I wasn't overtaken with anxiety, I would practice non-stop, before and after coming home from work. I owned this Yamaha SG-800 guitar and a Yamaha two-by-ten solid state amp, and I would play along to BB King tapes, over and over. I'd also sing along to the tapes, obsessed with trying to sing like him. I considered his voice the gold standard if I was going to sing the blues. I thought the same of his guitar playing. It was all so emotional, but with a kick-ass band backing him up. BB King was slick, smooth, and sincere. I'd sing his tunes, record myself singing them, hear the flat or sharp notes on playback, adjust, then start over. This was my ritual, day in, day out, until my singing had the least flat and sharp notes possible. I was also consumed with his bends on slow blues and shuffle songs. I'd practice them relentlessly, rewind those tapes until I got it good enough to be satisfied for the night.

Along with BB King, I also devoured The Beatles. They were songwriting *masters* and I had to learn their secrets. I soaked in Paul's natural sensibilities trying to absorb his vocal prowess, while loving John's lyrical depth and ability to write outside the box, making his chord progressions and ideas sound like they belonged. For me, he stretched how far a pop song could go and still capture the listener. He was also lucky to have a George Martin as a producer. Ringo and George were unsung heroes, always coming up with the most perfect concept for each song. The Beatles were the most Zen band of all time. The support team was just as important as they were, because it was all timing.

All I cared about was kicking ass, and that required practice. I'd sing for hours as well, and God bless them, I don't know how Terri and Maureen tolerated my singing. My screaming voice was nails on a chalkboard when I hit those high notes! Maybe they thought I was improving.

Nevertheless, I kept on practicing. The time with them on Walnut Street was one of the best periods of my life. It was a safe haven where I could be a young, confused, budding artist who felt supported. With that, my fear of panic attacks slowly left as spring entered.

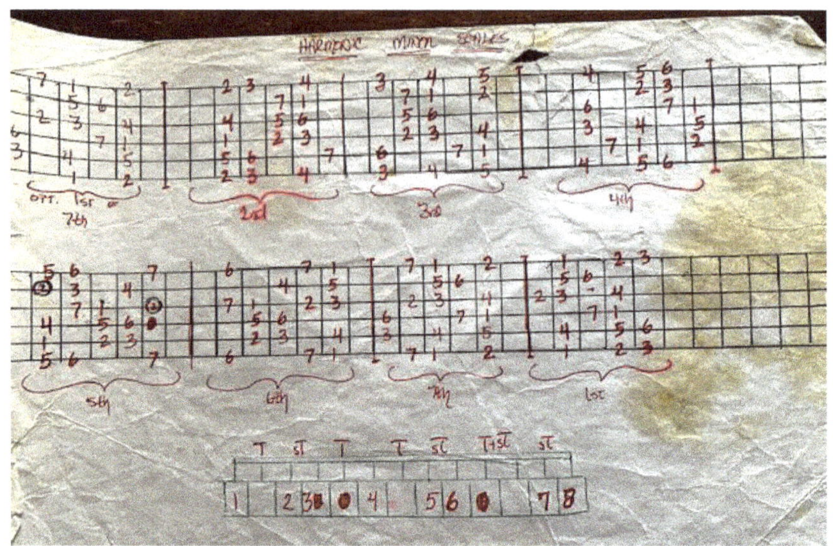

Harmonic Minor Scale I created to practice on guitar.

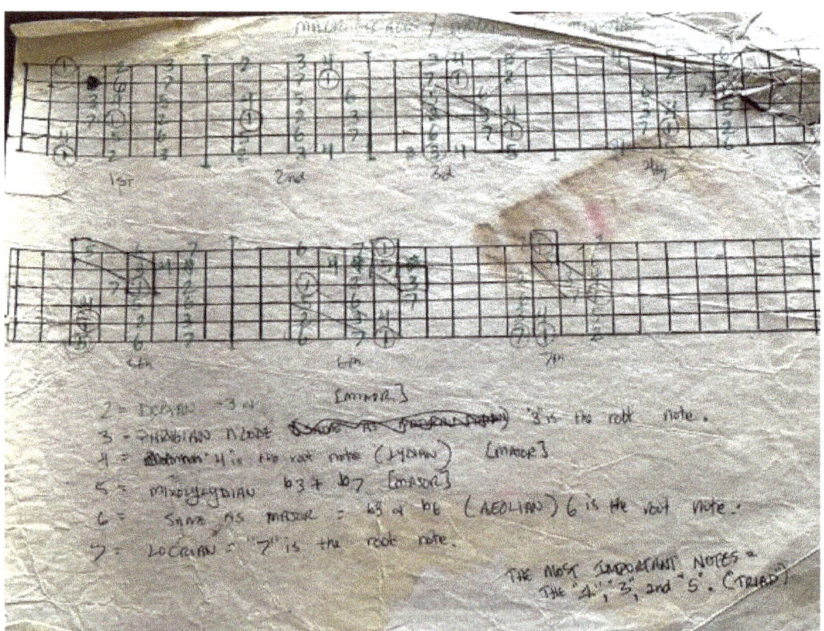

Another minor scale chart I created to help memorize the fretboard.

My Intervallic Relationship Chart I created to understand music theory no matter where I was on any given note. I couldn't find anything like this in the library, and there wasn't the internet in those days.

SARAH DELANO, HEALER

After some time trying to deal with my sense of dread on my own, I finally reached out. At first, I went to Maine Medical Center and talked to a general psychologist, dished out details of my sordid past to her, only to have her response boil down to "Well, it's no wonder you're having panic attacks." I'm sure she meant well, but I just wasn't feeling it with her.

So, I asked Terri and Maureen if perhaps they knew anybody that could help me with the panic attacks, or quelling the anxiety of anticipating them, which was worse than an actual attack. Since they were deep into the spiritual circle of healers in Portland, they immediately recommended Sarah Delano.

Sarah was a tiny woman, barely five feet tall, but filled with wisdom and a natural positivity. I think she was Irish, or perhaps Scottish? A full head of wavy ginger hair. She married a man who had studied Chi Gong, and then he moved to China to study further. Later, she also moved to China for ten years, studying and practicing Chi Gong, Kung Fu, and energy healing. She returned to the United States when she felt she had learned what she'd wanted to learn. She came back to Portland, Maine as a powerhouse. She was a skilled and intuitive woman, so I called her.

I was a little nervous at first, but she put me at ease fairly quickly, asking what, to me, were the right questions. A couple weeks later, I went to her office for the first time, which was a beautiful room in a brick home on Deering and State Street.

When I arrived, she asked the same generic questions that the previous therapist had, but she reacted differently to what I shared, and I liked that. I sensed she was calm and clear-headed. After getting the info she needed from me, she asked me to get onto her massage table, face up. Which I did. She did some cranial work, which felt great. Then she forewarned me that she was going to do a kind of breathing to help separate herself from her body, if you will, in order to go deeper with our session, and I was comfortable with that.

She practiced a breathing method that, to this day, I've never heard again. I could try to replicate it, but it came from an otherworldly place. I trusted that she had been trained to do what she did, so I just kept my eyes closed while she did her breathing method. After about a minute, her breath became more subdued, and it felt like her hands were searching through my mind for hidden artifacts of pain. Not in an offensive way, but as if she was trying to extract the traumatic energy that my mind had been hiding from my soul all my life. I know, it sounds really eccentric, but something was happening, and my anxiety was leaving.

I was on that table for about thirty minutes. She utilized acupressure and some Reiki. I had no idea what that was at the time, but whatever she did, I left feeling emotionally lighter. She helped me find hope, that I wasn't forever trapped in the never-ending dread. If I continued working with her, I was confident she'd be able to lessen the overbearing weight of my past. I thanked her profusely, paid her, and left.

I returned weekly a few more times. The second time, she did her breathing thing, then added some crystals to certain areas on my chest while she did acupressure. When she was done, and came "out of her spell" if you will, she told me that I was, "a very, very old soul, and had thousands of followers in my previous life." This obviously shocked me a little, but also made me feel validated in some way, as if I'd always known my past life experiences could help me work through the anxiety I had been holding onto since childhood. Sarah treated me as an equal after that, as if she had traveled to the past, and seen what I had done to help others.

I know there's many people who consider this kind of talk bullshit, but I don't. I believe that energy is the binding force of us all, and it can shape itself however it wants in the spiritual world, so long as your brain and attitude are open to it.

After about five weeks with Sarah, we decided that I'd gotten what I needed from her, and she was able to extract enough pain from my past for me to no longer suffer from panic attacks.

Granted, I also had to do a few other exercises in my life in order to keep them at bay, but I could not have moved forward with my life without her help. She was instrumental in helping me become a man who could manage his fears. For that, I am forever grateful for her wizardry.

I ran into Sarah a couple years later on Congress Street while there was an art festival happening in the street. It was so great to see her. Her eyes lit up when she saw me. She actually called out my name as she passed by, and then I recognized her. Her eyes twinkled with a natural radiance. She was so happy to see me, and I her! We made small talk, but it felt like it mattered. She acknowledged in that brief moment that we'd always share a spiritual connection. It meant the world to me. She was a special spirit. I wish I could've spent more time with her. In previous lives, maybe we did.

PHOEBE

The first time I saw Phoebe was at some random West End party in the summertime. She was a pretty wild one, making out with another girl on the stairs, not giving two shits about what anybody thought. I admired that. I was leaving the party by that time, bored out of my gourd, but she caught my attention with her brazen, sexually liberal attitude. She was a true *broad*. I smirked, and went home.

Sometime later, I went to a party at her apartment. My girlfriend at the time, Sarah Darling, told me to go there. So, I did. We met almost offhandedly, her coming out to smoke a cigarette on her front porch just as I arrived. I introduced myself to her, and she said something to the effect that of her not expecting me to be as good-looking as I was. That was a funny introduction, I thought, but I was fine with that. We talked as she smoked her cigarette. After hanging out for an hour, I left the party, finding it quite boring Except for her.

July arrived and I went to a party on Peak's Island. Phoebe was there. I didn't hang out with her at all during the party. After a couple hours, as I said my goodbyes to everyone, she pops up in front of me and intimates that I should stay. I say no, then I proceed to hug her, which transforms into a kiss, and the kiss intensifies into more than we both expected until Phoebe looks up at me and says, "Oh shit..." with a smile of destiny on her face.

We had quite the summer, one of the most memorable of my life. We fell in love so quickly and passionately. She was very artistic and sensitive, with a wonderful sense of humor. We didn't stay together past late fall, even though we'd still hang out occasionally. It took me a long time to get over her but time seems to soothe the pain of breakups, and my memories of our time together are mostly wonderful.

WORKING ODD JOBS AND SINGING AT INN BY THE SEA

At age twenty, I had a challenging time finding steady work. It was a tough time for the job market, so I signed on with a temp agency which kept me busy enough, while also working for my previous girlfriend's older brother David Darling at his landscaping company. In August, I was even hired as a garbageman for the city of South Portland for three weeks, literally holding onto the back of a garbage truck and tossing trash in at each stop. The first week was actually pretty fun. It had kind of a rebel vibe, working a job nobody in their right mind would ever want to do, but feeling a sense of liberation as I held onto the back of that truck and felt the breeze hit my face and cooling me off during those hottest of summer days.

August heat in Maine can be quite stifling, and as the heat rose, the maggots built up steadily in the bottom of that truck. Actually, the pile became so enormous, it looked like a pool of maggots you could jump into and swim around in – a very vile vision I immediately erased from my head whenever it crept in. The hours were decent. You'd still be paid for eight hours of work even if you only did five or six, which were most days, and we always had weekends off.

Of course, by the second week, I'd had enough. On the very last day, on the very last stop, we drove into this fairly large division of condos where this little group of preteen boys came up to me, asking me benign questions, which turned into asinine questions, then questions that were clearly designed to patronize and annoy the shit out of me. It eventually got down to them throwing shit at me as we turned the corner and me giving them the middle finger and telling them to fuck off while laughing at them. They still might hold the title of the most hated boys I've ever met. I've never been so relieved to leave a job as that one.

Since bills don't pay themselves, I had to find another job pronto. So, my pal Matt Beal drove me out to his job at Inn by the Sea in Cape Elizabeth. It was a beautiful hotel next to the ocean, obviously, and I filled out an application. I met the manager, an attractive older blonde woman, who asked me a couple questions, looked me up and down, amazed that I'd come to an interview in torn jean shorts and a t-shirt, but apparently dug my calm confidence.

I was hired on the spot - as their laundry guy. Absolutely perfect job for me. I worked alone and could bring all the music I wanted to work, crank the songs up on the tape deck and sing along to them.

I'd bike to work five days a week and blast the Beatles and BB King for the entire eight-hour shift, singing to my heart's content, playing the same tapes over and over. This was some of the best vocal practice I got in at any job I'd ever had. I'd sing so fucking loud and couldn't give a shit.

I thought nobody could hear me – until the housekeeping manager told me one day that I was a songbird. Ha! She actually meant it. Apparently, half the wing of the hotel could hear me sing, but they didn't mind it! I consider the six months at that job an incredibly important part of my vocal development. My voice grew stronger and my pitch got better.

The property grounds and separate cottages were spectacular. I loved pushing the giant rolling tub filled with sheets and towels to the housekeepers every few hours. The fog would roll in a few times a week and the smell of the ocean was intoxicating. Despite it being a job, it always felt peaceful.

I especially appreciated my bike rides back into Portland. The weather for the first few months was perfect. I'd take the back roads into South Portland, where it was mostly downhill and traffic was light, so I'd just take my time, breathing in the fresh air; really appreciating the rarity of those moments.

Unfortunately, winter came a few months later and the job became too difficult to keep. After all, it was seasonal work. So, when December hit, I was out. By then, I was biking to work through snowstorms, which was a little dangerous. I'll always cherish that job with that sunny little laundry room, singing along to "Til There Was You", "Hold Me Tight", and so many other Beatles tunes. I also got to read Miles Davis's autobiography during that period. Talk about an eye-opening book. He passed away around the same time I was reading it; I always found that interesting. Onto the next job, where new experiences awaited me.

WALNUT STREET, WRONG BROS, MIDNIGHT SHIFTS AND TAO JONES

As early fall arrived, I moved into a place right next door to Terry and Maureen's house. I was living with a few other guys: Neil Carroll, Chris Henry, and Sean Brilliant. I was close to turning twenty-one in January, just a few months away. Jobs were scarce as we were in the midst of a major recession, and I was having a hard time getting work to pay the rent, let alone food and money to pitch in for gas and heating.

I worked odd jobs. Once, when I borrowed Neil's bike to go look for a job at the unemployment center, it was stolen. They somehow took the bike but left behind the lock! I still don't know how they managed that. *And* I was collecting city food stamps; a lifesaver.

I scraped by with food stamps for a couple months, getting work with Neil at the docks on late and midnight shifts, working for this man named Richard Slaughter a few nights a week, cleaning and packing up fish and shrimp. Richard seemed like a very fair and decent man, then we found out a couple months into working for him that he was actually a serial stalker. His story had gotten written up in the local newspaper, *The Portland Press Herald*, and we could never look at him as our boss again after we read that. Sure, he was super nice, but he had been accused of killing his previous wife, found not guilty and released, and then found guilty of attempting the same pattern with his new fiancé.

It obviously didn't go as planned, and his tactics didn't work the second time. Even worse, he was exposed to the world. In a nutshell, that was the end of that job. Neil found us another midnight shift doing some shrimping a couple docks down from our previous post. This guy was a seasoned pro; he had a team of workers and he knew how to make money with shrimp.

The work was hard and backbreaking, literally. We began at midnight. They suggested we wear layers to work as the average temperature of our job was forty degrees. We were all bending over a conveyor belt, looking at gobs of shrimp coming down, and cleaning up any excess shells and other bullshit (barnacles, small fish, etc.) before the shrimp went into a tub at the end of the conveyor belt. We would stay in this position for hours on end, hardly moving, wearing white overcoats, hairnets, masks, and cotton gloves with rubber gloves layered over those. It was brutal on the upper back. After a few weeks, we actually became conditioned to that terrible posture.

On pay day, we'd walk into the bank after a shift, smelling like shrimp and fish, everybody looking at us, and making facial gestures to express their dislike of our scent, and we didn't give two fucks. We'd just worked all night, were cold as shit, and just wanted to cash our checks so we could get some beers, drink 'em, and go to bed.

This gig lasted for a couple months, then I couldn't do it anymore. Besides, I was waiting for the chance to get my job back as a busboy at Cap'n Newick's Lobster House, and in late spring, I did. It paid well and I only worked four days a week, so it gave me a lot of time to practice, and decent money to pay bills and buy some music gear as well as weed, beer, and food, in that order.

I was making almost five hundred in cash, plus another couple hundred dollars from odd jobs, which combined was a decent weekly wage back in 1992, about twelve hundred per week in 2022.

During that summer, Neil and I decided that we wanted to start a band called Tao Jones. All we needed was a bassist. In came Jeff Brown. I don't know how we met him. I think Neil ran into him somewhere and he mentioned to Neil that he was a bassist. The rest was history. We practiced a couple times a week in Neil's bedroom, learning our originals as well as creating new songs along the way and just jamming, the good ol' fashioned way.

After a few months of hard practice, we became pretty damn good. We were a young power trio; our goal at that time was to get a few originals down and play them at Raoul's Roadside Attraction at Wednesday night open mics, and Wrong Brothers at Tuesday open mics. That would be our testing ground.

We practiced diligently, and each night we played these venues, our confidence grew. My confidence grew more as a singer, which was very important. You have to sing with confidence.

There was one memorable Tuesday night at Wrong Brothers. We had just learned my hard rock song "It's Not Me" as well as Frampton's "Do You Feel Like I Do" - without the voice wah - which we knew was a crowd pleaser.

We knew we only had time to do those two songs. So, we began our Tuesday night open mic slot with Frampton's tune. I think Chris Henry played the lead on that as well. The song ended and the entire bar was cheering and whistling. We were pretty fired up. Once the dust settled, we counted in "It's Not Me" which is such an AC/DC-Sabbath sounding song, the crowd in the front went nuts. Some of them were actually putting their hands on their heads and saying, "Holy fucking shit!" Long story short, we killed it that night.

Wrong Brothers had a killer house band, with John Jacques as the bandleader. He was about 10 years older than me; tall and lanky with hair similar to Huey Lewis, but dark. He'd give us thirty minutes, knowing we were going to play some good original music that would get the crowd to dance or headbang in true hard rock form. He even asked to learn some of my tunes with his band so I could sit in with them.

We rehearsed a couple of my songs with his bassist, who was top notch. He played a Fender Precision Sunburst and had a mustache and a mullet. Somehow, he got away with that look.

We actually learned and performed my song "Silver-footed Queen" and it was only because his bassist took the time to get it down that his band could do that song justice. Man, I wish I could've hung out more with John.

I also remember a guy in the audience who observed how I'd played our first open mic night, shy and green, then became a little cocky once I grew more comfortable onstage, absorbing the attention, months later. It was a little hard to accept his critique, but it also helped me to find the balance between confidence and being full of myself. He helped me check myself at an early age. I wish I knew who he was; I'd thank him. I can still see his face. Granted, he was drunk, but his words were solid. I never became too cocky ever again.

HAUNTED HOUSE ON WALNUT STREET

The house we lived in was haunted. I mean, I had my early suspicions, but I'd brushed them off after a few months. The first signs I observed were while practicing drums in the basement. Most people would consider it paranoia, but I knew I'd felt a presence staring at me when I was practicing sometimes. We had this translucent tie-dye sheet hanging down to the right side of the drum set to cut the noise. On the other side, there was nothing but darkness.

While practicing, I'd sometimes look over and just feel somebody staring at me, or even sense a figure there. The hairs on the back of my neck would stand up, I'd stop playing and say out loud, "OK, I know you're staring at me, please stop doing that." Then I'd resume practicing, but I'd still feel what I'm sure it was a male spirit staring at me, so I'd stop again, now pissed, and start swearing at it. "Ok, cut the shit. I know you're there, so *stop fucking staring at me*." I'd try to resume practicing but the certainty I was watched would be too overwhelming, so I'd just say, "fuck it" and put down the sticks, every hair on my body standing up, and walk upstairs, a little freaked out but also a little pissed off.

The most indisputable haunting event happened when my roommate Shaun and I were watching TV in the living room. We heard a bedroom door open upstairs and figured it was Chris waking up from a late afternoon nap. By now it was about 6PM. As we heard footsteps coming down the stairs, we both said, "Hey dude" or "Hey Chris" but neither of us got a response.

We plainly heard the footsteps reach about halfway down the stairs, and turned around. There was nobody there. We still heard footsteps continue all the way to the bottom, then *saw* the basement door open, and the sound of footsteps stopped. We just looked at each other and I said to Shaun, "Must've been the ghost." He smiled and said "Yuuup" and we resumed watching TV, but were definitely tripped out by it.

Shortly afterward, we went upstairs to discover that Chris wasn't even home. About half an hour later, he walked in the door and we told him what happened. He just laughed; eyes wide. We all just took it in stride since the ghost was obviously not malevolent.

Shortly after that, Neil confessed that he'd seen a face in the sun-porch window of my room one night, but had brushed it off. Again, we figured it was the ghost, and it obviously lived in Chris's bedroom. Chris couldn't have cared less. In fact, he had a hearty chuckle about it and blew it off. Just another day in haunted Portland.

BARBER FOODS AND ITS VIETNAMESE COMMUNITY

This was a very interesting little moment in time. It was in the heart of winter, and for an entire month, I would bike in the slush and snow over to Barber Foods, sometimes under pretty dangerous conditions, almost being hit by cars, but I had to get to work and that was the only mode of transportation I had. I'd been hired by a temp agency to work at Barber Foods, a frozen chicken processing plant.

The plant was always cold, a consistent forty-five degrees. I always wore boots with two pairs of socks, two shirts, a windbreaker, and a sweater over that. All this was covered by a white smock, hairnet, cotton gloves and – once again – rubber gloves over those if working directly with non-frozen chicken, which would then get flash frozen. Sometimes I even had to wear earplugs to block out the noise from all the machines. It could get quite loud.

It wasn't a huge plant, but enough to employ a few hundred people per shift. The owner was known to hire a lot of immigrants from Africa, Central and South America, and Southeast Asia, mostly Vietnamese. He sponsored dozens of workers as well, helping them out of very adverse or even war-torn conditions. He was a real positive figure in the Portland immigration community. They worked hard for him and he knew they were grateful for the jobs.

One time, while standing in the line, inspecting frozen chicken going down the conveyor belt, an older Asian woman was throwing frozen chicken pieces at me to get my attention. She definitely got my attention. There were a couple young pretty Asian girls beside her, whom I learned were related to her.

She was their aunt. In Asian tradition, the older woman spoke for the younger women, so as not to be improper. The aunt was trying to get a read on me, to see if I was single. "You married?" Me: "No." Her: "You have girlfriend?" Me: "Yes, I'm dating somebody." Her: "You very handsome. You have pretty eyes."

Her nieces start giggling into their white cotton-gloved hands, hiding their mouths. Priceless. I just politely smiled and said, "Thank you very much." We continued to work and she never asked me again.

That job provided some consistency during a really tough time in Maine. We were still in a recession, and I didn't have much education or experience outside of basic labor.

One day, I went into the break room and noticed a lot of Vietnamese hanging out together. I didn't want to intrude, but this older Vietnamese woman took a liking to me, waving me to come over. She reminded me a little bit of my mom if she was that age. She held out her hand and asked me if I wanted a piece of candy. "Candy?" Not wanting to be impolite, I said, "Yes, please. Thank you." She handed me some classic Vietnamese candy. I loved it.

She then asked me what my name was. I told her Son Vo, which is as Vietnamese as it gets. The other Vietnamese guys looked at me with approval, warming up to me a little bit. This chatting went on for a while, then we all returned to work.

The next day, I saw them all in the break room again, waving me over and saying hi to me. I learned a few of the guys' names, and they told me, in very broken English, that they wanted to pick me up on a weekend day and spend some time with me, get to know me. I didn't quite understand the entire exchange, but apparently my response was "Yes."

The following weekend, they showed up at my home where I was living with Terri and Maureen in their little Cape house on Walnut Avenue, and stayed there for a couple hours, waiting for me to return. I had no idea this was going on until I got a call from Maureen, telling me a group of young Vietnamese guys were waiting at the house for me. I informed her I wasn't going to be coming home, and they stayed for another hour, finally realizing that I was blowing them off.

I felt awful about that, but I was actually frightened to get closer to them, and also embarrassed that I couldn't speak my native language with them. It was easier to just ignore them and hope they'd go away. That's exactly what happened.

I never saw them again, and to this day, I'm a little bit ashamed that I chose to deal with the situation in that way. They were embracing me into their community, and I straight-up ignored them. It was all out of fear. If I could redo that moment, I wonder what I would choose now?

Regardless, I squandered a wonderful opportunity to integrate myself into the heart of Portland's Vietnamese culture. I heard that word got back to the grandmother figure who had initially welcomed me and she was very disappointed and saddened. That's what hurt more than anything else. I disappointed Grandma.

NATIVE AMERICAN TALKING CIRCLES AND THE FORUM

Terri and Maureen invited me to be part of a talking circle that they were involved in. We would all get together when we could, which was usually once a month, but I only went a few times at most. The elder Native American was a Sioux Indian, and she would often remark how much I looked like a Sioux with my long black hair. I also had the facial features – the high cheek bones, the half-Asian eyes and the golden red skin tone when summer came and I tanned. I would sometimes sit in her lap, which I'm sure creeped out some members, but I didn't give a shit.

Terri and Maureen also convinced me to do a weekend intensive called "The Forum." They had just participated in it themselves and were convinced it would help elevate me spiritually. They even agreed to pay for half of it.

For reference, it cost about five hundred dollars, meaning I had to squirrel away two hundred fifty in order to do it. It was a rough feat in those times, much to the chagrin of my bandmember Neil, who thought it was a bunch of New-Age horseshit, understandably. Still, I raised the money, applied for it, and went.

On day one, the lead speaker did a lot of introductory talk, then got us to partner with someone to work through the concept that life is basically an interpretation of our interpretation of life, which immediately created confusion and miscommunication issues. The speaker also preached that life is essentially an empty vessel, an onion that you peel until you get to the middle and find nothing. They analogized Buddhism in their teaching often. All of this resonated with me deeply and caught me at the perfect time in life to absorb the concepts. I also had to call and make amends with someone whom I had hurt and ask for forgiveness. Very AA, and that's O.K., I did it and it helped heal a wound within a friend. I came home feeling like I had gained more perspective on life and had been reset. I'd recommend it if asked; however, I couldn't help but notice a definite cult-like potential for people who would continually attend their seminars. It could easily become addictive to those who were searching too hard and defeat its whole purpose. I got what I wanted from it and gracefully left. Others I knew stayed on and learned the hard way.

FORTY SONGS IN FOUR DAYS WITH RODNEY

This moment sticks out in my memory as it was the first time that I had to learn forty-plus songs I hardly knew, and had to learn them within four days for a Friday night gig. One morning, I met Rodney Sturdee at Green Mountain Coffee Roasters. My roommate Neil Carroll was playing with Ken Grimsley around town, and somehow, I found out that Rodney knew them. We struck up a conversation, he found out I played guitar, and asked if I might be interested in playing with him. He had a Grateful Dead cover band, and there wasn't a keyboardist for this one gig they had in Kennebunk or Old Orchard Beach.

Anyway, I agreed to play with him on a couple gigs. I had to learn at least forty tunes, mostly Dead or cover songs that the Dead played. I had just turned twenty-one, and I wasn't really versed in the Grateful Dead repertoire, despite living with Deadhead roommates for the last couple years and hearing their music incessantly. I leaned more towards The Beatles, Pink Floyd, Zeppelin, Talking Heads, and The Police at the time, so I had a lot of work ahead of myself.

Rodney was patient with me. We'd get some coffee, head over to his place, and for the next four days, go over dozens of songs which we'd tape for practice use when I had the time. On the final day, he was confident that I had learned the setlist as the rhythm guitarist. Some of those tunes were pretty tricky if you'd never heard them before: "Scarlet Begonias", "Eyes of the World", a bunch of Motown tunes, some Clapton, Stevie Ray Vaughan tunes, and other bands as well. But he deemed me ready! You gotta understand, I was as green as you can get. I had never played in a cover band, let alone a Dead cover band, and I had to fake being Bobby Weir for a couple gigs. Luckily, I had some good chops for a young kid and practiced like a motherfucker, so I was as prepared as I could be. After all, I wasn't going to make myself look like a fool, especially in front of Rodney. He was a funny guy, too. He rode a motorcycle about town but had a van for gigs. He had these huge fingers and super strong hands that could wrap around the fretboard. I'd trip out looking at his technique. He made playing the guitar look easy, and his tone, from what I can remember as a young musician, was good. He played a Strat and I think a Deluxe Reverb. Maybe a Super Reverb? I forget, it was so long ago. Regardless, this was my first experience in preparing for a gig, learning so many new songs. It was a quintessential moment in time, something I've only ever had to do maybe a couple other times, but this was the *first* time. Good for the mind and soul.

After playing a second gig with his band at The Treehouse, which Adam Powers and Phoebe showed up to for support, we met up the next morning at Green Mountain. He rode me home on his motorcycle afterwards and told me that he was no longer going to use me in his band since the keyboardist he'd been wanting to get was finally able to join. He felt bad about it, but he did me a huge favor that day. He told me that I was too talented to be playing with him and that I should start my own band. I was kind of bummed, but we parted on good terms. He was straight with me and I respected that.

What's funny is about a year later, he ended up seeing me on Fore Street in front of Leo's Pizza late one night, knowing he still "owed me" for one of those gigs I played with him, so he ran back to his motorcycle and comes back, handing me this Fuzz Face pedal. It was worth the equivalent of the gig's pay. I took it and thanked him, then we parted ways. Had I known how valuable that pedal is now, I would've kept it forever!

So, thank you, Rodney. You came at the perfect time in my musical development while in my early twenties. It's almost shameful that I didn't know the songs we worked through! Alas, I know them still, and I'm pretty sure I've played them all countless times out here in California. But you showed me that I could meet a goal that seemed unattainable.

BEBOPS CAFE

I was twenty-two years old when I decided to help my friend, Jim Dorian, open up a coffee shop. He had a local talented artist design the logo, and from there it was basically a fly-by-the-seat-of-your-pants operation. What's funny is that he was only twenty-six, but I considered him so much older. His wife just had a baby, so they were always exhausted. So many times, I'd come in and was opening that place up alone, making the muffins, coffee, etc.

It was pretty fun, except that he was messy and never cleaned up after himself. From working in so many kitchens, I was taught that good chefs always cleaned up after themselves. Jim wanted to become a good chef, but that attribute seemed to allude him, and frustrate me.

It was a good gig. He treated me fairly and always paid me on time, so I had very few complaints. In fact, he'd let me, Max Kay, and his friend practice in the basement a few times, until I screwed that up by somehow forgetting to lock the store up after we rehearsed. Damn it. Oh well, it was kind of creepy down there anyway.

We played a lot of jazz records as well as Latin music while the store was open. It was great to expose one another to our influences. During that time, I was deep into learning jazz. I listened to some great Latin jazz records, with some fantastic Cuban bands, though I don't remember their names now.

It was a fun summer. This is where I met my future girlfriend Rita and my still good friend Laura. They'd come into the café before going off to work. We hit it off, and we all started hanging together outside of the coffee shop. This was when I was playing drums for The Rhythm Section of Shame. We began as a cover band that changed its name for every gig and promoted the hell out of those gigs, then that band would "disappear." Suddenly, a "new band" would appear, which was just us again of course, but with another clever name.

I left at the end of summer. Apparently, I was supposed to work in the morning during a street art fair, but I showed up at noon. Jim was pissed at me, we got into an altercation, and I handed him my keys. I was finished! After all I had done for him, I didn't need this crap, so I quit and walked out, enjoying the art walk on Congress Street. I enjoyed a few days off, but I'd have to find employment fairly soon.

VAL MOLLINEUX, JAZZ GUITAR TEACHER

I had reached a point where I felt like I'd hit a wall and couldn't go any further without jazz guitar lessons. I had heard about this guy named Val, who taught private lessons on Vaughn Street.

I called and arranged to meet him, telling him I wanted to learn jazz guitar. When I arrived, I recognized him from the days of taking drum lessons on Forest Avenue with Bill Timms. At first, he was very polite and professional with me, even slightly cautious. He was a black man with blue eyes, one of those combinations that always intrigued me. I loved that look.

He began by teaching me the Berklee College of Music Jazz Method for Guitar. I was a diligent student, and within six months, I had gone through the entire course, as well as learning standards and learning to improvise on the I-II-V, a staple jazz progression. I practiced diligently for hours every night, singing at the top of my lungs. I had to get my voice strong and nail that BB King growl.

After about half a year of lessons, Val told me he couldn't teach me anymore and suggested I go to this other jazz teacher who could take me to the next level. He had reached his limit with me. I was sad to see my lessons end with him. Many a time, we'd be playing together and we'd get the giggles, and they wouldn't stop. I'd make some kind of face that made him start laughing, and from there, the giggles kept coming. He had these two front teeth that would come out like a chipmunk, his dimples would get exposed, and he'd chuckle like Santa Claus, with his shoulders bouncing up and down.

It was a sight to be seen. We'd have to stop until the giggling ended, then he'd say, "Maaaan, you're a trip." He'd look at me with his eyes smiling, the mood all light, and we'd go back to jamming. I'm glad I had my time with him. He was one of my biggest influences. When he got really comfortable being around me, he shared some of his own history and what he overcame in his days as a shoeshine boy in Harlem.

He'd met all the jazz greats as a kid and he told me some incredible stories. Once he reached fifteen years old, he started touring around the country as a guitarist with R&B bands. It wasn't easy work, to say the least, being treated like a second-class citizen while being all smiles on stage, pretending everything was A-OK in the world of the black man. Far from it. But he always had a good attitude. A little cautious, but that's par for the course. When Val became older, he gave lectures throughout New England on Duke Ellington, a figure whom he had studied and idolized throughout his entire life. He'd get so excited telling me facts about him. Studying about the Duke once I became older, I quickly figured out where his respect and appreciation came from.

One day, Val became so comfortable sharing things about himself that at the end of our lesson, he looked at me, paused for a couple seconds, then said, "Hey Son, I got something I wanna show you." His eyes lit up.

We walked out of the lesson room and into what I can only consider his man cave, where he displayed his prized possessions. First, he showed me all these scale-correct model cars that he'd collected for decades. He absolutely adored them, sharing the details of each one, showing how the doors opened and the wheels turned. He became a little kid right before my eyes. Then he said, "Now, I've got a big surprise for you." He seemed a little cautious at first, but he trusted me enough by now to share this treasure that he'd been hiding. We both walked down to this little basement level and he brought out this big guitar case. We walked back upstairs with it to his man cave where he unzipped the first case, which revealed another guitar case beneath that.

He then took out the second guitar case revealing his prized possession, a 1948 Gibson L5-C hollow-body guitar. At the time, it was valued at ten thousand dollars. I'm sure it's worth even more now. I was in awe. At first, I didn't dare touch it, nor did he. However, I eventually held it for about thirty seconds, then promptly handed it back to him.

He played it for a couple minutes, wiped it down with a cloth, and put it back in its case, which got placed back into the outer case and zipped up. This was his pride and joy, and I'm so glad he shared that with me. Hopefully, one of his children inherited it.

Years later, when I lived in Santa Monica, I talked to him over the phone. He was delighted to hear from me. We talked and talked, all excited to reconnect. I mailed him an autographed CD of my band's first album, *Life Is Illusion*. Unfortunately, that was the last time we talked. But I knew that CD was proudly displayed for others to see. After all, I was one of his favorite students. I miss him dearly, that goofy grin and chuckle, but I smile every time I think of him. Thank you, Val, you were one of a kind and I'll always love you for the invaluable information and love for jazz that you shared with me.

GO BUTTON

When living on Peak's Island, I'd occasionally go to the Porthole Café, literally next door to the Peak's Island dock, a fisherman's dive bar. Nothing fancy, smelling of fish and the ocean, and catering to fisherman who are going out at 4AM. When not cooking breakfast for fishermen, they had live music on weekend nights.

One Friday night, I hung out there and watched a band of total geeks set up. The banjo player stood out the most. He was wiry with dirty blond hair, he wore cut-off light-blue jean shorts, and he was full of energy. And he had all these pedals!

For a banjo? Well, I had to stay to see this! Their bassist was this nerdy, glasses-wearing female. O.K., that's very cool. The bandleader also seemed interesting, not that excited about the gig but focused. And the second guitarist, I knew!

He worked at the comic book store on Exchange Street, where I bought my cigarettes and also played pinball. He had this electric Ovation twelve-string guitar. I was fascinated. I don't know who the drummer was. For some reason, I still don't know.

I watched them play what I considered "hokey" music, but with a unique edge. The bandleader strummed his Tele while talk-singing through his verses, and the banjo player basically had carte-blanche to noodle through each song, but he was very inventive and brought the listener along for the ride, which felt like an adventure you wanted to be a part of. They were all just an interesting and quirky bunch that I felt compelled to meet, so I introduced myself during a break and told them I was a drummer. I don't even remember if we exchanged numbers at that point. It was probably another couple months before I got together with them. At the first rehearsal, we got along pretty well, although they told me I played pretty loud. I was surprised by that but said, "O.K." I did work on volume and learned to play lighter. It was a good lesson in dynamic playing, thanks to them.

We played around Portland at outside events, parties, and small venues. I was really psyched to finally be a part of the ultimate band of geeks. It made me feel legit, like I was in the club now!

RHYTHM SECTION OF SHAME

I was living at the Lafayette Square apartments with a Vietnamese guy who worked at a small restaurant named Saigon Tinh Tanh, a few blocks away on Congress Street. I was playing in this band called The Rhythm Section of Shame. We came up with it after putting all the names used throughout the summer on a dart board, donning blindfolds, and wherever the dart fell, that was to be our name. Luckily, it didn't fall on "Shit Sandwich," our way of making fun of a local band named "*Shark Sandwich*."

The band consisted of Chris Goetz - vocals, guitar, bandleader, promoter, alpha male, Max Kay, bassist, Tony Payson, lead vocals, and myself on drums. We were a very dynamic group with lots of energy and a fun, eclectic song list. We decorated the town, up and down every street, with visually intriguing posters. We were shameless. We'd practice right beside Moose Alley Music, which was above Bebop's Café on Congress Street. We went through countless gallon jugs of Carlo Rossi Paisano. The empty bottle collection added up quickly in a week's time of hanging out and rehearsing. It was a fun, fun summer with those guys. I also hung out a lot with a new friend I'd met while working at Bebops, named Christina. Super nice and intellectual young woman. She ended up first dating Chris, then Max, then realized dating band members wasn't all that, so she just stayed friends with us and went to shows.

There were many nights when we'd climb to the roof of my apartment building, Lafayette Square. It was seven stories up, with the last being accessible only by fire escape. We liked hanging out at the corner, where Park Street met Congress Street. We'd smoke our cigarettes and weed, drink our Paisano, and just shoot the shit for about an hour before heading back down.

One night, we discovered a closed-off section of the apartment building on the second floor that looked like it was once filled with stores. The air changed the second we opened up this secret door that clearly read *"Do Not Enter."* Of course, we opened it and, behold, were dumbstruck by this view of a long, eerie hallway, lined with abandoned storefront windows on each side. They were still decorated with mannequins and furniture placed just-right, untouched for seemingly 20 years. The street lights illuminated these abandoned storefronts, while behind the fixtures was complete darkness. It was provocatively creepy. If there was any place that was haunted, I would put my money on this place. We roamed this hall a few times after discovering it. To this day, I wonder if it's still there, untouched, as if rearranging anything would invoke unwanted and trapped spirits to awaken.

Summertime turned to fall, and fall turned to winter. Max tried to help me get a re-entry permit with my green card so as I could tour with them in Switzerland in February, but the permit didn't come in on time – ironically, it arrived on the day their planes left for the tour.

By then, I was moving to Bingham with Rita. The tour was apparently abysmal due to the drummer not being a good fit. They were clearly bummed I wasn't a part of it. When spring arrived, we did one final Rhythm Section of Shame Circus, inviting all the hot acts to perform with us at Geno's, a legendary punk rock club. It went off like wildfire and was a great way to end a great thing, out on top.

GRAVEYARD SHIFT AT THE YMCA

After working at Bebop's Café, I found a job as a janitor for the YMCA on Forest Avenue in downtown Portland. It was a five-story brick building that housed a couple hundred men. I first began working there five days a week, mopping the floors of the housing wings and vacuuming the basement preschool, as well as doing miscellaneous jobs, like cleaning the smudge marks off the walls from racquetballs, redoing the gym floor, which took an entire week, and replacing the lights thirty feet up.

Ironically, I found out that my previous drum teacher Bill Tims was working there as one of the activity directors. I finally "graduated" from mopping duties after months of doing grunt work, and the manager asked if I wanted to take the night shift. I'd work from 9PM to 5AM.

I took the job. I wasn't playing out much and I had to make money before Rita and I moved up to Bingham to live with her mom and younger sisters.

The night shift was actually pretty cool, even though somewhat creepy. The floor where the gym and locker rooms were had blood red halls, making it a little creepier than necessary. There were also a few activity rooms, and of course, the basketball court, which was huge, and echoed.

I always had to keep the music on fairly loud while I vacuumed and mopped the halls and lockers rooms. The female locker room was a bit creepy as well – I've just seen way too many horror movies where bad shit happens in women's locker rooms. It wasn't my favorite part of the night.

The *favorite* part of the night was the last couple hours. I had nailed down my duties where I'd finish everything within six hours, sometimes five, so I'd have a couple hours of down time. I'd rush into the men's locker room, which was more spacious and had a little restroom section with a locked door connecting to the swimming pool room. There was this huge gap beneath that door, which is where I'd smoke weed, leaning down to blow the smoke under the door because of the natural draft provided. It was perfect.

After I was nice and high, I'd wander back into the main locker room, where there was this huge television and a pair of lounge chairs. I'd get myself a soda and snacks from the vending machine, then plop myself down, turn the TV on, and watch some movies on HBO.

It was the best. There was nobody there to bother me and I was high as a kite, getting paid to watch tv for the rest of the shift. Toward the end, I think my boss suspected something was going on, but he could never pin down exactly what it was. I got my work done, so there wasn't much that could be said to me. Besides, by the time he suspected anything, I had given my two weeks' notice. It's still one of my favorite jobs of all time.

MY LAST YEARS IN MAINE

BINGHAM AND WEST FORKS, MAINE

Bingham, Maine was one of the trippiest years of my life. Rita and I had left Portland, Maine in February, and had decided to move into her mom's house, who even picked us up and moved our stuff up there.

Her mom was nice to me, considering that I wasn't the average guy that you might want to see your daughter dating. Add to that how she had just had a miscarriage days before the move up there, so the dynamics had shifted. I was no longer the father-to-be, I was back to being just her boyfriend. The whole premise of us moving up there was to have family support when our child was born. That obviously changed.

It was fun to get away from Portland, or city life, if you will, and slow things down. I got to practice a lot, even though if I had been Rita's mother, I'm sure I looked like a complete slacker. It was so cold and there were so few jobs, I literally didn't work for months, until April came and I was hired by Crabapple Whitewater Rafting Company. The owners, Chuck and Sharon, were great. I loved those two. They hired me on the spot after the interview. A week later, I started working – first doing odd jobs, then once the snow really melted away, I became their groundskeeper.

Rita and I rented this little log cabin up the hill in West Forks and we lived there for a couple months, then moved into town in this little room in the attic above Rita's job, which was photographing the rafters and then developing the shots to sell to them. We had it pretty good. After work, I'd do a decent amount of practicing. We didn't own a television, so a lot of progress could be made, writing and practicing scales.

Throughout all of this period though, I wasn't happy. I no longer wanted to be in a relationship. I wanted to leave the scene and get back to playing live music again, in front of an audience, and to interact with more artistic people. No offense to those who were in West Forks,

I needed more artistic stimulus, which I wasn't getting. I couldn't shake the feeling off, and I had to do something about it, even if it meant hurting the ones I loved.

LEAVING RITA

One morning, I called Matt Beal, broke down and told him how I'd been feeling, and asked for his help to get me out of West Forks, Maine. I didn't have a vehicle and was basically trapped up there. He simply asked me when I wanted him to come up, I said on pay day, and he said he'd be up that day.

Well, payday arrived, and right at 11AM, he arrived. We threw my few belongings into his VW Rabbit, and like a dream, we drove off. Before leaving, I wrote Rita a goodbye letter and stuck it on the standing ashtray alongside two fat joints. It was about the most cowardly thing I've ever done in my life and I regretted it for years. I didn't even talk to her for four days, and when I did it was because she'd figured out how to get Matt's number, and I finally relented and talked to her. The poor thing was so confused and had so many questions that I couldn't answer without sounding heartless and cruel. I felt like I'd ripped her heart out of her chest, which I'm sure is how she felt. I'd wake up for months with that heat in the back of my head, feeling guilt-ridden and not morally right. Rightfully so. I vowed that I'd never do such a chickenshit thing to another woman as long as I lived. Thankfully, I haven't been that stupid to this day.

MUNJOY HILL WITH MATT

After leaving Rita, I had a surge of songs come flying into my head. I was so wrought with guilt; it fueled me inspiration to write it out and rid me of the terrible feelings I harbored. At the same time, I was hanging out with a female friend named Rebecca Stubbs, who I had a little crush on.

She had no idea, or at least I don't think she did. I wrote "Within Our Reach", "Drifted Apart", and a few other songs in this two-month span that late fall and early winter. I continued with the odds-and-ends jobs, being hired by that same Pine Tree Temporary Agency that saved me many times in the past from unemployment. I did a couple weeks at a paper company and impressed them enough for them to offer me a job, but I just couldn't do that kind of thing long-term.

I ended up working at Victory Deli on Congress Square. The owners were really good guys and I'd always admired them. They had a good team of people working for them, many of them in their early twenties, which was perfect for me. I was a dishwasher, which served me just fine. I also did some catering with them here and there, and the following year, I worked down at their Forest Avenue store as a sandwich-maker and order taker. It wasn't my favorite job, but it certainly wasn't a dishwashing job.

The crew was much smaller down there. There was one guy that never really liked me. He found any excuse to chastise me, sometimes even writing lengthy letters, breaking down every little thing I didn't do and making me out to be a lazy ass. He quit a few months after I arrived. I had ruined the little world they had built. Granted, I did try to infuse myself with their daily customer-questionnaire-routine. Many of the clientele were University of Southern Maine students, so they could get quirky and imaginative. Well, my participation ruined the fun for that one guy who quit. Good riddance. I even had a little fling with this one really pretty girl whose artwork I convinced the owners to post, though her art horrified the manager, Patrick. I kinda didn't care, so long as I got to go out with this cute artist girl.

On our first date, she brought along her older sister. Once her sister realized she was a third wheel, she left. We walked up to this venue where Sarah McLaughlin was actually singing and playing piano. I don't know how we got in for free. We were trying to be quiet, but we'd keep cracking each other up because we were highly amused at how animated she was when she was playing. And the lyrics were just killing us.

Frankly we were pretty rude, and eventually had to leave because we couldn't stop laughing. Sorry Sarah, but that first date just gave us the giggles at your gig!

THE OFF-BEATNIKS

The Off-Beatniks began with me and Max Kay, the bassist I played with in Rhythm Section of Shame. We had a rapport, and he wanted to play my original music, so the formation of the band began. Next up was a conversation I had with Bill Hamilton while walking down Congress Street back to his workspace. I thought he did music editing, or overdubbing, or commercial work – I wasn't exactly sure, all I know is that he was smart, kind of geeky, and wanted to join a band. I told him I was putting together a band to play my original music, and I was looking for a lead guitarist. I had heard he played guitar but wasn't sure if he could fill the seat as lead guitarist. The more I described what I was looking for, the more he convinced me that he should be playing with me. In fact, he was a little bit insulted that I initially didn't consider him. That quickly evaporated when he officially became the lead guitarist of my band – all before we even arrived at his workplace. I honestly didn't know if he could pull it off, but I was enamored by his enthusiasm.

We spent a lot time together at his workplace, going through my songs. Some of them weren't easy mind you, like "Silver-Footed Queen" and "10 Million Miles". But he learned them and excelled as time went on.

Next up was getting a drummer. Luckily, that fell into our laps. Max Kay and I both knew Jason Stewart, a talented young drummer in the Portland scene, and I happened to catch him while he was looking for gigs. He was well-versed in many styles, fearless, and had great meter. He also had an all-around great vibe.

He was quick, witty, unabashed in giving his opinion, and had a perfect mix of punk meets ska meets jazz, while still being able to flow from one idea to the next. He was a songwriter's dream drummer – he listened to the song, then did what was appropriate or needed in the moment during a live situation. I believe our conversation was very quick. I asked him if he wanted to play in our band and he said yes.

We rehearsed at Max's place on Congress Street, next door to Moose County Music, on the second floor. After a couple rehearsals, we were ready to gig, but we didn't have a band name yet. Somewhere down the line, Beatniks came to mind, probably because our collective musical influences brought up conversation that steered us into that world. The Beatles of course came into play, then the concept of my songs being a little off-beat. After some cleaver word-play, Bill and Jason came up with The Off Beatniks. I initially didn't like the name, but it was the best name we had so far. I didn't hate the name, so the more the guys leaned towards it, the more I warmed up to it.

Shortly thereafter, Bill came up with a logo with some Beatnik guy and a special font, and we were off looking to book gigs. We successfully booked a gig at Granny Killiam's, a very respectful club in L.A. We didn't bring in many people for a Thursday night, but we knew the club owner, and he respected us and thought we had potential. It was one of only two gigs we ever played as The Off-Beatniks, the other was a battle of the bands at a church on Congress Street, we kicked ass.

Had the stars aligned and we were able to promote and continue to book this band, The Off-Beatniks would've been a powerhouse. The lineup was full of talent. However, life dictated our paths and the band split up after a few months. I remember those gigs with deep gratitude, knowing I was playing with musicians I first considered my brothers, and second considered incredibly talented musicians who were willing to put their time, energy, and enthusiasm into learning and playing my songs.

GO BUTTON GIG BEFORE GOING FOR GOOD

The last show I played before leaving for Venice, California was with Go Button as well as my pals Chris Goetz and Max Kay, at the Free Street Tavern.

There were select musicians in the audience, like Dave Noyes, who I was working with at the Victory Deli on Forest Avenue, before his band The Rustic Overtones, started getting notoriety. My dear friend Rebecca Stubbs was also there, which made my heart skip yet feel sad, since I knew I'd be leaving and most likely would never see her again. I remember Dave Noyes being impressed by my drumming when I filled in for a couple tunes with Go Button. Being that I was their drummer for some time, it wasn't that hard to pull off their tunes.

We ended the night with me being egged on to play an original song only on the acoustic guitar and singing. It was this stupid song I wrote, that was actually kind of funny, titled "In the Can Again, John." The title speaks for itself. It was a slow blues shuffle that got everybody riled. I mean, the lyrics were so juvenile but perfect for the moment. By the time it got to the last chorus, I was singing at the top of my lungs, everybody cheering me on, shellshocked that I could sing like that, so they kept me going and going, until the very last few notes with that classic 5-4 turnaround. I screamed the last words using every bit of breath, and got a standing ovation for my final show in Portland, Maine, amongst the people I cared most about. It was an unforgettable send-off.

After the show, a few of us went over to Peter and Karyn's place on Sherman Avenue, just to have one final hang together. Rebeccah Stubbs also came. I'd always had a huge crush on her but never revealed it because I didn't want to jeopardize our friendship. Besides, I was leaving and she was staying, so it wouldn't have worked out. Nevertheless, we exchanged gifts out in the hall right before I left and gave each other a huge long hug. She was very special to me, and still is, despite little contact.

I was really going miss this band of geeks. I just adored them. They were so weird and quirky, but quite genius in what they were doing. I left knowing that I held their spirits in my heart, and was so happy they were the ones I got to hang out with on my last day in Portland, Maine.

LEAVING PORTLAND, MAINE TO VENICE, CALIFORNIA

The next afternoon, I went down to the Greyhound Bus station on the corner of Congress and Saint John Street, got myself a fifty-dollar ticket to Los Angeles, and was on my way to California. It was a special they were advertising and I couldn't pass it up. It took four days and four nights to get there.

Unfortunately, I lost my beloved pot pipe, Ginger, in the Greyhound toilet somewhere near Chicago. How it fell in there, I haven't a clue. It just slipped out of my hands, and that was the end of that beautiful mahogany work of art. What a disgraceful end to a short and storied life. I'd been sneaking puffs of weed to make the ride more pleasant. My green Army duffel was stuffed with clothes and my beat-up acoustic guitar. That it made the journey in one piece, I'm still amazed. I met great people along the way and saw many a small town out those Greyhound windows. There were many hours the bus was fairly empty, so I was able to move about from one side to the other, taking in the scenes as the bus coasted from state to state, town to town. Some towns were literally two blinks big, then gone.

Starting from I-95 in Maine, we must've gone down to the I-80 to Boston, then N.Y. City. We then headed due west to Cleveland, OH, then onto the I-90 towards Chicago, IL, switching back to the I-80, driving through Des Moines, IA, then Omaha and Lincoln, NB.

We switched over to I-76 towards Denver, CO, then the I-70 through little Colorado towns, and I slept through much of it; I had no trouble sleeping. In fact, I've never had trouble sleeping. I can actually fall asleep within seconds once I'm tired. Somebody can be in midsentence and I'll be Zzz'ing it before they're finished.

Anyway, we finally arrived in Las Vegas in the morning around 7AM. There was a layover and a bus switch. This was the final leg before arriving in Los Angeles. I got to walk around for a couple hours in the casinos and caught a cheap breakfast, then I headed back to the bus, and we were off to the City of Angels by 9AM.

This final portion of the venture felt like an eternity. My stomach was in knots with anticipation and excitement. We started driving down this steep hill where we could oversee the city far away, or at least I thought it was Los Angeles. It was just the Inland Empire. I had no idea how expansive the entire metropolitan region was. It took what felt like hours before we actually saw downtown Los Angeles. Once inside it, I couldn't believe how dingy and unglamorous it actually was close up. We arrived, long last, at the Greyhound terminal on Santa Fe Avenue, and were met by homeless people in every direction, something I wasn't exposed to so invasively in Maine. It took a little getting used to.

Then I saw this funny-looking guy who asked me, "Are you Son?" and I, of course, said "Yes." It was my new roommate, Robert Mollineux. He was twenty years old and quite the character. Full of humor and confidence, and lots of I-don't-give-a-fucks, but in that frat boy kind of way. Completely harmless. Finally, I saw Regis and Neil through the crowd and we shared a huge hug. I had finally made it!

The car ride to Venice took about 30 minutes. Traffic was fairly busy. I just took in the skyline and chatted until we arrived at my new home, 216 Pacific Avenue, off Rose Ave. Half a block away from the beach.

CHAPTER 7
LIVING IN CALIFORNIA

WELCOME TO VENICE

Finally, I'm here! Yoo hoo! Half a block from the Pacific Ocean and the craziness of the Venice Boardwalk. It was a dream come true. I actually was able to leave the cold winters of Maine!

Now for the unglamourous part – in order to live there, I agreed to stay in Neil's closet as my "bedroom." I didn't mind the small quarters, for now, but my stupidity was in agreeing to pay equal rent. Oh well, I figured it would all wash out in the end.

As a welcoming present the first night there, I was greeted to a police helicopter literally hovering over our place, with its light beaming down on the empty lot beside us, looking for some criminal. He was important enough for them to use their loudspeakers, which miraculously can be heard over the whooping of the helicopter blades. I woke up to peer my head out of our bedroom window, look at the helicopter above, and wait for the scene to either escalate or die down. Luckily, it died down, and in spite of my welcoming gift, I immediately went back to sleep. Especially useful for my coronation night in Venice, CA.

MEETING JULIE FOR THE FIRST TIME, MY FUTURE WIFE

The next day, we all went down to the Venice Boardwalk around noon. We were apparently meeting up with Regis's girlfriend, Julie. We were all sitting outside, and it was packed. I wasn't used to this amount of people yet but I rolled with it.

About ten to fifteen minutes later, this groovy looking young woman comes up, wearing black everything, with huge funky sunglasses over her eyes, and bends down to introduce herself. It's Julie, Regis's girlfriend. I was taken aback. She shook my hand, and it felt like slow motion. We got along just fine. In fact, she ended up hiring me that day to help her make jewelry for her company, Seventh Muse. Regis was working for her as well. She was selling to Nordstrom and needed extra help. Perfect timing for me. Funny thing is, years later, once we were married, or dating, she told me that she had the same slow-motion reaction as I had when she met me, as if she had known me before. It was validation that we were meant to be.

FONTE COFFE ROASTERS, CELEBRITIES, AND COOL CO-WORKERS

Neil told me there was an opening at a coffee shop inside the Fred Segal building on Broadway and Fifth Street. I didn't need any experience, so long as I was open to learning how to make cappuccinos and lattes, which, coming from Maine, was a completely new world to me.

Fonte Coffee Roasters was born right around the same time as Starbucks and Peets Coffee. They were all from Seattle. Fonte was owned by Paul Odom, who's master roaster from Starbucks, Steve Smith, left them to roast for him, because he was fastidious about the roasting process. Of course, I had no idea about any of this when I first started working there, I just needed a job.

I also had no idea about the prestige of the Fred Segal buildings. He owned two buildings, on the West and East Sides of Fifth Street, hugging Broadway. This was where the stars and celebrities went to shop, incognito. Oh, the stars I met and made drinks for on a regular basis. What's funny is that I wasn't in the least starstruck. I'd hear about celebrities coming in and I'd think nothing of it. I wasn't ingrained in the culture yet.

Eventually, I started recognizing the "importance" of knowing who I was serving or who was coming in. It became fun. I mean, HUGE stars were coming in there, feeling safe to shop casually and drinking their lattes.

I worked and met some great people here, first being Casey Mallon, a transplant from Oklahoma who was bassist in a band. He had confidence and swagger, blue eyes that could cut through you just as sharp as a laser, and dreads that went down to the middle of his back. He was as hip as it gets, and I was glad he was part of the crew. And our birthdays were only five days apart. We were both Capricorns, important stuff in your early twenties.

There were other characters like Justin, who was this super mellow blond hip-hop dude who had a lot of talent and was very cerebral and expressive. I liked him a lot. Then there was Philip, a half-black half-Native American man with blue eyes, a great looking combination (again). He was a trip. He was a fast talker, and he'd always talk about how he'd gained "half a step" in his jogging regimen every night while working his shift. Hysterical. And he always smelled like beer. He drank a six-pack of Bud Light every night, self-confessed. He was always seeking a partner. He seemed lonely beneath his friendly exterior. I always gave him slack for that.

There was also Antoinette, a very kind young woman who actually ended up giving me the job as manager when she decided to move on.

After about seven months working there, I indeed became the manager. My pay got bumped as did my responsibilities, but I still had time to do my music. It really was a perfect job for years. But like all good things, they must end, which this did.

But before I end this section, let's check out some of the celebrities I met or waited on! Talk about fun shit.

Arnold Schwarzenegger was a regular in the afternoon. He was surprisingly not as huge in stature as I thought he'd be in person.

Jack Palance would come in the early evenings occasionally, and he'd always have a joke to tell, in the form of a story. He was taller and larger than I imagined. He was older by the time I saw him, but he still had the mojo. I had respect for him.

Michelle Pfeiffer would order a half-caf, extra-dry cappuccino in a short cup. Personally, I thought I made her drink the best. Casey also did her drink accurately. She was always mellow and cool. Never a superstar vibe to her. Just a good person.

Jodie Foster was very down-to-earth. She usually just ordered a small latte or a cup of coffee. She once came in before we were closing, asking us to fill her dog's water dish, which we did dutifully. You couldn't help but to be starstruck by her presence.

Nicole Kidman came in once with her mom. Talk about intimidating. It was an hour before we were closing, they were dressed to the nines, and we could only make sure they got their lattes made perfectly. Nicole was still so young, but still she had an air of sophistication, and she was taller than I had imagined, especially with high heels. We did not want to disappoint them.

Robert Downey, Jr. came in for a couple weeks. He hung out there for hours on end, talking to random people. Once, when somebody spilled a drink on the floor during a morning rush, we brought a mop and bucket out and he quickly grabbed it from us so he could clean up the mess for us and we could keep taking care of customers. I found that to be incredibly nice of him. He was a very genuine and caring person. I enjoyed it when he was around.

Valerie Bertinelli regularly came in during the last couple hours of us being open. She liked to talk to Antoinette, the manager at the time (before me). They'd get into some very deep conversations. She was always very kind and unassuming.

Eddie Van Halen came in with Valerie one time but decided to hide in the men's room in order to smoke a cigarette. My pal Neil was working with me that night and had to go to the bathroom. As he was washing his hands, he smelled what he thought was a cigarette. As he looked to his left, he noticed a door stall opening up and out came Eddie's head, all suspicious at first, but with that classic shit-eating grin of his. Neil said, "Hey, is that you? Eddie Van Halen?" Eddie looked at him, still hiding in the stall, and confirmed that yes, it was indeed him. He told Neil that he just needed to sneak away for a butt break, then they both proceeded to talk about David Lee Roth and Sammy Hagar for about fifteen minutes. It was a colorful conversation, apparently. Even though this wasn't really an official Fonte Coffee Roasters customer, it was in the building, which is close enough.

The band No Doubt and the writers for South Park came in together, in total fanfare, like the rock stars they were. Unabashed and with complete disregard of their surroundings. They came in really quickly for a couple coffees, then went off into Fred Segal's to do some shopping.

Hugh Grant and Elizabeth Hurley snuck in for a couple days. They were both sporting baseball caps to evade the paparazzi. Don't know if it worked, but they hung out for a couple hours, flirting and happy as could be. It was early in their relationship. Very fun to witness.

Heather Graham came roller-skating a couple times into our place. This was during the filming of *Boogie Nights*. Talk about epic. She was just as pretty in person. Just a magical vibe to her. The roller-skates helped.

Bob Saget would order a small coffee at times, but not without always trying out his material to us right when he got to the register. We were a good soundboard for him. We'd either laugh or politely tell him through our body language that his joke didn't do it. He'd even say sometimes, "Not working?", then we'd say, "No, dude. Sorry." Then he'd shrug and walk away. It didn't stop him from trying out another joke on us the next day. His good jokes would have him walking away smiling.

Barbara Hershey bought a very nice espresso machine from us. Antoinette was over the moon, being the saleswoman for that purchase. Barbara came in fairly often, always unassuming and mellow.

Glen Ballard, a producer and songwriter for Allanis Morisette, came in almost every day for nearly a year, writing songs for the upcoming Grammy-winning album *Jagged Little Pill*. He was super mellow and easygoing – he'd order a coffee or latte, then he'd sit at a table closest to the door on the right side, or he'd sit outside occasionally. The outside noise probably distracted him, so he stayed inside for the entirety of writing songs for that epic album. Super cool and mellow guy.

Olivia Newton-John would frequent us. She ordered a medium or large latte. She had a friend who owned one of the stores in the Fred Segal building and they'd come in to chat. There were so many times I wanted to go up to her and tell her how much of a huge crush I had on her as a kid, but I never wanted to bother her. My brother and I would kiss the television screen when Xanadu aired and she was roller-skating in that flowing white dress all around the Venice boardwalk.

Candace Bergen would get her morning coffee before heading off to work to shoot Murphy Brown. Casey and I would chat with her for a couple minutes. She was always approachable and super nice to us.

Andy Summers came in a couple times. Neil had a good conversation with him and introduced me to him. He was a super nice guy. I was kind of starstruck and speechless while he was around, so I didn't really end up chatting with him. I regret that, because he was a really friendly guy.

Café Bene was right next door to us, and we'd frequently see George Harrison ordering food there often. He was almost always wearing a huge overcoat and hat to disguise himself. Nobody ever really bothered him though. We'd be craning our necks just to get a glimpse of the former Beatle.

David Spade would also eat next door at Café Bene practically every day. I never gave him much attention, but I found it amazing how much time he spent there. He was always reading or writing.

I'm sure there were more celebrities that passed through those doors, but the list above is more than enough.

MEDULLA OBLONGATA

This was the band that Regis, Neil, and I came up with. We rehearsed for a couple months before we finally booked a gig at The Blue Saloon in Hollywood. It was a trashy, dank bar, going lower than a dive bar. I can only remember the pool table and a stage that looked like it belonged in an elementary school, even with red curtains on the side. But hey, it was our first gig and we kicked ass, actually. We had assembled an act where Regis and I would switch off on bass and guitar, depending on the song we were playing. It was pretty bad ass and unique. No other band we'd seen before had done that. And our songs aren't easy ones to pull off.

Even though that was the only gig we ever played, I was very proud of our performance. We had a thing going that was unique, and we did it damn well. Unfortunately, we just weren't meant to be a band and dissolved.

FRESHLY BAKED

Once Medulla Oblongata split up, Neil found some other bands to play in, first being Act of Faith, which he somehow got me into playing with. This lasted for a few months, then we left that band.

The guitarist Christian was really talented but we couldn't hang with the lead singer for some reason. It had something to do with him screwing over Christian or wanting to fire him, and he was the only reason we were playing in that band. We left immediately after that.

The same time I was in that band, Neil found a jam band to play in called Freshly Baked. He was playing in it for about a month when he told me about it and how I should join since the bandleader, Rand, was looking for another guitarist. I auditioned and got the part. Ironically, the bassist, for his own odd reasons, wanted to just stay a trio, so he left the band, which now meant they needed a bassist.

Since there was a gig coming up within a week, I told Rand I'd be the bassist for the band. I practiced a shitload before the gig, learning a bunch of Marley and Dead tunes, learning my way around the chord changes and bass lines.

The first gig we played was at The Kettle Room in Manhattan Beach. Rand seemed to think I was good enough, so I kept on playing with them. From that point on, we played little clubs, bars, parties, and festivals produced by Howard Freiberg, a mover and shaker in the SoCal jam band scene.

The gigs started getting a little larger, but it was hard to get people out to our shows consistently. We weren't a Dead cover band, like the popular band Cubensis, who had a weekly residency at Moose Mcgillicuddy's in Marina Del Rey, where they let us open for them occasionally.

They were always very hospitable toward us since we were playing original music written by either Rand or myself.

We began work on Freshly Bake's second album, "Twice Baked". Rand lived on Market Street in Venice and had a little back shed that he turned into a rehearsal and recording space. We worked on that album diligently for about six months. Many times, I would go in on my days off and spend hours tracking songs on my own once Neil laid down the drum tracks. It was a real good lesson for me. Back then, everything was DAT tapes, so there was a lot of rewinding involved until I got the tracks right. I recorded most of my backup vocals, although Neil had a great voice and could pull off all the high harmonies.

I even helped in drawing the album cover. It was a fluke that the illustration I drew was even used. Rand scanned it into his computer and started coloring it in Photoshop. It looked great! Rand didn't know I had artistic skills at first, but once he saw some drawings, I became the de facto flier guy for the band.

Once *Twice Baked* was mixed, mastered, and pressed, we started aggressively touring the Southwest and Northern California regions. We did it as a trio for the first couple short tours but soon realized we needed a fourth member.

Enter John Jakubek, also the lead guitarist for another popular and signed band, Zoo People. They had finished touring and weren't as busy, so he agreed to work with us.

For the next two years, we kept increasing our tour lengths while our local gigs became less frequent. We began to play larger rooms like the El Rey Theater and the Coach House in Redondo Beach, opening for acts like Jimmy Cliff, Third World and Eek-a-Mouse.

We began a third album titled *Pirates of the Sun*, using a doodle I drew as the default brand for the band. It was literally a twenty-second doodle, but Rand liked it enough to use it for most everything including the album cover. The album was recorded at our friend's backyard house on Rose Avenue, which was converted into a recording studio. It wasn't fancy but it was more than adequate. After the album was finished and released, Freshly Baked actually got signed to the House of Blues record label, with a major producer signed on to produce our next album. They even created a greatest hits version of the previous three albums to release immediately. It was a couple weeks of bliss, until the parent company of House of Blues record label, Platinum Ltd., decided to dissolve House of Blues label, effective immediately, which dissolved our record deal immediately. Talk about a letdown.

At this time, that record signing had been the only thing keeping me from leaving the band. Since that was now gone, I decided it was the right time to depart. I had a great time and was forever grateful for everything I learned while being in the band, but it was time for me to move on.

I took a long break from performing, opting to stay home for about a year and practice the bass diligently, as well as continue playing guitar, writing music, and singing.

LIVING IN GHOST TOWN

Venice's "Ghost Town" was a notorious section where crack and the Venice Crips ruled about ten square blocks. It got its nickname because the crack dealers would shoot out all the streetlights, leaving blocks upon blocks completely in the dark. When the city would try to replace a bulb, it would just be shot out within days, so they just didn't bother for a couple years. Ghost Town was encircled by Rose Avenue to the North, Lincoln Boulevard on the East, California Avenue to the South, and Electric Avenue to the West. Within those blocks, there were a few gnarly ones: Brooks Avenue, Indiana Avenue, and Broadway between Fifth and Seventh Avenue.

I had just moved in with my friend Andrew Gross, who had found an apartment on Indiana Ave and Seventh while I was out touring for a month with Freshly Baked. We'd gotten the place for dirt cheap, but it was a decent apartment – no roaches, hot water, protective metal door, and cable. This was back before personal computers - imagine that! I loved the area despite its reputation. We actually got in at a time the area was trying to clean up – some would call it gentrification.

I would call it get the piece-of-shit crack dealers out of the neighborhood. I loved our next-door neighbor, who was a really nice black man and his family and an old-school Venice resident. He went to church a few blocks down the street and never minded me playing my instruments or singing. In fact, he loved it and encouraged me to keep doing it.

In classic fashion, my first night in that apartment was like my first night on Pacific Ave. a few years prior. I woke to the sound of a helicopter, a huge beam of light coming down from it, straight into my neighbor's front yard, with police demanding the perpetrator to surrender. Suddenly, I heard footsteps and a guy panting by my window! About thirty seconds later, still half asleep, I hear him running past my window in the opposite direction, and back onto my neighbor's front lawn.

By now, clearly awake, I looked through my blinds, to see a kaleidoscope of blue and red flashers added to the cacophony of sirens, courtesy of a dozen police cruisers. The chopper's spotlight was beamed down on a guy splayed out on the lawn, about ten officers pointing their revolvers at him. Welcome to the hood, Son! Ha!

The next morning, I walked over to Rose Avenue, looking for some coffee. I happened on a place called Gourmet Coffee Warehouse; a really hip-looking joint that looked like it belonged in the bayou. It smelled like coffee and burlap bags, a great combo.

Suddenly, I see my pal Casey Mallon, whom I had worked with at Fonte! We were pretty psyched to see each other. We did a little catching up, and soon I was asking him if they were hiring. He told me to talk to Nina, the manager, which I did, interviewed a couple days later, and got hired to do afternoon shifts a few days a week. I worked this job as well as at mornings and evenings at The Java Bus. Between the two, they paid the bills, bought me food and some weed; I was happy. The Java Bus would go around to movie lots and sell coffee to the workers and actors. I hated that job but it was fairly easy work.

After about six months, I picked up morning shifts, which tipped better, as well as suited my schedule. I'd work from 6:30am to 1pm, then go home and practice eight hours, four days a week. It was perfect. I'd work the Java Bus on other days and still squeeze in many hours of practice. This was one of the most productive periods of my life.

I wanted to start my own band, but I also wanted to hire myself out as a bassist. I felt like I needed more practice under my belt. After work, I'd do my general schedule of studying. There were days where I'd only practice jazz standards to my Jamey Aebersold CDs, along with their charts; another day, I'd study nothing but Motown, Stax, and R&B songs, playing the CD's over and over, practicing the licks until I had them right. I'd go through hours of Stevie Wonder, James Brown, Funkadelic Parliament, Solid Gold Hits, disco, and jazz funk tunes.

There were days where I'd do nothing but play along to Bob Marley's albums, writing charts and listening to their bassist (a.k.a. Family Man) obsessively. I started practicing a muted thumb technique as well. I'd have my classic rock days, interspersed with The Beatles, Zeppelin, Pink Floyd, David Bowie, The Talking Heads, The Police, and tons of other bands. Surprisingly, I didn't study much Grateful Dead, because I was already submersed in their music.

I stuck to this disciplined routine for a year, I hardly played out, and vowed that I wouldn't until I deemed myself good enough. Apparently, after that year, I deemed myself good enough, and started looking for bands to work with. I even had a couple live music jams in my apartment, with full-on drums and blaring electric guitars. It was a true Venice experience when we did that. Loved it.

Andrew Gross moved out after a couple years, pining to live in Maui. Soon came another roommate named Joel Dunning, who was a soon-to-be graduate of Yō San University, with a degree in acupuncture and Chinese Medicine. He was solely responsible for ridding me of my chronic allergies after a couple months of drinking the most heinous tea concoctions, which we brewed in the apartment day and night. What came out of my sinuses was beyond description.

What I do know is that from then on, I was able to live a more manageable life. I still have allergies, but they aren't debilitating. I could go through one and a half boxes of tissue in a day. Luckily, Big Lots was right up the street, so I could get tissue for cheap – it was cheap tissue that ripped my nose apart, but it was affordable.

Soon thereafter, Joel's acupuncture friend from Yō San moved in, Alex Wolf. They were both super nice and super mellow, fun guys. We had little moments where we'd get some time together, smoke huge joints, and watch movies or listen to music. I couldn't have asked for better roommates.

THE CRAZY CAR CHASE BREAKUP

During this time, I was also dating Lena, who was as sweet as can be. She literally saved me during the Freshly Baked years – buying clothes for the winter tours, buying me food, taking me out to restaurants and other events. She had a white half-wolf dog that she brought back from Japan when she was an ESL teacher. She was friends with Antoinette, and we had met during the Fonte Coffee Roasters days. We were still dating while I lived here, but I was falling out of love with her. I was actually falling for my friend Julie, while I had started to do some part-time work for her jewelry company again.

I didn't really plan to have feelings for her, they just developed. We got along very well, were hanging out a lot while working, had the same interests in movies and philosophies about life; it was just natural that feelings would start brewing.

Those feelings revealed themselves one night after going to a Harry Potter movie with her. I was still dating Lena, but I decided that night that I needed to tell Julie how I felt about her, so a few nights later, I just laid it out on the line when I visited her at her home. I think she was pretty shocked, but I wouldn't have done that if I hadn't thought I'd had a chance; hoping that maybe she had some feelings creeping in about me as well.

As luck would have it, I was right. Now I needed to break up with Lena. I ended up doing that on Christmas Eve. Really classy, right?!

She came over to my apartment, and I couldn't hold it in any longer. Something she did just triggered me and I blurted out that we needed to talk and that I was no longer in love with her, had feelings for Julie, etc. This didn't go over as well or as smoothly as I'd imagined. Go figure.

The breakup went into Christmas Day, with very little sleep, if any at all. We went to a Chinese Restaurant (the only place open, of course) and I continued to confirm to her that this was it. She had a really hard time of it.

Despite that, I was certain she left knowing that we were finished and broken up, while in her mind we were "just taking a little break." Boy, was I ever off on that one.

A little over a week later, Julie and I went to another movie, *Lord of the Rings*. As she was about to drop me off, I notice Lena's SUV in the rear-view mirror. Instead of getting out of the car, I told Julie to just drive so we could get away. Lena recognized her car and caught up to us. She started driving closely behind us, honking her horn and putting on her brights, almost bumping into Julie's car, which was very disconcerting. This happened on Main Street in Santa Monica. It was really fucking scary. Lena temporarily lost her shit.

Julie remembered some sage advice from her dad, which was to drive to the police station if you're in trouble, which is exactly what she did. It was only a few more blocks away. When we got there, Lena was right behind us. She fumed over, cursing at Julie and I, trying to drag me out of Julie's car, all while her dog was barking wildly out the passenger window.

Luckily, a police officer walked out of the police building, noticed the altercation, and asked us if everything was O.K. We immediately responded with "No! She's harassing us and followed us here to the police station." He asked if we wanted him to separate her from us. We, of course, said, "Yes!" He also asked if we wanted to press charges. I felt that was going too far as she was having a bad enough night. This went on for about fifteen minutes, with Lena being put into her car, the poor dog being calmed down, and her finally driving away. We thanked the police officer and got back in Julie's car.

We headed over to Chez Jay, where I promptly ordered a dirty martini. We stayed there for about an hour. When we walked out to the car, we finally had our first kiss. Julie had to initiate it. I was still too shy, and also on edge from the night's experience. We drove off shortly afterward and she dropped me back at my apartment.

When I arrived at my door, I noticed that the front door was unlocked. I must've said, "Oh, shit" under my breath, because I knew exactly what this meant – Lena had broken in. She had a key to my apartment. Not good. I slowly walked into my bedroom, and there she was, with her dog, on my bed. She was writing scornful notes on colored pieces of paper and tossing them onto my down comforter. She then proceeded to pour this bottle of massage oil onto my down comforter, worth many hundreds of dollars, ruining it. I sure was going to miss that comforter.

After about an hour of my attempting patience, I finally reached Level Pissed, told her to get her box of things she had there, grab her dog, give me her key to the apartment, and get the fuck out. I must've repeated this for a full fifteen minutes. Finally, she did just that. I helped her with the box, put it in her car, watched her look at me one last time with the saddest face I've ever seen on a woman, then I walked away screaming at the top of my lungs, "I don't ever want to fucking see you ever again!" She turned her SUV on, put it in drive and slowly limped away. I was too pissed to feel sorry for her.

During this time, Julie had been trying to call me for over an hour if not more, but I couldn't pick up. When I finally could, I did so with had a glass of Ketel One on ice. We were on the phone for the next hour. I told her what just happened, which of course came with a response of shock.

Looking back at this event, I feel incredibly bad about it. I never talked to Lena again, even to this day. I actually left her a message on Facebook Messenger, but I never checked to see if she read my words of apology. She was one of the sweetest and kindest souls I've ever met, with a great sense of humor and a heart of gold. It certainly wasn't the best way to end our relationship, but Julie and I have been married for almost twenty years. I had met the woman of my dreams, Julie, and nothing was going to stop me from marrying her, even if I didn't know it at the time.

MEETING TONY DEPIANO

After having taken some time off from playing out, but practicing in my bedroom after work for about a year, I finally decided it was time to start my own band. By now, Freshly Baked was far enough in my rearview mirror that I felt I had the courage to move on. First course of action was to place an ad on Craigslist.

After a couple days, I got a phone call from this boisterous guy. He'd just graduated college on the East Coast and came out to California to become a rock star. He played lead guitar, had lots of energy, wanted to join a jam band, and liked what my ad said. I was about thirty years old and he was twenty-six, just a baby in my eyes. After more chatting on the phone, we decided to meet up, and he came over a day or two later.

It was early evening on a weeknight, probably a Tuesday or Wednesday, and I see this stocky dude, knocking much more loudly than was necessary on the screen door, carrying his guitar with a shit-eating grin, white teeth shining through. He had this funny Italian accent, was obviously high-energy and excited about meeting up. I heard, "Yah, it's me" or "Hey, it's me" and this funny little "Heh..heh...heh...heh" chuckle that can't be replicated, and includes a little back-and-forth movement of his head. O.K., he's already in and I haven't even heard him play guitar.

So, we sit down, do some small talk, but I can tell we're gonna get along just fine. He wants to get down to business and start playing. He takes out his Taylor acoustic, I take out my cheap ass Takamine, and we start jamming. It sounds great. His teeth are showing, so that's obviously a good sign. I start playing some of my originals, and he plays along with me, flowing without any lack of confidence.

We probably only played for about forty minutes together, but we also talked and cracked jokes, asked questions about each other, and at the end of it, we both knew it was the beginning of a partnership that would last for years.

There was an instant and true brethren vibe. We cliqued immediately, musically and emotionally. I liked that his spirit was light, extroverted, full of energy and enthusiasm, something to counteract my slightly introverted character at the time. I was more internally intense, mellow and amicable, and still a little shy around the edges. Tony was the furthest thing from shy, exactly what was needed in order to turn people into fans.

So that was the beginning of a new band. Now all we needed was a band name.

WOODSHED FORMS

Tony and I had been playing with this drummer named Niel Shukla in a band called Not Enough. They had a female singer named Patty, who was Tony's girlfriend at the time. We realized we had the core to create the jam band we wanted – we just needed a bassist. Tony responded to an ad on Craigslist from a bassist named Larry Breedlove, who had also just moved out to Los Angeles "to become a rockstar" although I think he was actually more realistic and would be happy to just be a working musician. They met, and Tony liked him, so he brought him over to my place where we all jammed together. I liked his quirky personality and more importantly, his bass-playing. Since I was playing bass for other bands here and there, I was going to be more discerning as to who would play that role in my band. The final step was to get together with Niel at a rehearsal space and see how we gelled. Well, we did, and we sounded fantastic. We were kind of loud, but we'd work on that. I was the lead singer and Tony played lead guitar and guitar harmonies.

We began rehearsing regularly, tightening up a setlist for a show. We had to get at least four songs tight enough to make a solid demo, which we did in a month's time.

Soon thereafter, I called Molly Malone's and got us booked on a Friday night, which was no easy feat, considering we were a new band. I just said the right things, utilized my credentials from being a former bandmember of Freshly Baked, who had good draw when we played there. We made posters and fliers and passed around our demo; I created artwork consisting of a woodshed with a rocking chair and a barrel on the porch, a smiling sun, and some critters on the grass. This became our official design. It looked awesome.

We soon hired some nerdy website kid from downtown L.A. to create an interactive website based on the artwork I did. He finished it halfway, then we never saw him again. He just disappeared after a couple months. With the website half finished, I approached my good pal, A.J. Dagger, and he put the finishing touches on it, making it interactive. You could click on the window, the barrel, and other items in the graphic, and something would pop out, or sounds would play, some of them with sayings I'm known for - even a cow mooing when you shot at the barrel! Brilliant!

Everything was in place, but something seemed to be missing. We could live without a keyboardist for now, but that seat would soon be filled (Marshall Thompson). What Tony and I decided after a few whiskey-fueled nights was that we needed a female singer. Tony was adamant about this, and I was totally fine with this idea. I needed help with harmonies and none of them could sing. It was a no-brainer – we needed a singer and a damn good one.

MEETING HALINA JANUSZ

Finding Halina is a pretty funny story, only because Tony was involved in finding her. If you ask Halina or myself to tell that story now, it's going to be pretty identical, with the famous phrase "Don't move or I'll kill ya" added to it.

One Friday night, after a Woodshed rehearsal at this classic dumpy rehearsal space right off Highland Avenue, we knew David Nelson and Cubensis were playing at a venue a couple blocks away, so we decided to go over there, with fliers in hand. Tony and I drove the two blocks over there and since we arrived so late, we didn't need to pay to get in. Very cool. We walked in and there's a couple hundred Deadheads walking around, swirling about and dancing to David Nelson's band. I got up close to check them out for a few tunes. They were definitely hot shit, top-notch musicians. But that wasn't the point of our being there – we were there to promote and to find a lead singer. Tony told me that he was going to walk around and find a female vocalist for the band. I kind of chuckled a little bit while he was all gung-ho determined to find a female singer, handing out fliers to those who were receptive.

Literally five minutes later, Tony came back and said excitedly, "Hey dude, I found our female singer! Follow me..." He grabbed me excitedly and I followed him.

A few seconds later, we're in front of this long-haired female who's looking at me, then Tony introduces us amidst the blaring music of the David Nelson Band and we shook hands, saying hi to each other with a smirk. I think I asked her if she was a singer, even though I already knew the answer because of her speaking voice. She told me that if I asked around this room, that many people would tell me she could sing. She seemed confident and friendly enough to me. I shook my head in acknowledgment.

She also knew of me from my Freshly Baked days, which is how Tony introduced me to her. Which is also what enticed her to check us out at Molly Malone's when we handed her a flier for our show the following Friday night.

The Molly show comes, and we're playing our asses off, sounding pretty bad ass. Halina showed up as well, which meant she was serious. Tony was pretty psyched that she showed up. So was I. After we finished, she told me that when we were performing, she could hear so many harmonies that she could do with me as well as some lead singing. She was really buzzed about it. Shortly after that, we decided that she should come over for an "audition" - Ha!

It was a weeknight when Halina knocked on our screen door. We lived on Indiana Avenue in Venice This was before the neighborhood got gentrified and the gangs were still selling crack right up the street. She came in with her guitar and we made small talk.

After getting ourselves some beers and whiskey and puffs of weed, we started singing together. I swear to God, the very first notes that we sang were like magic. We both instantly knew this partnership was going to work. I'm pretty sure we both smiled and thought the same thing. I tell Halina to this day that it was a "Bambi Moment" – my roommates, Joel and Al, came out of their rooms, either sat down or stood around, and just listened to us, completely mesmerized by the sound of our voices together, kind of like how the forest animals gathered around Bambi. I could almost see birds tweeting and flitting around our heads. The moment was magical, to say the least. I wouldn't be surprised if I said something like, "Well, I think you passed the audition." Woodshed had officially found its female singer. Onward and upward!

MOTHER JONES BAND

Woodshed officially played only two gigs under that name: Molly Malone's and Canter's Kibitz Room, Halina's first gig with us. Canters was also the first gig I played with Marshall Thompson, our keyboardist, whom I had met at Gourmet Coffee Warehouse, my workplace. He came out to rehearse with us and was sold on the band. One of the finest keyboardists I've had the honor of playing with even to this day.

Halina was a little nervous, but she sang well and we had quite a few heads that came to support us. The Kibitz Room is very strangely shaped – narrow and long. You're literally playing to a row of restaurant tables lined up against the wall, with the bar directly to your right, and more tables lined up against the wall across from the bar. There are windows beside the tables where you can peer into Canter's, the actual restaurant.

We did pretty damn well, but as the night progressed, Marshall started nodding against the spinet piano. The thing about Marshall is, no matter what state he was in, he could *play*. Didn't make it out for the cigarette, but he was back in his seat and on his game when the next set began.

When it ended, we all packed up and I let Marshall sleep it off for a little while until it was time to leave, then woke him up and took him home. He left his car at the restaurant and picked it up the next day. Those were the drinking days! All in all, I consider that a great last rock 'n roll gig for Woodshed.

As the weeks progressed, we realized that another California band was called Woodshed. Well, it would just not do, having two Woodsheds in California. Time for a name change. We had one of those classic brainstorm nights, coming up with names that were almost good but not "it." Then Larry started talking about Mother Jones and who she was, what she was about, and said he thought that would be a pretty cool name for a band. We all agreed. Mother Jones officially became our new name.

From that point on, we busted our asses. I played the role of web maintenance, chief songwriter, booking agent, bio writer, poster and art designer, and many other intangible roles. I got very little sleep, always doing something in my spare time for the band. The time, money, and effort it took just to create promo kits was staggering. Calling the bookers for venues, convincing them request a kit, convincing them to actually book you, then to contact local media in the towns you're performing... It was staggering. Add to this rehearsing twice a week and you've got a mass collective effort in moving the band down a successful path.

Larry held on as long as he could, but he couldn't hang after our first tour to Flagstaff. He realized this wasn't a lucrative situation, nor would it be for some time. Kevin Smith, a super nice guy and talented keyboardist, would fill in for Marshall, who was in demand and available only part-time.

Neil Shukla also didn't last past the first couple months, but we were lucky to have found Albert Estiamba, a fantastic drummer of the highest level, then getting David Abercrombie on board as the bassist. Add Marshall Thompson on keys to the mix and you've got a powerhouse the likes I've never played with before, even to this day. It was an all-star lineup.

ALBUM #1: LIFE IS ILLUSION

Halina's mom, Leslye, was instrumental in getting the first album off the ground. Halina got in touch with Barry Conley, the sound engineer, as well as scheduling time at Paramount Recording Studios in Hollywood. Julie's parents also gave us some money for our wedding, which helped to fund the album. It was all coming into place. We split recording the album between three places: Steve Janowski's home for drum and bass tracks for four songs, Paramount Recording Studios, and Chuck Maithonis' apartment to record the four songs with drums tracks from Steve's home. Larry played the bass for four tunes, then Abercrombie played bass for the other five tunes.

Once inside Paramount Recording Studios, we were placed in our separate spaces and tracked the songs completely live, onto two-inch reel-to-reel, with only vocals and a couple guitar solos overdubbed. The studio was beautiful and the drum room was huge, with the grand piano about thirty feet away, tucked into the corner.

Tony and I tracked in one separate room, the bassist, David Abercrombie tracked out with the drummer, Albert Estiamba, and Halina was in a small vocal booth beside the control room with a Neuman U87 mic.

We probably did two to three takes of each song, but we were so well-rehearsed with them, most of the tracks were just one-takes. Right to the point. Barry mixed them and those songs were set to be mastered.

I went over to Chuck's place for months on end, bringing five-pound bags of Ethiopian Yirgecheff coffee as payment, as well as some money on the side and some lunches. We spent a lot of time tracking, making sure it all sounded just right. Chuck did a fantastic job, besides having his computer crash and me having to re-record everything I had done again, it was all a good time. Once finished, we had this guy named Elvis master the album. Perfection! We released it and had Barry Smolin play it on his radio show. After a celebratory dinner at Hamburger Hamlet in Hollywood, Halina and I got into her car just as Barry was spinning our song, "Get it Right from the Start" - how exciting to hear *your* song played on the radio. We looked at each other in disbelief, filled with pride. We did it!

ALBUM #2: UNION

Right before the second album had begun, I had gotten an acupuncture treatment by my previous roommate, Al "Alskie" Wolf, who'd treated a few acupuncture points on me, creating this incredible feeling, like a point of light was coming straight into my head from outer space. I got a sustained jolt of inspiration and information that I couldn't control.

From that point on for the next few weeks, I ended up writing six songs for our next album. The songs kept coming, and I'm talking complete songs, not fragmented ideas or bits and parts of songs to store away for later. Sometimes I'd be working on a few at a time until they were hashed out and completed, then I'd play them to the band members.

I remember finally inviting Halina and Tony over to hear a few of my tunes and their jaws were on the floor. Tony was so excited at one point, he was jumping up and down, saying, "Dude, what the fuck?! How the fuck did you come up with this shit?! This is fucking awesome, dude!" or something close to that. All I know is I was filled with complete information from a source beyond me that kept feeding me these songs until they were truly complete and we had enough for our second album. It was a moment in time that has never happened before and is highly likely to not happen again. I give my pal Alskie full credit for bringing it out in me, because of those acupuncture points. He helped bring out an album's worth of songs.

Mother Jones was able to sustain a full-bore schedule for about three and a half years, until about 2006-07. That's when Tony had to leave the band to go back to the East Coast. It was a mental blow to us, and I was going to miss him dearly, but we moved on, bringing in Ted Kraut as our full-time guitarist, while having other talents like Kenny Kasman, Spiro, and Doug Monteith fill in when he couldn't play.

Not having Tony around to record the songs I had written and shown him for this second album – the songs he was so excited about – was really hard. But Ted did a great job and was a consummate professional in the recording sessions.

Halina's mom, Leslye, loaned us money upfront for the recording and manufacturing of the second album again. I was very grateful. She really believed in the band and her daughter, and had grown fond of me as well - I was kinda the son she never had, as she likes to say. Whatever Halina and I were pursuing, she believed in us and wanted to support it. Our next album was officially in the works.

The name of the album came one night while Halina and I were looking over the rehearsal space while standing on the bridge of Seventh Street in downtown Los Angeles on an unusually foggy night. Steven, our bassist, had just finished taking photos of the bridge overlooking the railroad tracks beneath us. The bridge was in front of us, also shrouded in fog; it was a fantastic shot.

We went through a couple names, then we started talking about Mother Jones, the woman, then started connecting the dots while looking at the tracks, and suddenly, Union came into my mind. I asked Halina what she thought of that name. She said it a few times to herself, and the more we thought about, with Mother Jones being a supporter of unionizing, it was a no-brainer. We found our album name, "Union."

By this time, Mother Jones was becoming pretty well-known regionally and had gained respect in the Southern California jam band scene as well as gaining national attention. We dedicated a lot of time and a fair amount of money into promotion and radio airplay. We did our best, considering we didn't have any management. That didn't deter us, but it certainly made the onward grind challenging. We did get some people who "managed" us, but it was more like just helping us get gigs here and there, a little bit of promotional help, but nothing that was legit or backed with a healthy budget, certainly nothing organized with departments in booking, promotion, and distribution. But we kept on.

ALBUM #3, BETTER DAYS

Around 2009, Mother Jones Band took a little time off, then reconvened for one final album. We took our time with this one, which was nice. It wasn't being crammed into a set time. John Jakubek helped us produce it at our friend Leslie's house in Marina Del Rey. We invited many friends in to record with us: Jennifer Palomba, Jeremiah Roiko, Nate LaPointe, David Pierce, Dave the saxophonist, Billy Yates, Chris Nyquist, etc.

We finished and released it around August of 2010, titled *Better Days*. I remember when Darrin Brenner, an incredibly skilled artist who designed posters for other top jam bands throughout SoCal like Cubensis, came out to Brennan's one night to help us with the album cover. I had the idea of having a hand holding a kaleidoscope, so Darrin came by to take photos of my hand holding the empty cardboard section of a toilet paper roll. Hysterical. But it worked! Darrin and I had a good laugh over it. The back side of the CD would be a photo of the entire band looking into the kaleidoscope, getting both sides of the kaleidoscope perspective. It looked great. Once that was completed, we pressed the CD's and set our big CD release party at none other than – you guessed it – Brennan's Pub.

REPRESENTING INDIE INTERNET RADIO IN WASHINGTON D.C.

Halina had been working with a coordinator to bring a collective front of musical artists to Washington D.C. in order to influence U.S. senators and representatives to not increase rates on independent internet radio stations. They would die on the vine, if you will, if the monetary increases were enacted.

About a dozen musical acts from the United States were chosen to perform in front of the Capitol and to lobby Congress members for two days. We even had a hearing before Congressional members, and I was the representative for Mother Jones. They asked us prescient questions, ultimately trying to figure out the pros and cons of this bill being passed. It was an honor.

At this time, internet radio stations were in their infancy. Regulations weren't set, and music was being downloaded and shared like the Wild West. There was justifiable cause for concern.

However, the bill that Congress wanted to enact was to increase royalties to such a level that the stations wouldn't be able to exist. Hence, music from unsigned and independent artists would've been too expensive to play on their stations, which numbered in the thousands nationwide. It would've collapsed the entire internet indie radio infrastructure.

What was so ironic, and almost counter-intuitive, was that we were being asked to lobby Congress to charge *less* for the plays of each song of indie artists so that indie artists could still have a promotional platform that FM radio stations couldn't provide.

On the day of questioning, about half a dozen acts were chosen to represent this alliance. I was one of them. It was exciting and nerve-wracking at the same time.

When it came my turn, I actually mentioned that music was going back to promoting singles as it was a more affordable option for artists and indie labels, and because of that, it was even more important to not charge indie radio stations more to spin a song.

Walking through the halls of Congress and trying to convince senators was a very interesting experience. It challenged my abilities of persuasion. In the end, as a collective unit of artists, we ultimately succeeded in convincing our senators and representatives not to pass this bill increasing internet radio fees. It was one of the most eye-opening experiences I've ever had in terms of seeing how procedures in D.C. work.

CHAPTER 8
MARRIAGE AND MUSIC

MY WEDDING

As you know by now, Julie and I kind of began with the "Crazy Car Chase" involving my previous girlfriend. Mind you, it wasn't set in stone that we'd be an item. Sure, we had some real feelings for each other; I was madly in love with her already, but that didn't necessarily mean were going to go the distance. After that car chase, we actually took at least a month off from seeing each other, because we were freaked out that my previous girlfriend might come in and pull a Lifetime movie stunt on us. We also had to see if our feelings for one another really were going to stick. We stayed in touch and talked on the phone during that time, which was a good sign. Time passed, and we decided it was safe to start seeing each other again. We still had some slight PTSD from the car chase event, but it was clear that we felt a solid, soulful connection and that we were truly in love with each other.

About a year later, I decided to move out of Indiana Avenue and in with Julie. It was a big deal. I was going to miss my acupuncture homies, Alskie and Joel, but they knew it was destined to happen. They knew she was special. We had many conversations about it.

So, Julie and I made a go of it and soon after, we decided we wanted to get married. It wasn't even a formal event. I didn't get down on one knee and ask for her hand in marriage. I was too naive to do that. Plus, that really wasn't our style. It was a casual question she asked me in the car as we were driving, something to the effect of if I would want to marry her. It barely took a second for me to immediately reply, "Yes!" *Of course I did –* it was a no-brainer.

I wasn't able to see the smile on her face as she turned away to look out the passenger window she told me about a year later, but she was pleased with my answer. From then on, we started making plans for our wedding.

Julie's parents were especially nice to me. Here I am, a musician working at a coffee shop, a classic cliché, about to marry their second daughter, but they treated me with respect, knowing this was the man she wanted to spend the rest of her life with. Julie's mom luckily already adored me, and her dad knew I was a hard worker, so he respected my work ethic, and knew I truly loved their daughter, which was worthy enough for him to accept me as his son-in-law.

We decided our wedding was going to be intimate and simple. We didn't want complex. We also knew what was involved with a bigger wedding. No thanks. Keep it simple. We just didn't know where to have it.

One evening, we were walking around our neighborhood and found this tiny and serene park on Ashland Ave. in Santa Monica. We fell in love with it, and thought this was it, this would be the perfect place for our wedding. We invited only our closest friends and family: Julie's parents, her sister and sister's husband, their adorable three-year old daughter, and Julie's best friend Brad. I invited my little sister Zeland, her partner Mike Martel, and my dear musical friend Neil Carroll. Plus the minister, of course. She was the perfect person to do our wedding. She was non-denominational. Neither Julie and I are bound by any religion, even though we were both raised Catholic – Julie much more than myself, we're just influenced by many spiritual ideas.

On the day of the wedding, we all gathered at Ashland Park. Julie's three-year-old niece Olivia came fully prepared, in her perfect little dress, clutching a basket full of rose petals to throw with a kid's joy onto our wedding pathway. She was very excited to have this responsibility. We were all involved with small talk and my sister, her partner, and Neil getting to know Julie's family. It was a perfect day in Santa Monica. Then noon came, the time of our wedding.

Our minister began with her most wonderfully-prepared nuptials. About a minute into her speaking, a garbage truck drove up the hill from down the street.

As she kept speaking, it got closer and closer, until it was across the street from us, about a couple hundred feet away, making such a ruckus that she had to stop speaking. We all looked over at the truck and saw the driver looking at us, mouthing the words, "Sorry." We all just had a laugh, while he gritted his teeth and shrugged his shoulders, slowly waiting for the noise that his truck was making to end. Our minister cleverly added into our vows how the garbage truck represented the throwing away of the past, and moving forward with a clean slate or something to that effect. I don't remember her exact words, only that they were very clever. It certainly made for a memorable moment.

Julie looked so beautiful, wearing these amazing burgundy shoes and a vintage black dress with a spectacular print. I looked like a hippie who was trying to not look like a hippie, wearing this funky print shirt with black pants and shoes, but no tie and jacket. I was trying to keep it simple and I was also nervous as hell. Julie's parents were at least polite about my wardrobe choice.

I had my closest people beside me. I was so happy to have my sister Zeland at my side. She's the epitome of the endless optimist, despite having endured so much in her own life. Her then-partner Mike was a kind and loving man whom I also loved dearly.

Then of course, there was Neil, my best friend who I've experienced so much with, from Maine to Los Angeles and back, and now back again. To have him there was icing on the cake. I could've lived without him showing me all those "Stupid Videos" clips on the internet, hours before our wedding, while Julie and I were getting prepared, but that's another story. He's a soul brother whom I'll cherish to the end.

I had also become close to Eric, Carey's husband, over the last year. He was an accomplished guitarist, knew rock music like a historian, and we had the privilege of nerding out over music and music gear when Julie and I would go over to their place to visit. The connection between Julie and her sister Carey was just short of psychic. They were close as can be. Julie, Carey, and their parents were also really close to Brad, who was Julie's best friend. He was a real trooper as he was ill at the time, but the moment was very important to him, so he made sure he was there to witness our union.

We placed rings on each other's fingers, kissed, and became officially bonded for life. Now it was time for our wedding lunch, then to prepare for the party at our neighborhood's café. The band came to play: Tony Depiano, Larry Breedlove, Halina Janusz, Albert Estiamba, and Kevin Smith. We lasted about thirty minutes, then a neighbor called the cops and that was the end of live music. The only thing I remember is that we ended it with my song "Get it Right from the Start."

We immediately shut it down and told everybody that the party was moving over to our place on Twentieth Street. Wow, what a fun time that became. The keg and booze got transferred, and our neighbors endured a long night of wedding festivities. All my friends and coworkers from Gourmet Coffee Warehouse came over, making it a scene to remember. Julie smiled so much; her face hurt in the morning. I doubt we got more than a couple hours of sleep that night.

I woke up tired, but I knew that I had married the woman of my dreams.

COWSPACE AND BRENNAN'S PUB

I met Jeff Cleveland at Brennan's Pub. He was a pretty trippy dude. He managed The Grill in the Alley in Beverly Hills, a very prestigious restaurant, then wore cargo shorts and a t-shirt on his off days, performing live music whenever he got the chance with his band, Cowspace. He had an ad on Craigslist looking for a bassist, so I responded, and he told me they had a weekly gig at Brennan's. He respectfully declined my playing in his band after listening to Mother Jones' first album, telling me he thought I'd be bored playing in his band. I was a little shocked to be honest, but I respected his decision.

Almost a year later, the chance to play with them came up again, and I, again gave it a shot. I first came and sat in for a few songs. I met Alan, the drummer, and we hit it off right away. I knew I could hang with them!

A few days later, Cleveland and I met up at a bar near my home and I convinced him to let me play in his band. I promised him I wouldn't be bored. He had prepared a CD of songs to learn (back in the day when there weren't any links to songs online) along with the band's setlist. I learned all the songs in a week. However, it took about a month before I became the full-time bassist. The current bassist, Doug (a super good guy and great bassist) was leaving, but was finishing up his last stints.

I ended up being the bassist for Cowspace and playing at Brenan's for eight years. We played every Wednesday night, with crowds that spanned from a hundred plus fans to just the bartenders, and everything in between. We played on St. Patrick's Day and Halloween as well as other holidays. Brennan's was our home base. The cast of characters also included Bosco on the lap steel, Geoff LeDoian on guitar, then Chris Nyquist on guitar, Alan Combies on drums (love this guy), Marshall Thompson on keys and vocals, Cleveland on guitar and vocals, and myself, bass and vocals.

The very first gigs I did with them, I noticed nobody came early to help Cleveland with the PA system. I was horrified. I was also horrified at his PA. It was barely usable. I promised him from that day on that he would never be setting the PA system alone as long as I was in the band. I also promised him I'd be bringing in better gear. Let's just say I brought the gear up a couple notches.

A few months in, I bought a large Yamaha mixer, tons of cables as his were breaking down, about 3 huge Peavey monitors with Black Widow speakers (loved these monitors!) and I introduced him to Shure Beta 58 mics. I earned his respect. From that moment on, we became close friends, playing countless and memorable gigs together. Around seventy-five gigs a year for eight years, then I became a part-time bandmember.

Mike, the owner of Brennan's Pub, also let me have at least one show a month to book bands on a Friday or Saturday night. I produced shows under "Rising Sun Entertainment", bringing in other jam bands throughout Southern California, or even other non-jam band acts. I just wanted to bring in talented acts, not just jam bands, although my main focus was on the jam scene. It was a successful gig for years, but I started getting burnt out. The amount of work it involved got to me, so I had to take a break. I just didn't have the stamina I once had.

My final gig with Cowspace was, fittingly, a few days before Brennan's Pub closed. All of our closest musician friends came up and played with us throughout the night. It was a very bittersweet show. Lots of tears were shed but damn, the music was good and that last gig with Cowspace at Brennan's will always be remembered.

JEREMIAH ROIKO BAND

I was about thirty-six years old, looking for a blues band to work with. This guy named Louis had an ad looking for a bassist, so I responded to him. We talked on the phone for a little while, I liked what I heard, and he mailed me a CD of songs that he performed. We talked some more and he invited me to do a jam one night down in Torrance. I went down there and we started playing, then this young guy who looked like he was still learning to shave came in, plugged in, and started playing the living shit out of his guitar. My jaw dropped a few times that night. We gelled immediately. After the jam, I asked Louis, "Who the hell is that?!" He told me, "Oh, that's Jeremiah Roiko." I immediately shook his hand and heaped praise on his playing. He laughed and was very cordial about it all but was definitely pretty psyched to play with me as well.

Ironically, I never did play with Louis because of some health issues that came up, but I kept in touch with Jeremiah. He wanted to get a band together, so I told him about a drummer I knew who was available, Perry Ostrin. Soon after that, Jeremiah introduced us to Philip Clark, a singer, keyboardist, saxophonist, and songwriter – a very talented guy, and a nice guy to boot. As was Perry. In an instant, the Jeremiah Roiko Band was formed.

We started playing at The Starboard Attitude on Saturday afternoons at the Redondo Beach Pier, then Friday and Saturday nights. It became our residency for a year or two. A lineup change happened a couple years into it; Philip and Perry parted ways. My good pal, Doug Lloyd, filled in for a couple months on keys. Stephen Riddle, who had just moved to L.A. from Georgia along with his brother, Jeremy Riddle a talented songwriter and colorful character, became the drummer. They had been playing in their town as an act for a number of years but wanted to take a crack in the City of Angels. Stephen immediately fit in and we got very tight as the rhythm section.

It took about six gigs, but after that, we were pretty much anticipating all of our moves and ideas. Jeremiah kept kicking more ass, and this lineup lasted for about three years. With each gig, the energy we created was infectious and huge. It's still the strongest power trio I've ever been a part of, and I'm sure they'd both agree.

Eventually, Stephen moved away, other factors came into play and we stopped performing together. It wasn't until in February of 2022 that we did a show together again in Steamboat Springs, where Jeremiah lived. It was a show for the ages. We kicked royal amounts of ass.

Jeremiah and I became really close friends and remain really close friends. I love this boy dearly, and he's one of the special guitarists that I've had the pleasure of playing with on stage in my lifetime. I'm sure we'll have more gigs in the future.

SARAH GOFF AND THE ELIZABETH KILL

I also played in another band with Jeremiah's girlfriend and future wife, Sarah Goff, who was a very talented vocalist, lyricist, and songwriter. She wrote great originals, decided she wanted to have a band, instead of just an act that backed up her name, so her band became the new band name for us. We became "The Elizabeth Kill". It consisted of Jeremiah on guitar, me on bass, Phil on drums, Marshall on keys for about six months, and another guitarist who was fantastic, but played loud as hell.

We practiced weekly and played out about once a month. We were an Indie Rock Showcase band. We recorded an album while I was in the band, which I thought had some damn good songs. After about a year, the drummer, Phil (Flip) left the band, replaced by Corey, who was a juggernaut and was influenced by Neil Peart.

He brought a positive new energy into the band. The other guitarist left as well, so it became a compact trio with Sarah in the middle, belting out her lyrics. Unfortunately, I didn't stay for too long after that. I played one gig at Molly Malone's with Corey, then abruptly left the band. At that time, I was burning a candle at both ends, playing in too many projects, but also wasn't feeling the music anymore. Getting a DUI soon thereafter kind of sealed the deal with my leaving as well.

MID-LIFE CRISIS, DUI, AND THERAPY

This was a very interesting time in my life, to say the least. I was almost forty, playing in five different bands, working five days a week, and only home three nights a week. Julie and I had been married about eight years, and we were starting to feel disconnected because of my schedule.

Granted, we were both used to my not being home much, but it was starting to catch up in subliminal ways. It's strange how we can acclimate to situations we're in and create justifications in our minds to ease the unspoken tension, even though we know deep down something isn't right. I was on a hamster wheel, hoping that one of the bands I was playing in or something I was a part of would break open and become successful. None of it was happening fast enough, and I was starting to feel and to act a little desperate. I was sick of working so much, but the bills had to be paid. I was also sick of playing in so many bands but couldn't lose the possibility that one of them could become lucrative. I had a hard time saying no to any project that came my way, a huge reason for my predicament. Yes, they were all fun to play in, until they no longer were. None of the bands satisfied me. I didn't know what I was looking for anymore, except for a way out. I just felt trapped.

This was also a trippy period where I was resembling Johnny Depp, believe it or not. It's not like I was *trying* to look like him, it just kind of happened. I wore similar hats, the same kind of facial hair, similar glasses, and at certain angles, my face looked like his. It actually started to get to a slightly disconcerting level.

Women were occasionally stopping me at Whole Foods or CVS, telling me that from down the aisle, they swore to God I was Johnny Depp and were starting to get all nervous and star struck. I'd get A LOT of double takes when I was walking around, even from guys. Jeremiah and Jeff Cleveland started calling me Sonny Depp on stage, which was more for a laugh, but it showed how much that became a part of my persona during that time. It also contributed to my getting a false sense of confidence, looking in the mirror a lot more, thinking I was the shit. Then it got tiresome and was no longer fun. It became distracting. I was literally walking around with my head down towards the end of this period.

I was also starting to drink a lot more at home and at gigs. Not a smart thing to do, and the drinking became progressive. I had been driving home pretty damn buzzed, or truthfully, drunk, quite often and my luck finally ran out. One night, after a show with Jeremiah and Stephen at The Big Fish in Glendale, I didn't follow the other guys to the freeway. Instead, I decided to take an alternative route. I didn't see a cop car as I was taking a left while approaching the freeway entrance a few blocks away. They immediately turned on their lights, and for some reason, I instinctively drove into a gas station, hoping that might steer them away from suspecting me of anything – I was just getting gas, after all!

Ah, what a drunk brain thinks makes sense! I pulled in, walked out of my car, and asked them what I had done. They said I was driving slightly off and they decided to investigate. I immediately knew I was fucked, even though I had stopped drinking at 11:30PM, I had drunk a couple big shots of Jägermeister and a couple light beers.

They pulled me aside and wanted to do a sobriety test on me, which I did willingly. I actually did very well with the alphabet, the counting, the walking backwards. It was when they gave me the breathalyzer that I knew I was in trouble because of how they looked at me. After the second breathalyzer, they confirmed I was actually twice the legal limit. They immediately read me my rights and brought me towards the squad car. How humiliating. What was I going to tell Julie?! Before I was handcuffed, I had about thirty seconds where I was able to call her and tell her the mortifying news. It was about 3AM by now, so she knew something had happened. She had been reading the tea leaves for the last few months anyways, wondering if this would happen, and it did.

I was first brought to the hospital, had a blood test done, and was then brought back to the Glendale Police Station. I did the standard stuff: the paperwork, taking off my belt and shoelaces, and just stayed in a little holding cell until I was able to get my phone call. I called Julie and talked to her for a few minutes. Told her where I was being held in Glendale.

She was tempted to make me stay the entire weekend; she was so mad. But she didn't. She picked me up sometime in the late morning. I basically wept like a baby once I was in the car. We also had to go over to get the car out of the police pound, where it was filled to the brim with music gear, boiling in the sun.

From that point, a lot of changes happened fairly quickly. A DUI isn't cheap, either. It cost nearly ten thousand dollars after all was said and done: fines, court fees, programs that I had to attend, which were actually very healing and rewarding, as far as the recovery process was concerned, car insurance rate hikes, a blowing device in the car for six months in order for me to be able to drive. Not to mention the strain this created on my marriage.

I had fucked up big time. I tried to do everything as well as I could, going to all the classes, not drinking, literally quitting every band I was in, and slowing way the fuck down in order to eliminate any temptation.

It was embarrassing, because my inner circle friends knew exactly what had happened. Jeff from Cowspace was pretty affected by it. The previous bassist, Doug, filled in for me for that year and was gracious enough to share the gig with me when I felt like I was able to start playing music again. He was a real gentleman.

I don't wish a DUI on anybody, but I have to say, it helped to straighten my ass out. I can't say it does that for everybody, but I got the message, loud and clear. However, it still wasn't quite enough for me to get real healing.

I did AA meetings for about a year, and they were good, but I couldn't really connect with them. It was hard to constantly hear stories of others doing heinously idiotic things to themselves. I understand it helps a lot of people; it just didn't connect with me after a year. I needed more.

I decided that I needed to see a psychotherapist. I needed to work through my childhood crap. It was obviously affecting how I was behaving as an adult, and I wasn't making wise choices. I needed serious help to work through the pent-up anger I had been holding onto all these decades.

The therapist I had was fantastic. She knew exactly what to ask me and paced her questions wisely. I went to her weekly, for over a year, and I finally purged the anger I had been holding for my foster mom. I got really pissed, and just let it out finally.

For years, I had always given her some kind of out or justification for the way she had treated me as a child, and I justified my mom's death, and my childhood situation. I had never allowed myself to really get pissed off and let out the anger and unfairness I deserved to feel. It felt so damn good to let it out.

I stayed angry for a long time about everything, but it felt like a healthy anger, something I could process, not harbor. It was a new approach to observing my past, and it was helping me to heal.

I had some really amazing breakthroughs with that therapist. She single-handedly helped to shift my life away from feeling like a victim toward gaining emotional control of my past. I'll always be grateful for her help.

About a year and a half after my DUI, I started coming out of my shell and slowly reintegrated myself back into performing again. Being in bars wasn't such a trigger for me anymore. I wasn't drinking how I used to, I was being responsible and feeling like I had more control over my life. I had developed healthier habits to replace the bad ones.

RECORDING SINGING BOWLS AT BODHISATTVA TRADING COMPANY

I was looking for a steady job. Julie and I were kind of in a desperate position. My previous job had just ended abruptly, so I needed to find something sooner than later.

One morning, I saw a job listing by Bodhisattva Trading Company on Craigslist that seemed interesting. I had to read it a few times before I got it right. It entailed learning how to play singing bowls and recording them. I honestly had no idea what a singing bowl was, but I was intrigued, so I responded.

I had forgotten all about the job, then I got a reply two weeks later from the owner Shakti, asking if I was still interested in the position. I said "Yes" and came in for an interview. Apparently, they liked my answer to their final question, which was "Why do you want to work here?" I replied, "I just want steady work" and that sealed the deal.

It took me a good couple months before I even felt marginally comfortable saying that I could play a singing bowl decently. There were so many different types of singing bowls and sizes that I had to learn how to play in a short time. They didn't rush me through the process, but it was obvious that knowing how to play them and recording them was key in helping to sell them. What set this company apart was how much they cared about the recording quality. I respected that. Since I also cared about those factors, I made sure my recordings were of the highest quality singing bowl recordings anybody could hear.

Nearly fifteen years later, I'm still working for Bodhisattva Trading Company, having recorded at least fifteen thousand bowls and hundreds of singing bowl sets. Little did I know that I'd become a premier singing bowl playing artist. My ears have become so much more sensitive, differentiating Western versus Indian keys, since most singing bowls are not concert-pitch based 440 Hz.

CHAPTER 9

FINDING MY DAD

For a number of years, I would go on these searches on the internet looking for my dad, Jimmy Soto, or James Soto, and he served in the Air Force. From what my mom told me as a kid, he was from Texas, so that's where I'd do my searches – or states close to Texas. I'd look up his general age, since he'd have to be eighteen to twenty-two years old on average while serving in Vietnam. Oh, and he was also Mexican-American. I'd get on these tangents off and on throughout the years, looking and looking for him, but I never got anywhere. Julie even asked a friend who was in the Air Force if he had access to a database to search for members named James/Jimmy Soto. He told her he did and he searched extensively, but he never came up with anybody who could fit all the above criteria. After hearing from her friend, and doing our own Hail Mary searches, I finally looked at Julie and said I wasn't going to look for him anymore. It was obvious that it wasn't meant to be, so I resigned myself to the reality that I'd never know who my dad was, and I completely let go of the notion that I'd ever find him. And it was O.K. I just surrendered to the facts and moved on with my life. I couldn't say that I was content with my decision but letting go took some emotional burden off my shoulders.

A few months later in early December of 2015, Julie and I were looking at Ancestry.com ads online and thought it would be kind of fun if she got me a DNA test for Christmas. They were also having a twenty percent off sale, so what the hell, why not? I was curious as to my Mexican-American roots and any other lineage mysteries that would be revealed. When it arrived, I immediately did their test and mailed it back to them with my DNA. My results came back a few weeks later on their website, so I logged in and eagerly looked.

Shockingly, there wasn't a trace of Mexican or Native American blood in me, at all! I had a good laugh about that. I'd been telling my closest friends that I was part Texican – ha! But I found out that I was 11% Irish, 30% British, 11% Indonesian, and the rest Asian stuff. It was a lot of fun to get the results and no longer be in the dark about my general ancestral background.

ANCESTRY.COM MATCH MESSAGE

For a couple weeks, I kept getting these emails from Ancestry about a "Possible Match" they just found. I had been ignoring it as I figured it was another sixth cousin. No offense, but that was something I didn't have time for.

Finally, I got tired of seeing that reminder coming to my email almost daily, so I finally logged in and looked up their message.

It was Tuesday, May 3rd of 2016, sometime in the morning around 10AM. The message first said it was a possible Father/Son relationship, the likelihood of the match was something astronomically accurate like 99.99997% accurate. I kept looking at the "relationship" part and couldn't quite understand it. I must've stared at the words "Most Likely Your Father" about ten times before I was starting to get what it was telling me.

Was it for real? They were telling me that they fucking found my *dad*? Really? I actually looked around my work room for any potential cameras and shit, honestly thinking I was getting punked, that maybe I was being filmed. The emotions I had were mostly of shock. I was kind of laughing it off because it was too kooky to be real. This shit happens only in the movies, not to real people.

Once the reality of the message starting sinking in, and the feeling of getting punked no longer seemed a logical choice, I decided I needed to message my father.

Oh, and his name was definitely not Jimmy/James Soto. It was Robert/Bob Nore – so far off what my mom had told me when I was 5. Wow! I was nervous as hell after I clicked on the Send button. Would he respond? Will he give a shit? Is he a loser drunk or an addict, or some super far-right extreme conspiracy theorist whack job? Will he even respond?!

I called Julie from work about it. She was in as much shock as I was. She told me I should probably message him. I told her I just did. When I got home, I showed her the message I sent him and she approved. We just sat there in amazement, wondering if he'd reply.

It was the longest two days of my life. Then, finally he did. My message was very polite and noncommittal, trying to make him feel like he had no obligation to respond, and that I was only reaching out as I had just gotten this very shocking news. His response was just as polite and respectful as mine. He had been waiting for a month after getting the same message in his email, hoping I'd message him. He didn't want to interfere in my life, so he waited for me to respond. Very respectful. I was elated to hear from him. I read it to Julie after work and she was in complete awe, soaking in the seismic shift of this new situation in my life. I had just found my dad, and he wanted to be in touch with me! It could've gone so much worse, but it didn't. In fact, it was a dream that was coming true, one that I had given up on months ago. Amazing what can happen sometimes when you let go of expectations – the world has an uncanny way of surprising us.

The following week, we continued to email each other on our personal emails, not on Ancestry.com's message platform. We were getting more comfortable with each reply.

What I noticed immediately was how similar our writing styles were; our responses, the way we'd approach questions or subjects. It was almost like reading something that I would've written back to myself. It was just more affirmation that yes, he was my dad. We finally decided that it was time to talk on the phone. We both chose Sunday at noon. Sunday arrived, and boy, was I nervous as all shit.

I wouldn't doubt if I'd had a whiskey in one hand. He called and we started talking, nervously for some time. Then I told him that I was a musician who played and wrote a lot of country music, which made him instantly excited. He asked me what instrument I play, I said bass, and he immediately said, "That's what I played!" That was the moment he knew I was his son. Ha! The nervousness lifted for the most part, and he started telling me about the family history, about my great-grandmother and how the family would perform at barn dances in North Dakota and she was the music director; that my grandfather (his dad) was also a musician who played guitar as a younger man but but when he was older heplayed accordion and sang at a small venue every weekend. I was blown away to say the least. Now I knew why I loved country and folk music so much – it was in my blood! We talked for a good hour, then we both started getting nervous and emotionally exhausted, so we decided it was time to go and to talk again soon.

He called a week later, and after about fifteen minutes of talking, he told me he and his wife Debbie, had been talking about inviting us out to Huntsville, Alabama to visit them and to meet the rest of the family. We decided that the best time to come out would be Fourth of July weekend.

By this time, I had learned that I had two brothers and two sisters. I had already had a couple phone calls with both of my new sisters, Mandy and Audrey. They were both awesome, open-hearted and we connected immediately. Our conversations seemed to be effortless. Mandy was elated that she was finally no longer the oldest sibling, a perspective I never even considered. I was so honored to be her "Big Brother". The very first thing Mandy wrote to me when we found each other on Facebook was "Well, it's official – you're my brother from another mother!" I immediately laughed my ass off out loud. Perfect. Absolutely perfect.

Audrey and I also had a cool connection that was immediately obvious. We must've talked for an hour and a half on our first phone call. It was at once like we had known each other for years, but we were also learning about somebody who was an unknown sibling until now. The significance didn't get past any of us. I must admit, I didn't contact the brothers, James and Justin. I didn't want to fan the flames or make them uncomfortable. Guys are just different. Plus, I figured I'd be meeting them once I went out there and we could go at their pace.

THE BIG NEWS AND THE BIG CRY

The first people I mentioned finding my dad to (besides Julie) were Jeremiah Roiko and Stephen Riddle at Sonny McLean's. Sarah Goff was also there but she left after about thirty minutes, so she only got the news later from Jeremiah.

I had been chomping at the bit all night, wanting to tell them the news, but this was more about a reunion with Stephen, Jeremiah, and myself – or JRB; Jeremiah Roiko Band. It was a good hour into the night before I ordered a round of drinks then told them, "Hey, I've got some crazy news to share with you. And I mean crazy." Their eyes got huge. "What is it?" I told them, "First, we have to sit down for this." We found a table in the side room, had our beers, and I started in on the story. I told them how Julie got me the DNA kit from Ancestry.com as a Christmas present, how I did it and sent it in, how I got the results back. Then I told them how I kept getting these messages from Ancestry.com, which I kept ignoring until after about the third time. Once I told them I found my dad; they sat there open mouthed, in complete shock. Another round of drinks!

The "Big Cry" came after a Scruffy O'Shea's gig in Lomita on a Sunday afternoon. I was hanging out with Sarah and Jeremiah at the end of the gig and I was talking to Sarah a lot about the whole event since we hadn't really had a chance to chat about it. She had some great things to say about it that stuck in my head. We all hugged then went our separate ways.

As I was driving, I just kept thinking about my newfound dad and the gig, how great it was, and then like a fountain that got turned full blast, I just starting crying, then weeping, then bawling. It just didn't stop. It was full-on water works. I was releasing all these emotions I didn't think I had been holding onto, but apparently, I had. It was such a multi-tiered level of emotions I was crying through. I was letting go of what I thought I'd never find and embracing the depth of what I didn't necessarily find. Moreso by letting go, I had opened up the door to what would find me, which was my dad. It was one of the most incredible experiences I'd ever had alone.

And on the freeway. And I missed my exit. And I had no idea where the hell I was. I was literally crying into my phone, asking Siri to give me directions to home. Because my glasses had fogged up so much, I actually had to roll down my driver-side window to help defrost them. Kinda funny.

I finally started calming down so as I could follow Siri's directions. Man, I had gotten onto a completely different freeway and had to go up the 101, to the 5, then to the 10 West to get back home. Crazy but hilarious.

I kept the window open for a little while as well – the fresh freeway air felt nice. I told Sarah a couple days later what had happened and she admitted to me that she had done a prayer in her car, asking the Powers That Be to help me release my burdens and to replace them with this new amazing moment with my dad.

I finally got home to Julie and barely made it past the door before I completely lost my shit and heave-cried on her shoulder for what seemed like ten minutes. She just gently patted my back and said, "Let it out, sweetheart. Just let it out." They weren't tears of sadness, not in the least. They were tears of joy, tears that I can only imagine an Olympian medalist might cry when they've crossed the finished line and realized they not only won but beat the world record. All those years of training, all those years of isolation, focus, living with their inner doubts, and so many other intangibles, were erased in a split second, replaced by the most amazing feeling of knowing that everything they had gone through did matter after all. Now they could let go of all that effort and just bask in the glory of what they deserved and had earned, whether that was their intention or not.

It was the most glorious bawling session I've ever had in my life. I hope everyone gets to experience that just once in their life. It will change you, for the better.

FOURTH OF JULY WITH DAD AND MY NEWFOUND FAMILY

The weekend of all weekends finally came. Julie actually got footage of me meeting and hugging my dad at the airport for the first time. It was very nerve-wracking yet calming, because the day finally came where it could happen and we could get to knowing each other. We walked a little way to the hotel, which was literally next door to the airport, then met his wife Debbie at the little hotel coffee shop, where we all had some beverages, hung out, and got the formalities over with. The good news is that they loved Julie, and we loved Debbie. We were all going to get along quite well. Nothing off at all with our exchanges. It felt good. We got tired after about thirty minutes, so we decided to head to our respective rooms and reconvene in the morning.

Morning arrived and my dad drove us back to Huntsville, not without first going into Nashville to show me the sights really quickly and to get himself some Starbucks coffee, of which he was a complete fan. We then drove to Muscle Shoals Sound Studio, where I proceeded to buy two t-shirts, and we took a few pictures of each other there.

For the final hour drive, we just stared out the window and I mentioned how many churches there were out there. I mean, depending on what stretch of road you were on, there could be six churches for every mile you drove.

You couldn't drive a mile without seeing at least one church. It was high-level Bible Belt country. I had missed being surrounded by so much healthy greenery and fresh air.

We headed over to first meet Justin and Audrey for about an hour. Justin was in a slight state of shock over the whole thing, justifiably. Since Audrey and I had talked a few times on the phone, we had a more natural flow of conversation. We finally arrived at my dad's home, which was absolutely beautiful and spacious. After we had some time to decompress and take a nap, we got to meet Debbie's mom, who was absolutely precious, then her son and their family. In between visits, I brought out my guitar and my Beatle's songbook, and my dad and I began singing a bunch of songs. It was a helluva feeling to be singing with him for the first time and sounding pretty damn good.

Shortly afterward, we headed over to Mandy's home, where we had a huge feast and I also got to meet her daughter Sammy. James was there as well, his eyes big as saucers and full of amazement at the moment unfolding. He was meeting his half-brother for the first time! It was all kind of a huge whirlwind of a day and slightly overwhelming, but we all trooped on. Later that night, we went over to James's house to hang out and we also met his wife. We all just played some board game and talked. She was super nice and loved to laugh. It was a good family I was coming into.

The next morning was the Fourth of July, and we all headed over to Mandy's home where the big celebration was happening. My dad decided to bring his little Karaoke machine, apparently a tradition he does every year. It was the first time I'd heard him yodel to a Hank Williams song. It actually got me teary-eyed, with the help of a couple glasses of whiskey. That was my dad over there, yodeling! That's where I come from, right in front of me! I stood beside Audrey and she noticed I was all emotional, which got her teary-eyed as well. She needs little help to start crying, a family known trait! As the day and night wore on, more people came in. I met Justin's wife and kids, and my sibling's mom. After a couple hours, they asked me to bring out my guitar so my dad and I could sing some tunes together. We began with songs we had rehearsed, like "Bye Bye Love" by the Everly Brothers. It got welcome hoots and hollers. We kept going and my dad looked like he'd never had so much fun in his life. He'd never had the chance to do this with his other kids. On the flip side, I'd never had the chance to sing with my dad, until now. As I write this, it still feels surreal that this all has happened to me. Just otherworldly. That Fourth of July was one of the greatest days of my life. I was so happy to have Julie be a part of as well.

WASHINGTON POST AND OTHERS WRITE ABOUT OUR STORY

Word got around about our story. I initially contacted Ancestry.com's media department, and they almost got us onto a national Sunday morning television show, but our story was beat out by another story. Oh well. They passed us along to a journalist from *The Washington Post* named Tara Bahrampour, who was fascinated by our story, so she interviewed both of us by phone, then released her article on October 12th, 2016. Lucy Berry from *The Huntsville Herald* where my dad lived, approached us shortly after and wrote an article on us. They featured some wonderful photos of my new family with me.

About a year later, we were approached by a film crew who represented IBM Industries to create a four-minute film on how technology and the internet has changed society for the better. Now that was a forty-eight-hour gangbusters session! Wow, it was exhausting, but I loved every minute of it. They paid for our plane tickets, as Julie came along, of course, and hotel room, food, and a check at the end of the shoot. I prepped my dad a month before it all went down, telling him that I had been approached by them and asking if he was willing to take part in this short. He was a sport about it and said yes to it. I think he also wanted our story to get out there a little bit.

But once the lights and cameras were set up and the shooting began and we were being directed in how to talk and what to do, the reality definitely kicked in. It was fun and challenging. Huge props to the team. They had been working together as a unit for some time and it showed. They were a family. I had some great conversations with them, especially with the audio tech, of course! We nerded out on his awesome Schoeps boom mic. I was drooling before the first take.

They asked some really engaging questions, to the credit of the female director, who was a whirlwind of energy. Everybody was truly awesome on that team. And the final version for sure encapsulated our finding one another, and what feelings and dynamics were involved with our new relationship.

The most beautiful thing about this video is that we were able to gather most everybody in the extended family to come together at my dad's place and to use the community center in the neighborhood where they lived to have this amazing gathering documented by them. We had a huge dinner, the kids were filmed running around, I was joking about how "terrible" the ribs were while chomping away at them; some of the best ribs I've ever had in my life, bar none. At the end, they got a shot of the entire family in front of the pond, which was used to begin the film. It really was so well done. I applaud them, not only for their vision, but for their stamina! It helps to be young in the film business!

What's so funny is that at the end of the night, when everybody was leaving and my dad was slumped into his recliner, I hardly hugged him goodbye because I was so exhausted, and I knew he was spent. We just said, "O.K., love you" and Julie and I left shortly thereafter. I was all good. Debbie (my dad's wife) totally got it. She was exhausted too, having been the planner of the dinner and getting all the relatives together for the shoot. The video, *A Chance of Two Lifetimes*, was released the following year on October 20th, 2017. It can be found on my website (sonvosongs.com) and YouTube.

We had about a year's respite of press, then *Guideposts Magazine* approached us for an interview and an article on us, giving us a three-page spread. Julie and I met my dad and Debbie at a hotel close to LAX in Los Angeles in between their vacation. This was their last leg before going home. The interviewer and tech set up the camera and lights in my dad's hotel room, and we were interviewed together. It was a fun interview. For some reason, I was very giggly for that. Maybe it was nerves. Who knows. I can also be a giggly, silly guy.

We did our interview, then we all went downstairs and they took photos of us outside in front of the hotel. They thanked us, then went their merry way. It was very efficient. We then all went to get some food. We were hungry.

Then Julie and I bid my dad and Debbie goodbye. My dad and I were secretly hoping this would be the last of the press for a while. Not that we didn't like for our story to be out there, just that it can be a little bit exhausting to deal with that kind of thing when you're not used to it. Granted, I've done a fair number of interviews on camera, but I'm no veteran. After that interview, things died down. We were fine with that.

However, I did happen to get an interview last year (2021) with *The L.A. Times* Opinion Section. It was when President Biden decided to exit Afghanistan, and footage of all those refugees clinging onto the airplane emerged. The visceral reaction I got from watching that instantly brought me back to being at that airport in Saigon.

I felt like I had to share my own experience, so I went to *The L.A. Times* website, found where I could submit my story to the Opinion section and I began writing. I wrote about the sounds I heard when watching that footage, and despite it being a different language, I remarked on the fact that the sound of desperation was just the same as in Saigon. I couldn't get it out of my head. I also remarked on what message we needed to send to the Afghanistan soldiers, that was their work was not for nothing, that they were appreciated, and moreso appreciated by the Afghans.

I sent off my opinion piece, then thought nothing of it. A few days later, I got a personal email back from Paul Thornton, Editor of the Opinion Section, telling me that he read my letter and that he was very moved by it, so much so that he had shared it with his kids, and that he wanted to use it. He also told me that *The L.A. Times* had also created a new department where they bring out a videographer and interviewer to document stories for their website. Of course, I said I was very interested and that yes, they could tape me. So, they got me in touch with Karen Foshay and her camerawoman, who were both top-notch pros, asked all the right questions, and nailed the footage. Once all was said and done, and edited, my interview went out on October 22nd, 2021. The funniest part of all that was getting messages from my friends telling me how they just saw me on Spectrum TV! I had no idea they had a thing with Spectrum, and it was getting aired several times a day for a couple months. This video also recently won a journalistic award for best 2-minute documentary piece. Incredible.

The fifteen minutes of fame from that felt really good. It hit close to home. It's also what jump-started me to really take writing my book seriously. In a sense, it was the final push to motivate me to the finish line. And here we are!

SINGING WITH DAD ON STAGE

My dad and Debbie decided to come out to Santa Monica in 2017 during Thanksgiving to visit and check out the sights. We all had an amazing Thanksgiving gathering and they got to know Julie's family a little more. It was uncanny how much in common my dad had with my father-in-law. They had both worked as engineers and geeked out about it during the meal. The rest of us just soaked in the moment, and the amazing food and view.

Before this trip, I had asked my dad if he would be O.K. if I booked a gig where we could sing together. It would be at Brennan's Pub, my home away from home. Mike, the owner and bartender, instantly gave us the day. Because my dad's a consummate gentleman, he said O.K., even though he was nervous about it, but also excited. We had sung together before, and sounded incredible, considering the lack of rehearsal. Our tones sat well with each other's, and we knew when and how we were going to sing the next word. It was the most natural vocal experience I've ever had. Now we get to do it in front of my friends and family.

I was nervous as all hell. Apparently, we had both downed a couple of shots of whiskey before getting on stage. I wanted to make sure everything was perfect for him: the mic height, the chair height, if he could hear himself perfectly in the monitors. He told me he was all good.

The moment came. I sat on the bench next to him. There was enthusiastic clapping, then it was whisper quiet. You could hear a pin thinking about dropping. We looked at each other, I said nervous stuff, then he said, "Let's try it" and that's just what we did. I don't remember a damn thing that I said, I just know that anybody who was human in that place had a tear in their eye, and they knew something incredibly special was happening. The first song started off a little rough, but we got on point toward the end of the song. It was the most special night of my life, bar none.

How could anything top singing with my dad, in front of all my closest musician friends who I've played with for years, and their family members, who were there to witness it? I only wished that all my siblings from both sides of my family had been there as well. Nevertheless, whoever was in that room on that night, watched the most important and magical day of my life.

SON VO, UNITED STATES CITIZEN

If finding my dad wasn't big enough news for the year, I had decided it was high time for me to become a U.S. Citizen. I had begun the process before I met my dad, but it became more solidified as the year progressed. I took my preliminary tests and got my immigration lawyer all set to make sure I was doing everything correctly.

Working with the system also takes a great deal of time, and I wanted to make sure another presidential election didn't pass by without my being able to vote. Enough!

Once I took the final test where you have to speak to an administrator in person, I knew I had passed in flying colors. They actually let you know within the hour after the final test. I had passed. Granted, I've been living in the United States almost my entire life and I spoke English as my default language, so I didn't really have an excuse for not passing it. Nevertheless, the feeling was damn good. Ha! That drive home was a great one. Julie was with me the entire time and I'm so glad she was.

The inauguration was on September 22nd, 2016. My brother-in-law Eric, and my wife attended. I was so happy and touched that they came. The event was right beside Staples Center, so I was able to walk around and check out the statues of Kobe, Magic, and Shaq before it officially started.

I walked back in and was in a room filled with hundreds of other citizens-to-be. It was an amazing site to behold. We all received our official plaques and watched the official video being narrated by Barack Obama. Once the video was done, we were told congratulations and that we were now officially Citizens of the United States of America.

There was only one thing that my mom ever asked my sister and I to do for her, and that was to become American citizens. Over the years, every excuse in the book came to delay my citizenship application, but after all the obstacles were overcome, I finally did it.

This one's for you mom. We can both sleep well now.

EPILOGUE
PRESENT DAY

I've been working at my job recording singing bowls at Bodhisattva Trading Company for nearly fifteen years now. It's been an incredibly interesting job, to say the least. There are times I'm recording and photographing 16th or 17th century bowls. It's mind-boggling to think that it reached my hands after hundreds of years, that these bowls have their own stories and experiences which stretch back so far.

My life is fairly routine nowadays but satisfying. My wife grounds me and is my confidant. We talk about most anything and are complete horror movie addicts. Great television programs are a large part of entertainment, as well as our two large and very fluffy cats, Louie and Sally-Tomato. Their personalities couldn't be any more different. Both are rescue cats.

Louie is an orange Maine Coon who came from Ensenada, Mexico, filled with complex emotions and a huge vocabulary of sounds. We're convinced he was an actor in his previous life due to his overly dramatic moments. He's a cross between Nick Nolte and Clint Eastwood meets Faye Dunaway. You'll know when Louie's in the room – he'll announce his presence.

Sally-Tomato is a fluffy black mix of Maine Coon and Ragdoll Cat with huge vampire-like canines. He was saved from a kill shelter and came into our possession shortly after. He has the best disposition of any cat I've ever had and is incredibly playful. Unfortunately, he's also an excellent bird hunter. What little opportunities he's had (they only have a back patio space since it's the city) he's jumped on, literally.

When I'm not working, I record and write music as often as I can. Over the last few years, I've been able to record an impressive amount of my originals. Granted, I play most every part, sing them, arrange the songs, mix then finally master them. It's a long process at times but I've become pretty adept at it by now.I even made a silly music video last year with my niece, Olivia, for my song, "I Want a Hamburger". My young nieces and nephews as well as all my friends' kids absolutely love it. The kicker is the fireplace intro – I wanted to depict an old-school SNL meets old-school MTV. I think the video achieved that.

I perform live nowadays with a few bands, mostly playing bass, although I occasionally bring out my guitars. I feel more at home as a bassist. It's less of a headache for me to play and has more feeling for me, while requiring me to listen to everyone on the stage. I love having to be constantly present.

Playing guitar live, on the other hand, requires so much mental acuity, I start losing the sense of why I'm playing music on stage because I'm thinking about everything I'm playing and not feeling it as much.

I currently play bass for Jerry's Middle Finger, which has become a very popular Jerry Garcia tribute band, performing at very nice venues up and down the Western coast of the United States. I also play bass alongside my good pal John Jakubek, a prolific songwriter and incredibly talented guitar player, as well as my super-skilled and talented drummer pal, Perry Ostrin. We've put together a lot of pickup bands throughout the years, performing countless times in all types of situations and venues. I recently reunited with my old pals Jeremiah Roiko and Stephen Riddle, playing shows in Colorado and scheduling future shows either there or close to where Stephen lives. It's easily the best and most dynamic power trio I've ever been a part of.

Aside from that, I keep in touch with my dad and relatives in New Hampshire, Maine and New York. We can lose perspective on how important family is, especially living in such turbulent times. My wife's family is very special to me as well. They're wonderful individuals. Her parents, Tom and Norma Saywell, have always been so kind and generous to me. Her sister, Carey, is also cut from the same cloth – selfless and thoughtful, and with a great sense of humor.

Carey's husband Eric and I are also very close pals. He's an incredibly intelligent man with a wicked sense of humor, and a really talented guitarist to boot. We've gone down the rabbit hole talking about music gear too many times to count. And their daughter, Olivia is just as thoughtful and kind, with a twist of silliness and a great sense of humor. I love them all dearly. And like my father said in his video, family is the most important thing in life. As I've gotten older and satisfied many of my goals in life, what he says rings even truer.

Last year, I was finally able to connect with my nephew, Justin, my older sister's son (Mychele). He's an incredible personality and brimming with musical talent. He was out here in Los Angeles, so we got to meet and shoot the shit while shooting shots of Patron Silver. He also has a sister, Cara, who's as sweet as can be and recently got married. I felt terrible for not being at their wedding as I was hardly there as an uncle for them when they were children. Having the chance to visit with Justin carried weight due to my absence as a younger man, and to see him grown and developed such musical talent has created a bond with him. I couldn't be prouder of him and my niece, Cara. My sister Mychele did a damn good job along with their dad, Dennis, raising them to be kind and thoughtful human beings that I'm very proud of.

Family is what gets you through the hardest parts in life and gives you a reason to share yourself when it's good. Family doesn't need to be blood; it's all about connection, sharing and who you trust.

MY APPROACH TO SONGWRITING

Since I'm ultimately a songwriter first and everything else I do falls in line behind that reality, I look at the song as the base idea and the arrangement as the foundation of every song. It is the most important aspect of all songs, but it's entirely dependent on excellent performances that are emotionally-rooted. What you'll also find is that only the greatest musicians and songwriters have an impeccable sense of meter; meter is the unsung hero.

Which brings me to the next most important aspect – my vision of where I want a song to go. This part can be tricky, because many songs can start with just a beat or a rhythm or a simple lick or a vocal melody, then any of those ideas can be cultivated and mature, growing branches that reach out to create more ideas until finally, you look up and it's a fully grown tree. You either start with a melody that has lyrics, or a beat that lays down the vibe of what you're trying to express. Music isn't rocket science; it's based on emotion. Interestingly, many rocket scientists love to play music, but that's another story.

Then there's the other perspective, which is where I come from, which is having most of the ideas of the song already arranged in my head: the rhythms, melodies, chord changes, arrangement, harmonies, etc.

My songs don't have a long gestation period. I usually have most of the song worked out before I start recording it, because I've either obsessed over the parts to make sure they sound just right, or the ideas were already there. They rarely come from a place where its piecemeal, ideas trickling in, etc., they're pretty much fully-realized concepts, then I decide to record them. Sure, accidents and ideas can enter randomly, but then again, I don't consider those ideas random. They came in at exactly the right moments.

As far as solos, I'm not the most prolific soloist, but I play with emotion and like to keep the solos in my songs within that realm. I occasionally have really complex solo ideas, which require more practice time. Solos are the one exception I have as far as not having a clue for the most part as to what I want. Having solos with harmony parts is one thing, but a straight-up improvised section is a completely different beast. I prefer to keep my head empty and to let my fingers and ears bring me to the ideas that they think will work with the song.

HOW I RECORD SONGS

I begin recording a song one instrument at time, at least nowadays, since I'm playing all the parts at home or tracking instruments one at a time. I usually begin with an acoustic or electric guitar (or piano, depending on what the lead rhythm instrument is) played along to a click track. I then record the drums, which take the longest and will most likely be refined as other instruments are brought into the song down the line. After the drums, I'll add the bass, then finally the vocals. I might switch that around - vocals, then the bass guitar. I may need to redo the vocals if the song seems to need that. Next comes the percussion instruments; tambourine and shakers. After those are recorded, I bring in the piano and/or keys (organ, Rhoades, Farfisa, etc.) and start in with the backup vocals. I need to make sure all the other instruments are in play and that they don't get in the way of any instrumentation, only complimenting them. It's also much easier to mix and pan the vocals once everything else is in play. Finally, if there are any horns, I'll invite them in. By this time, everything's laid out and I'll know for sure whatever horn lines I've created won't be in the way of other ideas. If they are, no biggie, just adjust the arrangement. And to top off the final instrument(s), I record the strings and/or any extraneous instruments (glockenspiel, vibraphones, etc.)

I've given you the rundown on how I record my songs, but the most important aspect for me is the vibe of the song, which is where the arrangement comes into play. If the vibe that I hear in my head and feel in my gut doesn't translate, then it's not good enough to bring out to the world.

Luckily, for me, my songs don't seem to fail my own judgement test, because I'm my own worst critic. Interestingly, I've never released a song that I consider just good. It has to be excellent on every level: its vibe, lyrics, arrangement, performance, and production, just for starters. If all those elements collide to make a song that makes *me* feel something beat in *my* heart, then I know it's something that will touch other hearts. It's just that simple.

Another critical important aspect that a songwriter has to have is the ability to gut-check themselves while writing or recording an original song. You can't be afraid to say, "Nah" or "Nope, do it again." It has nothing to do with you. It has everything to do with the vibe and bringing out the best in the song. You serve your song, not the other way around. You do *everything* you can to make sure that your gut, heart, and ears are seamlessly synced with one another, unafraid of being critical, in order to bring out the best in each song.

Of course, there's the other side of this, which is to not overthink what you're doing or get overworked and stressed to the point where you're no longer making good decisions. Just drop what you're doing and come back to it later.

If those aspects above *are* synced, you'll be fine to give it a rest and analyze the song when you're in a better headspace.

Then other aspects of songwriting come in: the chord progression(s), meter, harmonies, singing and playing on pitch. Those aspects, of course, are necessary in order for the song to even sound like a respectable song. Don't get into the habit of thinking you can cut corners. Strive to give the best performances you can. If it isn't good enough, do it again. And again. Dig deep into what you're trying to express.

Interestingly, songs are no longer songs once you delve deep into them. They become expressive fragments, like a jigsaw puzzle, slowly piecing together parts that keep on making sense as you connect more pieces together. What you play or record makes sense only within the spectrum of the song, and when you're deep into it, every note – and how it feels and sounds – matters. You become obsessed with playing "the perfect parts". And those perfect parts actually happen. And they make you feel like a king when you finally nail it, even if it takes twenty or seventy-five takes. It's about playing for spirit of the song.There's also the mixing aspect of songwriting. This is where the rubber meets the road. All songs need to be mixed.

Songs need to be mixed "well" and this becomes an interpretation, since we live in a time where there are people who dedicate their time and lives to mixing songs, record to a level of perfection, and who have learned the fundamentals of frequencies.

Then there's the artistic musician, who's learning how to mix their own music, either because they can't afford to hire a professional mixer or because they have a vision in their head that they feel that only they should control.

I fall into the latter category, due to financial constraints. I represent the musicians who have a limited budget, but own quality gear, and have dedicated thousands of hours to learning the art of mixing and mastering music, out of necessity. We no longer live in the world of record labels signing us, let alone, distribution deals. This has freed up many musicians who aspire to become good mixers and producers.

There are a lot of artistic choices the mixer and producer have, but there are also fundamentals that they need to know and have a solid handle on. It takes years to develop a good ear to mix, even if you are naturally gifted with good ears. I won't list those fundamentals – there are entire books and courses dedicated to mixing and studying frequencies.

To me, mixing is where the alchemy of skill, talent, and sometimes beautiful mistakes, amalgamate to make the song cohesive. Let's not even get into the world of mastering, the final leg of the marathon in which the song runs before it reaches the listener's ears. And once that listener sits down and hears that song, you want them to simply feel it, not think about how a certain part stuck out and didn't feel right.

They should only be feeling the vision that you had for the song, and if that vision was executed well, the listener will be smiling or dancing, or better yet, sharing your song. In the end, the songwriter has to be smiling at the final mix of their song. If my gut feels it, then it's passed the test.

COVID WORLD

Covid really turned the world upside down, to say the least. Any live performer who was making a living got hit hard, be it actors, musicians, the film industry, comics, Vegas, any touring acts – we were all fucked. And everyone else, too. Parents were hit hard. The elderly low-income people, children with disabilities, farmers, factory workers, teachers. The list goes on. It was an international shit show of the highest disorder.

Interestingly, our planet got a respite since traveling ground to a halt. Mother Earth was able to breathe for a few months, which gave us some time to reflect on our priorities. Unfortunately, that didn't last long enough. We're back to the mess that it was, sorry to say.

Paradoxically, this was one of the most productive periods of my life as a recording artist. I was grateful to still have a paying job working with singing bowls for Bodhisattva Trading Company.

It helped to pay the bills, and I was able to spend my weekends recording a huge backlog of songs I'd written between ages nineteen to forty, as well as newer songs that had been brewing. I must've recorded and released at least a dozen songs in 2020. Even in 2021, when the effects of isolation were taking its toll, I still released about eight more singles, which included a single for Halina that involved bringing in musicians, but we did it!

I became a better mixer and engineer. I studied videos from experts in the field. I kept playing around with my mixes, learning the nuances of EQ'ing reverbs, multi-band compression, panning delays, honing in on the plugins I preferred. To this day, I'm deep in the never-ending process of learning how to be the best mixing engineer I can be, given my limitations.

I might not have a multi-million dollar recording studio, but that's become unnecessary nowadays. We're so spoiled, with a myriad of top-notch plugins at our disposal to manage most any audio ailment that we come across, as well as great recording gear at fairly affordable prices, and with knowledge, we can get great recordings. It gets down to developing good ears and a willingness to being self-critical. With those two ingredients, you'll only become better.

ASIAN-AMERICAN VIOLENCE IN AMERICA

Growing up in Harrison, Maine, I surprisingly didn't get harassed much for being an Asian kid. I might've gotten stares because obviously, I was different-looking from the white-majority population. Sure, I had to endure the occasional stupid Asian jokes, but for the most part, I was spared of racist slander and abuse. Nevertheless, I always felt judgement and eyes on me because I was different from everyone else. That was just the reality.

I also had to take into consideration that I was going to always be hypersensitive about how I looked, no matter how much others didn't look at me as different, my mind would become fixated with the reality of my difference. However, my perspective would've surely become more negative had I been consistently harassed.

Most people are inherently good. I truly believe that. We're just caught up in our own worlds and trying to either keep our shit together or goals on track. Life is ultimately one-dimensional – we live life from our own perspective. And that's where societal issues can be exposed. More people than we'd like to admit are raised with or live in an environment where racism is just a natural extension of themselves, even to this day, 2022.

It's hard to break habits, especially racial habits. Humans naturally have a pack mentality. We hang out with like-minded people as ourselves. This makes it harder to break the mold, especially when dealing with generational racism.

The mold can be broken. But it takes empathy and education. Ironically, in a life-or-death situation, most humans forego their prejudices for the sake of survival, relying on those they previously demeaned. Let's hope that we can all get along before we're in that position.

I want to believe that hateful and angry humans are just "going through a phase" and acting-out based on pack mentality, then realizing that violence ultimately gets ends with zero positive results, no one wins. Being hopeful and positive are some of the hardest attributes to maintain as a human. But we must. We can never let ignorant aggression and anger get the upper hand. We're better than that.

THOUGHTS ON MUSIC

Yes, it's a cliché: "Music is the international language." But it's also a language based on emotion moreso than function. Is it a necessity? Absolutely. It surrounds our entire existence. It helps to fill the voids; it connects us with its nearly limitless options of tones and rhythms. It's at once mathematical and feeling-based. It utilizes both sides of our brain. Without music, we could very well be emotionless, or less able to process our emotions.

I've always considered music the perfect balance between the logical and spiritual. It gives every human what they need, in their own personal way. What's always tripped me out the most about music is that it's inanimate. You can't touch it with your hands or see it. It's an artform you create out of thin air, creating organized frequencies and beats. It has no physical form, yet it's arguably the strongest bonding force of humankind. Songs are stories that we can pass down to future generations, like the folklore of our ancestors.

We live in a very complex time and the music industry reflects that complexity, trying to adapt to a new business model of streaming and singles. Younger generations have become very adept at self-marketing, and the music industry seems to live in a world based on algorithms – a double-edged sword, in my opinion; it gives you what you want, but you're not as likely to hear something new by pure chance. I miss the days of walking into a record store and randomly looking through album covers of all types of music, taking a chance buying albums of bands I've never heard about while songs I've never heard are being blasted through the sound system. However, I can also go to YouTube and type in literally anything at all and find something I want to listen to or watch. It can be overwhelming, but also comforting and exciting.

Music will always be there to comfort us and remind us that we're all in this together. There's room for all types of music, personalities, and emotions to be freely expressed. Even if the world goes to shit, which seems to be its current path, music will persevere. Music will always be created, somehow, someway. Music and humans are inseparable.

LIST OF BANDS I'VE PLAYED WITH 1988-2022

1988-89 - Low Tolerance (88' Rock Off album, two live shows)

1991-92 - Tao Jones (demos, open mic live shows)

1992 - Fetus Mongrel (tape demo)

1992-1993 - Rhythm Section of Shame (live shows)

1992-1994 - Go Button (live shows, on air live)

1993-1994 - The Off-Beatniks (demo, two live shows)

1994-1995 - Medulla Oblongata (demo, one live show)

1995-96 - Act of Faith (Christian Rock, few live shows)

1995-96 -All-Access Album and Video (with interview)

1996-2001 Freshly Baked (recorded three albums with Rand, toured)

2002 Woodshed (recorded demo, live shows)

2003 Z-Rave (Art Rock, live shows)

2003-Present – Mother Jones Band (recorded three albums, toured)

2004-2015 - Cowspace (album, weekly shows)

2005-2015 John Jakubek/Elektrobek (originals, live shows)

2005-present - Jeremiah Roiko Band (funky blues jam rock, live shows)

2008-2010 Sarah Goff Band, The Elizabeth Kill (recorded debut album)

2007-2010 Chris Shoop Band (Christmas Album, videos, live shows)

2011 Stone Soul (classic R&B, a few gigs)

2015 The Dirty Martinis (jazz, a few gigs)

2016-2018 Jerry's Middle Finger (Jerry Garcia Tribute, live shows)

2019-2020 The Doggie Llamas (live shows)

2020- 2022 John Jakubek (recording originals, live shows)

2022 Jeremiah Roiko Band reunion (funky blues rock, live shows)

2022 Vo & Co. (live shows)

2022-2023 Jerry's Middle Finger (Jerry Garcia Tribute, live shows)

COMPLETE LIST OF MY JOBS

Just for shits and giggles, I decided to create a list of all the jobs I've had throughout my life. There are quite a few wacky ones. Mind you, there were some years where I had to work with a temp job agency during a recession, so I'd be hired for only a few days or a few weeks. Beggars can't be choosy, especially in the heart of a Maine winter. They certainly gave my life some color and many stories. Hell, I could write another book of tales with all my job adventures! Until then, have a fun time scanning my list.

Age 12:

Babysitting kid down the street from where we lived a few times.

Mowing the lawn for an author of the children's books, Maynard the Moose.

Age 14- 15:

Mowing lawns in the neighborhood, including my English teacher, Miss. Miller.

Gas station attendant at Getty Gas, Cottage Rd., South Portland, Maine

Age 16:

Dishwasher/Prep Cook at The Blue Moon, Fore St., Portland, Maine. Became short order cook after hours.

Delivery driver, paper company beside The Blue Moon, 2 days.

Night shift cook, Denny's Restaurant, 2 nights.

Age 17:

Housekeeper, then laundry room, Sheraton Inn Armory, Market St., Portland, Maine, 6 months.

Dishwasher, Psychiatric Hospital, South Portland, Maine, 2 weekends.

Dishwasher, The Baker's Table, 4 months

Age 18:

Canvasser, Greenpeace, SOHO, NY City, 3 months

Cook, The Elephant Room, Christopher St., Greenwich Village, 2 weeks

Flyer passer, Dial-a-Porn cards, Manhattan, Brooklyn, Queens, 2 months

Fry Cook, Cap'n Newick's Lobster House, Broadway St., South Portland, Maine, 4 months

Age 19:

Assembly work, Earth Care, Madison, WI, 4 months.

Dry cleaning presser, Madison, WI, 2.5 months.

Fry cook, pizza maker, Madison, WI, 3 weeks.

Busboy, Cap'n Newick's Lobster House, South Portland, Maine, 6 months.

Unemployed for 2-3 months. Collected unemployment and food stamps.

Fish assembly work for Richard Slaughter (who was actually accused of killing his wife then stalking his girlfriend while being employed by him, in the papers), Portland docks, 1-2 months.

Age 20:

Shrimp assembly work, midnight shift, Portland docks, 2 months.

Summer and fall landscaping work on beach front properties with David Darling, Cape Elizabeth, Pine Point Beach, Scarborough, Maine 5-6 months.

Dishwasher, small hospital, South Portland, Maine, 2 days.

Garbage collector for South Portland Waste Management, 2 weeks in July

Laundry attendant, Inn by the Sea, Cape Elizabeth, 4 months

Age 21

Dishwasher, Old Port Tavern, night shift, 4 months.

Dishwasher, Victory Deli, Congress Square, 3-4 months

Age 22

Counter help, Bebop's Café, Congress St., 5 months

Janitor (day then midnight shift for last 2 months), YMCA, Forest Ave., 4-5 months

Age 23

Landscaper, Crabapple Whitewater Rafting Co., 6 months

Pine Tree Temp service work – paper company, South Portland, 2 weeks

Victory Deli, Congress Square

Age 24

Counter help, sandwich-maker, Victory Deli, Forest Ave., 8-9 months.

Cashier, sandwich-maker, Vaughn St. Deli, Vaughn St., 2-3 months.

Barista, then manager, Fonte Coffee Roasters (Fred Segal Bldg.), Santa Monica, CA, 2 years

Age 26-27

Counter and customer service, Santa Monica Homeopathic Pharmacy, 7th Ave., 6-8 months.

Misc. Work for art dealer, part time, Santa Monica

Age 28-29

Barista, customer service Java Bus, Fox lot, Santa Monica, Los Angeles, 1.5 years.

Age 30-35

Barista, customer service, Sunday Farmer's Market, Gourmet Coffee Warehouse, Venice, CA., 4.5 years

Age 36

Customer service, custom bookings, My Concert Concierge, Beverly Hills, 6 months.

Age 37-present

Recording engineer, photography, office management, Bodhisattva Trading Co., 15 years.

PHOTOS

Classic photo of my mom

Corky and me, my favorite dog in the whole wide world. The happiest animal I've ever known when he saw me

Me and Danny Grey at the house-raising party

In our PJ's L-R: myself, Frankie, Zeland (front)

My sister, Mychele and myself – Olin Mills classic photo

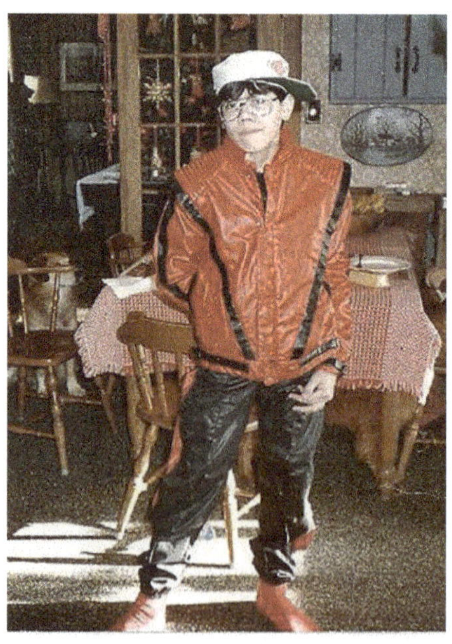

Chess king and break dancing!

Low Tolerance on Peak's Island, 1988 L-R: Regis McNicholas, Sean Kinney, me, Greg Kinney

Go Button L-R: Dave Naybor, Dave Burd, Karyn Jenkins, me, Peter Wool.

The Rhythm Section of Shame, day after Max's bachelor party.
L-R: Max Kay, Chris Goetz, and me.

Classic photo of Freshly Baked as a trio
L-R: Me, Rand Anderson, Jerry Dog, Neil Carroll.

Freshly Baked 1998-99, L-R: me, Neil Carroll, Rand Anderson, John Jakubek, Jerry Dawg

Mother Jones @ Pershing Square 2004-05 L-R: Albert Estiamba, Steve Janowski, Halina Janusz, Tony DePiano, Son Vo, Kevin Smith

Mother Jones @ Pershing Square 2005-06 L-R: Albert Estiamba, Mike Dwyer, Halina Janusz, David Abercrombie, me, Tony DePiano

Jerry's Middle Finger L-R: Garrett DeLoian, Rodney Newman, Lisa Malsburger, me, Halina Janusz, Jon Gold

Jeremiah Roiko Band 2009-10?

Back L-R: Perry Ostrin, me; Front L-R: Philip Clark, Jeremiah Roiko

Jeremiah Roiko Band, 2012 L-R: Jeremiah Roiko, Stephen Riddle, Son Vo

The Elizabeth Kill, 2009-10?
L-R: Phil "Flip", me, Sarah Goff, Jeremiah Roiko

The Hope Knots, an offshoot of Cowspace
L-R: Me, Jeff Cleveland, Alan Combes, Julie Gawkowski Fergus,
Bosco

My younger sister, Zeland and myself at my wedding

Frankie and myself, an unexpected visit

Collage of my newfound family, the Nores.

What a July 4th!

L-R: James, Justin, Mandy, Audrey, me, and dad

The extended Nore family during the filming for an IBM short

Receiving my US Citizenship, a very proud day.

Our wedding day L-R: Eric, Carey and Olivia Larson, Julie, me, Norma and Tom Saywell

Julie and myself at the Maypole

My best pal, Louie, one week into living with us.

Lickity Split. Loved this little girl kitty to pieces.

Sally Tomato with his toys

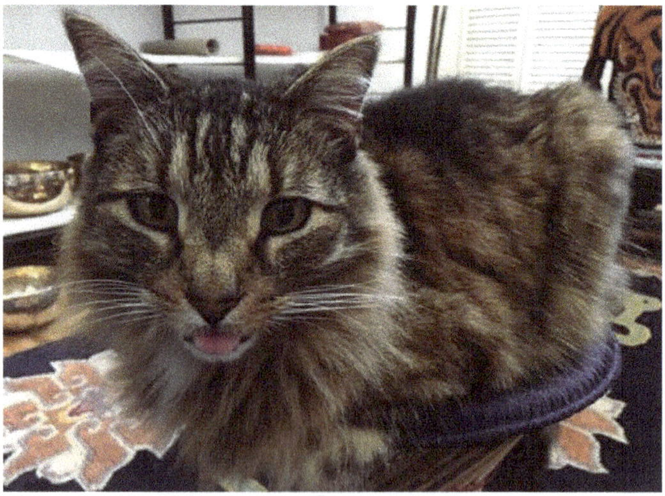

My work buddy, Boots @ Bodhisattva Trading Co.

Mrs. Vo and myself, watching the sunset on Santa Monica Beach. Love this woman with all my heart and then some.